A British Sub-Aqua Club First Class Diver and National Instructor, Gordon Ridley took up diving in the late 1960s, and has been writing about it virtually ever since. In addition to founding *Scottish Diving* magazine and regularly contributing articles to other diving publications, he has co-edited several highly regarded diving manuals including *Sport Diving, Seamanship for Divers,* and *Safety and Rescue for Divers.*

His fascination with diving in remote and challenging areas was reflected in his founding of the BS-AC Expeditions Scheme, which still sends hundreds of divers to relatively undived locations every year. As leader or organiser of more than a hundred major trips, his own expedition diving has taken him to Iceland, Norway and the Faroes, as well as all parts of Scotland. He has also been involved with running training courses for divers in places as far afield as Cyprus, Bahrain and Kenya.

Among his current projects is the final book in the ambitious *Diver Guide to Scotland* series, of which this title forms Volume III. Covering the Western Isles, the Hebridean Outliers including St Kilda, and Scottish freshwater dive sites, Volume IV is already well advanced.

D1437987

© Copyright 1992
by Underwater World Publications Ltd
55 High Street, Teddington, Middlesex TW11 8HA

Cover illustration by Rico
Maps by Suzanne Hall
Early Scapa Flow photographs courtesy of Peter Dean
All other photographs by Gordon Ridley

Typeset by Graphic Studios, Godalming, Surrey
and printed by Printhaus Book Company, Round Spinney, Northants.

ISBN: 0 946020 19 1

In the same series:

> *Dive West Scotland* by Gordon Ridley
>
> *Dive North-west Scotland* by Gordon Ridley
>
> *Dive Sussex* by Kendall McDonald
>
> *Dive Wight & Hampshire* by K. McDonald and M. Pritchard
>
> *Dive Dorset* by John & Vicki Hinchcliffe
>
> *Dive South Devon* by K. McDonald and D. Cockbill
>
> *Dive South Cornwall* by Richard Larn
>
> *Dive North East* by Dave Shaw and Barry Winfield
>
> *Dive Yorkshire* by Arthur Godfrey and Peter Lassey

Contents

Area maps accompany Chapters 1-9. Smaller maps, photographs, and drawings showing locations of particular interest are included as appropriate.

NOTE: The site numbers in this volume run on from those in Volume II, *Dive North-west Scotland*, which covers the area from the Sound of Mull to Duncansby Head. This numbering system will continue in Volume IV for sites in Western Isles and Hebridean Outliers, including St Kilda, and freshwater sites in Scotland. See *"How to use this book".*

Returning from a dive in the shadow of the towering cliffs of Foula, a little-explored island off Shetland. (See Chapter 8.)

Preface

HERE, at long last, is Volume III of the Diver Guide to Scotland. It is not the final volume in the series. When the books were planned several years ago, I had rather less information on the far northern and western areas. However, the intervening time has allowed much more information to be collected and has necessitated splitting the original third volume into two. Consequently, this volume will shortly be followed by a final volume covering the Western Isles and Hebridean Outliers, including St. Kilda, and freshwater sites in Scotland.

The plan of this volume is to describe the sites North from the border at Berwick on Tweed along the East coast to arrive at Duncansby Head (593 sites later). These are followed by the challenging and intriguing diving in the Northern Isles of Orkney (including Scapa Flow) and Shetland. An introductory chapter discusses how to select good sites.

When I planned the books in the early 1980s not too much was generally known about diving around the far northern and western islands of Scotland. How dramatically that has changed! My friends and I have made many expeditions to these island waters over the last few years. Many friends have contributed important information on remoter areas, and finally, and very satisfyingly, many of the readers of the first two volumes have written in with extra information. All of this has hugely expanded the coverage possible for Orkney (218 sites), Scapa Flow (154 sites) and Shetland (522 sites).

Many people have helped me with the dive site details. I plan to list them all at the end of the project. However, especial thanks must go to a relatively small number of people who have consistently provided information on many dive sites. In this volume these are George Brown, Andy Carter, and Eric Thomson.

Notwithstanding the large number of sites described in this volume, it must be obvious that there are huge numbers of dives just awaiting discovery. It should also be borne in mind that most of the dive sites are described from the information resulting from one visit by one diver under one specific set of conditions; due caution should therefore be exercised in their interpretation and application.

The author and publisher would be very grateful, therefore, to receive any information on extra sites and conditions, and for information that updates and extends those already described.

Launching down the slipway at Howton Bay, Scapa Flow. (See Chapter 7.)

How to use
this book

This work is divided into four separately published volumes. Volume I covers the West coast from the Solway to Fort William, including Islay and Jura; Volume II covers the West coast from Mull to Cape Wrath and also includes the North coast; Volume III covers the Northern Isles and the East coast; Volume IV completes the series and covers the Western Isles and their Outliers.

Each volume is divided into two parts – a detailed listing of dive sites, and a number of general sections. I must emphasise the point made in Volume I, therefore, and this is that the general chapters and the appendices of each volume are intended to be complementary. To help your understanding the dive sites are numbered consecutively throughout the four volumes.

The work represents a greater undertaking than the other books in the 'Diver Guide' series, so I have been obliged to considerably condense and restrict the information. In many cases I have extra information on many of the sites, (especially on some of the wreckings). There is space to include comprehensive information on only the outstanding sites. I will be pleased to correspond, on specific points; please use the site numbers in any correspondence.

Each of the chapters describing a specific area is prefaced by general information on that area, and concluded with details of relevant local facilities and emergency services. Note that I have not usually quoted details of the secretaries of local diving clubs, as these are changed frequently. The headquarters of the parent organisations (addresses in appendix) can supply current lists upon request.

Accommodation of various types is widely available in most, though not all, of the areas covered by this volume, and it is only mentioned when there are specific reasons for this. The Scottish Tourist Board publishes excellent annual booklets covering accommodation to suit all tastes. There are also accommodation guides produced by the local tourist offices.

Access to dive sites is only mentioned where it is not obvious. Generally access is via small boats; the exception is where there is access to shore dives from a road along the shore. Because of the complexity of the coastline and the fact that many sites are accessible by several routes, I

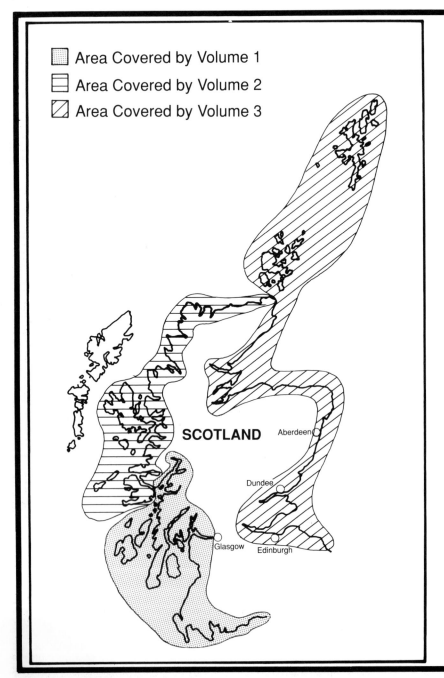

Area Covered by Volume 1
Area Covered by Volume 2
Area Covered by Volume 3

SCOTLAND Aberdeen

Dundee

Glasgow Edinburgh

Areas covered in Volumes I, II and III

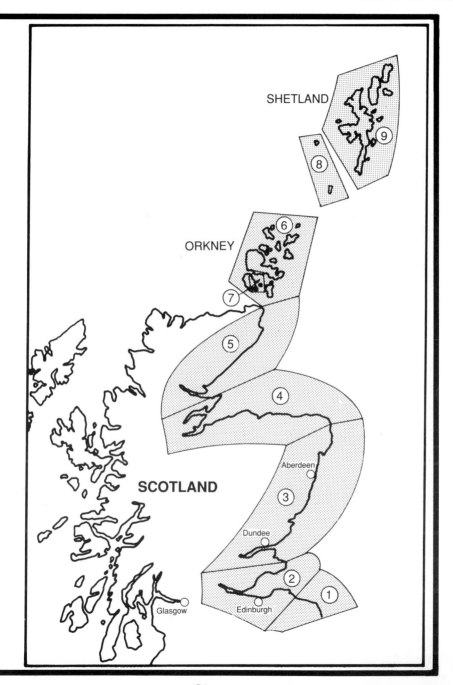

Chapter areas

Precipitous cliffs along the east coast of Fair Isle, which offers a number of magnificent, albeit challenging, dive sites. (See Chapter 8.)

have integrated the descriptions of small boat, charter vessel, shore, and wreck dives.

Sites are described from the Border, near Berwick-upon-Tweed, to Duncansby Head, at the East of the North coast. The Northern Isles of Orkney and Shetland are then treated. Scapa Flow is felt to be of such importance to divers that it has been allocated a separate chapter. A number of sites that have not yet been dived have been indicated where it is felt that they have importance. This is made clear in the text, and further information would be welcome. Similarly quite a number of wrecks are mentioned when their position may only be known approximately. These points of general information are still given site numbers for reference purposes.

Usually each numbered site refers to a specific point on the chart, but sometimes a whole area of coastline is covered under one site. Each site is described in terms of access (where this is not obvious), tidal stream data (if relevant), depth and bottom profile, unusual dangers, and any special precautions that may be necessary. Attention is drawn to interesting underwater features, such as rock scenery, marine life, and the visibility. Wrecks are briefly described, together with how to find them. There is obviously not the space to describe all the wrecks fully; however, I have included sets of transits where these are known to me and when they are appropriate. As I stated in Volume I, there is still some secrecy and furtiveness in this area!

Reference is often made to Admiralty charts and Ordnance Survey maps. The information contained in these complements much of the information given in this work and it is essential that you refer to them, and also to other sources of information, as frequently as possible. I have assumed, in fact, that you will use this guide in conjunction with the appropriate OS 1:50,000 map and Admiralty chart.

Six-figure national grid references are given for almost all sites, except those few that are well out to sea, where this information would be irrelevant. Considerable care has been taken over the accuracy of their details; they are mainly taken from the OS 1:25,000 maps where these are available. Additionally, latitudes and longitudes are given for most wrecks and offshore sites; the grid references given for wrecks are often approximate, and are mainly only intended to enable you to find the general area on the map. Note that a 6-figure grid reference specifies a square of side 100m, whereas latitude and longitude to seconds specifies a 31m square. (If quoted only to minutes then 1852m square is specified.)

Bear in mind that many of the areas, especially among the islands, do not lend themselves to ready division into chapters. It would be well to check chapters describing adjacent areas to find extra sites available from any particular base. The best way to deal with this is to examine the site maps for each chapter; these have all the sites numbered on them and should give a rapid cross check on relevant chapter contents. Most of the sites are given the title of the land features nearest to them.

Diving at Steggies Rocks, south Shetland: choosing a site appropriate to your experience and your equipment is a vital part of good dive planning.

Site Selection
in Scotland

TO MAKE the most of your time when diving in Scotland means carefully picking the best time of year to maximise the chances of good weather and good underwater visibility. It also means ensuring that your equipment – diving and boating – is prepared, and that your companions are similarly organised. If you have hired a charter vessel, you must brief the skipper adequately so that you both understand clearly what you would like to achieve. However, there is one factor that is even more important, in some ways, than all these. And that is the selection of the dive sites. One way of doing this, naturally, is to consult the four volumes of this guide. However, the Scottish coastline is enormous, and there are many superb sites yet to be discovered and dived for the first time. So how are good sites selected? My method has evolved over the years. It involves adding experience and knowledge to natural animal cunning.

Admiralty charts are the best source of all, but sometimes these do not exist at a large enough scale to be useful. I can let you into a secret here – there appears to be a second series of charts produced by the Admiralty and restricted to Services users only. These are certainly sometimes at a larger and more useful scale, and some of you, at least, may have access to these on occasions. Where large scale charts are not available, the Ordnance Survey 1:25,000 and particularly the 1:10,000 maps can be of some help. Obviously they do not give depths, though the fine detail of coastal features can sometimes give an indication. A further source of mapped information is the detailed 1:50,000 geological maps of Scotland.

Next come the Admiralty and other pilot books. These contain much background information, and notes about reefs, shoals, tidal streams etc., all of which are of considerable use in dive planning. There are a series of specialist publications – Scottish Mountaineering Club publications, mountaineering guides to coastal cliffs, canoeing publications, sea and freshwater fishing guides – which all contain odds and ends of useful information. And there are many general publications on the Scottish coast and islands which often contain snippets of information about coastal features and about vessels being lost. Additionally, there are several books published listing wrecks themselves. One of the primary sources of wreck information is the Hydrographic Dept's wreck printouts, though these are very expensive in quantity.

This is the only set of dive guide books to cover the Scottish coast systematically and comprehensively. However, there are a few smaller guides to some areas. There is also the Scottish Sub Aqua Club's guide to Scottish dive sites, though this has not attempted to be as comprehensive or as systematic as this work; details of 358 sites have been published in 33 parts (34 articles) since January 1979.

Of course, when you are visiting an area you should consult the local divers and branches, the dive centres (if applicable), and the local coach (BSAC or SSAC). You should not neglect to check through back issues of the diving magazines to consult articles that may have been written about your intended area.

A close examination of charts will reveal depths in general, and the sites of underwater shoals and reefs, where isobaths run close together or even disappear into each other, and the location of foul ground and wrecks. They will also give tidal data in narrows and round headlands. Large scale Ordnance Survey maps enable you to find and examine fine coastal detail; this is especially useful on some of the rugged and grossly indented headlands of the North. They will also enable you to prospect for launch spots that suit your particular boat equipment. Finally, they can be a guide when no detailed chart is produced.

The coastal sheets of the maps of the Geological Survey can be an unsuspected source of information for divers. If you compare these carefully with the Ordnance Survey maps of the same scale you may gain useful data. The rock type can be determined. Where this is soft and the coast is eroding without the presence of strong tidal streams, then it is likely that depths just off the coast will be shallow and the bottom covered with sediment; where the rock is harder then there may well be underwater cliffs, especially if tidal streams are strong. This of course, is also a function of the raised beach and submarine shelf phenomena, as these can also determine depths close to the shore.

Geological maps will also show where dykes run into the sea. If these are softer than the surrounding rock, then they will erode to form geos (Gaelic for a chasm or creek) and channels, which often make spectacular dives. Geological faults can also permit selective erosion and/or indicate the possibility of channels, gullies and tunnels. Conversely, if the intruded rock in a dyke is hard, then the dyke will form a rocky reef which, on a sediment-covered bottom, will present an oasis for the colonisation of sessile life, together with the shoals of fish that often frequent the larger reefs.

The angle at which rocks dip towards the earth can also indicate good dive sites. Inclined rocks can erode to provide ledges and crevices which marine life (of the nipping variety) is usually very happy to colonise. When rocks which are prone to erosion form the bottom they may well erode to form overhangs under which solitary fish can make their home.

The wreck diver will be well aware that wrecks will be best preserved in deeper water. Near the shore in shallow water wrecks break up. Wooden wrecks will break up and disappear faster than metal ones. Usually, when diving on old wooden wrecks, all you will see will be fragments and artefacts. As a general rule, the bigger, deeper and newer the better!

The process of locating wrecks breaks down into three areas – research, then the dry and wet searches. Initial research begins with a suspicion, which is then followed up by checking in books, wreck registers, old newspapers, local archives, old charts, and by talking to local fishermen and perhaps wreck survivors. As well as local sources of information one can check with the national organisations such as the Admiralty Hydrographic Dept (Beadon Road, Taunton, Somerset), the Board of Trade (War Risks Insurance Office, Parliament Square House, 34/36 Parliament Street, London, SW1), the Shipping Editor of the Corporation of Lloyds (Lime Street, London, EC3), Trinity House (The Secretary, Tower Hill, London EC3), and the Maritime Museum (Greenwich, London, EC10).

The dry search may merely involve following transits and bearings from locals and/or charts. Alternatively, various sophisticated electronic aids can be employed. Decca navigators and radio direction finding equipment can be very helpful if they are available. A low level aerial search can be useful if you have the funds. The use of side scan sonar is also excellent, though most of us have to make do with an ordinary echo sounder. The proton magnetometer can narrow down the area of search relatively quickly, though they are not the great panacea that advertisers make out. Then we get down to dragging and grappling for a positive contact with the wreck, before we finally commit divers to the water in the "wet" search. Time spent on research and in the dry search is never wasted. And a couple of hours on the surface is infinitely preferable to committing divers to the water too soon.

Divers especially interested in marine life have evolved their own criteria for good dives. Remember that life is richest where there is strongish tidal flow. Wrecks also provide an excellent artificial reef type of habitat for life.

The underwater photographer also has special demands. Usually he will want good underwater scenery, like rocks, boulders, cliffs, geos, and tunnels. Then he wants good visibility. The appropriate factors are discussed below, and remember the basic tenet – "further north west is best". He also wants good life and good wrecks, like all other divers.

We must differentiate between locating good sites in general, and making sure we arrive at the sites when conditions are favourable. The main variable factors are the weather and underwater visibility; of course, the latter is somewhat controlled by the former. Visibility is virtually always better away from sandy and especially muddy bays, near headlands and over rocky ground, and the further offshore the better. Fast tidal streams usually make for better visibility, as does the flood tide.

In estuaries or rivers visibility is often reduced by sediment-rich freshwater run-off. Near towns, industrial and human pollution can reduce visibility. Shallow shores facing the prevailing weather will stir up rapidly when the wind and swell increases. Finally, all the factors affecting plankton blooms can grossly affect underwater visibility. Visibility in freshwater is more predictable – lochs are always yellow/brown and peaty. Rivers are only clear at times of reduced water flow. This is usually in early summer, but the possibility of clear water under ice, when most incoming water is frozen, can also be considered by the young and hardy.

Diving in the St Abbs and Eyemouth Marine Reserve, which extends down to the 50m isobath in an area running from Greenends Gully to Pettico Wick.

CHAPTER 1

Berwick-upon-Tweed to Dunbar

LYING AT THE very South east of Scotland, the Berwickshire coastline includes two very popular diving areas – Eyemouth and St. Abb's. St. Abb's is 10 miles North of Berwick-upon-Tweed and only 4 miles off the A1 trunk road. It is reached from the South by turning off the A1 at Burnmouth, initially making for Eyemouth, then turning for Coldingham on the A1107; St. Abb's is just a short hop on along the B6438. From the North turn off the A1 just South of Cockburnspath along the A1107 to Coldingham, where you turn left for St. Abb's about 2 miles away.

The geology of the Berwickshire coast is informative for the diver attempting to understand the dive sites. From the Border a series of low limestone cliffs run North to the 300-500 feet high igneous felsite rocks of St. Abb's Head. These igneous rocks then decline in height and continue to Cockburnspath where Old Red Sandstone appears. Finally at Barns Ness, towards Dunbar, Carboniferous limestone forms the coastal scenery. The shore from the Border to Cockburnspath is one of the finest pieces of Scotland's (and Britain's) eastern coastline.

The geology, of course, controls access to the water either for boats or on foot. In many places the coastal cliffs prevent access to the water, but all the settlements allow access, and many have launching facilities. Shore access is also possible at many of the bays.

The wildlife is largely typical of northern farmland and moorland. Berwickshire between the Lammermuir Hills and the coast is an important farming area. The headland of St, Abb's is, of course, a significant seabird colony, with guillemots, razorbills and other cliff-nesting seabirds breeding in large numbers.

From the Border to Eyemouth the coast is low and quite sandy in places; little diving is done. The Eyemouth shoreline is low and rocky, with only quite shallow depths off the coast; the Eyemouth area has gained popularity as a nationally-known diving area only over the last few years. This has

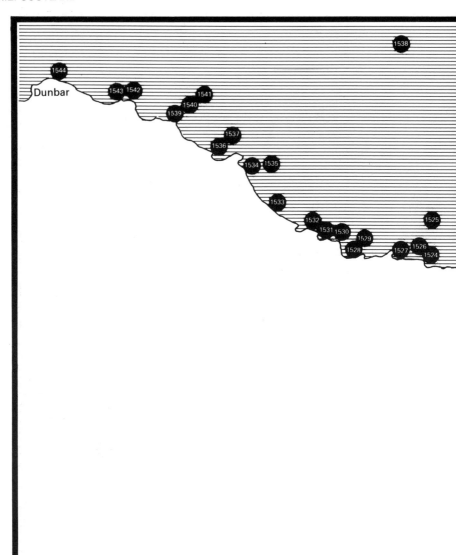

BERWICK ON TWEED TO DUNBAR

Dive Sites: Chapter 1

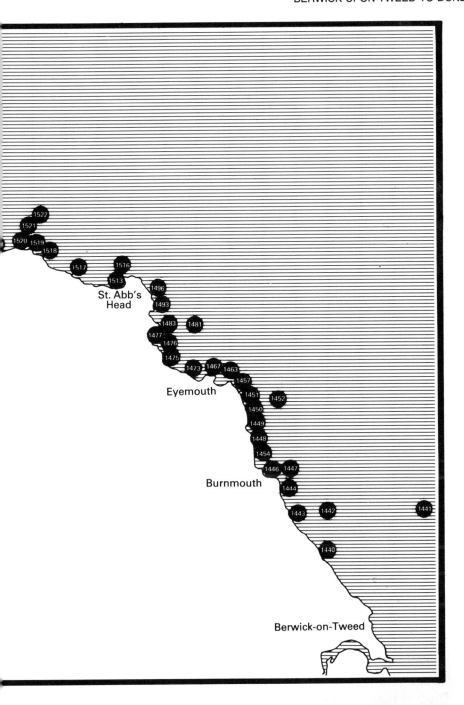

been very largely due to the efforts of one man – Lawson Wood – and his setting up in 1979 of the Barefoots Marine Reserve. Barefoots is a revolutionary reserve with very reasonable rules (don't remove marine life); as virtually all diving is from the shore, and as access to this is over land part-owned by Lawson (Northburn Caravan Site), he has pretty effective control. The curious name – Barefoots – originates from a garrison of French and Scottish soldiers who, roused from their sleep and in their bare feet, successfully repulsed an attack by English troops. Facilities at Barefoots include a fully-stocked dive shop, comprehensive spares, equipment hire, compressed air, caravan accommodation and bar food. An 8m charter boat can be hired.

Lawson Wood's initiative has now been followed by the creation in 1981 of the St. Abb's Head Wildlife Reserve, which has been set up to conserve the wildlife on the headland, mainly breeding seabirds, and also to prevent the removal of marine life. This grew into the St. Abb's and Eyemouth Marine Nature Reserve which was opened by David Bellamy in August 1984. The reserve extends from Greenends Gully in the South to Pettico Wick and has a seaward limit of the 50m isobath – the rules are simple – don't take or disturb any wildlife. There is a summer warden who will assist divers.

St. Abb's gives splendid rocky diving in fairly shallow water, though the boat dives off the Head itself can be somewhat deeper. St. Abb's has a very long tradition as a diving area, and particularly with English BSAC Branches it has been popular since the origins of sport diving in Britain.

The coastline from St. Abb's Head to Dunbar is a mixture of rocky headlands, sandy bays and rocky foreshore. It is not fully explored, though many sites have been examined; the area would amply repay more detailed investigation. There are also quite a number of offshore wrecks that would be well worthy of research by budding wreck detectives.

The diving of Berwickshire is frankly not typically Scottish in flavour, but it is very rewarding nonetheless. It has the great advantage of being relatively uncommitting, compared to many of the West Coast sites. Depths rarely exceed 15m, visibility is often 10m or more (though rarely in the depths of winter). Night diving is best from either Pettico Wick or Little Leeds; it is forbidden at St. Abb's and is unwise at Eyemouth. The sites are all exposed to winds from the North to East quarter and unfortunately the prevailing winds are from the North to North east – phone the coastguard or harbourmaster before making a long journey for a day's diving.

However, I can wholeheartedly recommend the area to you and, if you take an inflatable, you will find the more inaccessible sites on the headlands to be virtually unfrequented when the harbour areas are thronged with eager, fresh-faced divers. Tidal streams between Berwick and the Firth of Forth are generally weak, with springs rates not exceeding 1 knot. At Berwick LW slack at +0010 Dover, HW slack at −0605 Dover; at Barns Ness LW slack at HW Dover, HW slack at −0600 Dover; at the Forth LW slack at −0250 Dover, HW slack at +0315 Dover. Off the exposed headlands, however, springs tidal streams can reach 3-4 knots.

Although I have visited the areas covered in this chapter frequently since 1970, and dived many of the sites, I am especially indebted to Lawson Wood and George Davidson (both of Berwickshire Divers) for much additional information.

Berwick to Eyemouth

1440 Berwick to Burnmouth. Flat and sandy, though with the occasional kelp-covered reef at about 10-15m further offshore.

1441 Wreck of the SS "Egholm". A 1317 ton, 78m long vessel torpedoed by submarine in 1945 with the loss of five lives. The approximate position is 55 50N 01 52W, 5.5 miles North east of Berwick in a chartered depth of 64m with a clearance of 40m.

1442 Wreck of the "Barron Stjernblad", 1 mile South east of Ross Point. A 991 ton Danish vessel which sank in 1917 at 55 50N 02 02W in about 25m of water. The charted clearance is 15m.

1443 Hilton Bay. NT972572. There is strenuous shore access by following a culvert leading from the A1 under the railway and on to a steep grass slope leading to the sea. The diving over shallow, flat, kelp-covered rock split by a few gullies does not justify the effort!

1444 Ross Point, Burnmouth. NT966606. Shore access to shallow rocks while further offshore long, low rocky ribs rise above coarse sand. Lots of small marine life.

1445 South Carr. The rock strata have produced a series of reefs ranging in depth from 10-20m and running parallel to the shore. The seaward edges are vertical and are covered with hydroids. There is also a large bed of feather stars.

1446 Burnmouth. NT959611. A shallow training site beside the slipway among outcrops of rock at depths of up to 8m.

1447 Ross Carrs, Burnmouth. NT966608. Parallel, 1m-high reefs running North/South at a depth of about 15m on a sandy seabed. Lots of crustaceans and small fish in the crevices.

1448 Hawks' Ness. NT955629. The cliffs drop underwater to 10m and then give way to sand.

1449 Horse Head. NT955632. Three caves are visible from the sea. The centre cave runs well back into the cliffs and there is an airspace all the way. A pleasant dive, but only in calm conditions. Depth of seabed is 10m.

1450 The Cauldrons. There is a 7m-deep 5m-wide channel which ends in an amphitheatre where a hole gives access into a circular chamber. The wall can be followed out to sea and South through a large archway at 9m. This site rivals the well-known dive through Cathedral Rock at St. Abb's.

1451 Wreck of the SS "President", Agate Point. NT955642. A 1946 ton vessel that ran aground in 1928 at 55 54 00N 02 07 30W just off Agate Point. She became a total loss and the remains lie completely broken up and covered with marine life in shallow water. The wreck is owned by the Eyemouth Sub-Aqua Club.

1452 Unknown wreck, ¾ mile East of Agate Point. Charted at 55 52N 02 03W in a depth of about 35m with a charted clearance of 20m.

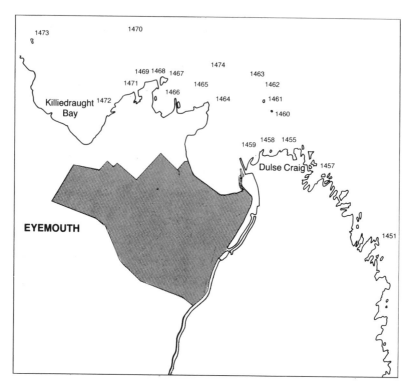

DIVE SITES AROUND EYEMOUTH

1453 Unknown wrecks, off Eyemouth. There are at least 3 more wrecks lying out to sea within 3 miles of Eyemouth. Another 7 wrecks lie within a 9 miles arc seaward of Eyemouth. They are all charted as position approximate and they all lie in water of 60m depth or greater.

Eyemouth Area

There is a profusion of dive sites hereabouts, many resulting from the efforts of Lawson Wood. They are all included for completeness and because of the nearby provision of diving back-up facilities. It should be noted, however, that in other diving areas the whole section might only warrant two or three dive sites. Shore access should be assumed unless stated otherwise.

1454 Fancove Head. NT956627. A boat dive on an exposed headland. Depths to 20m with many overhanging rocky outcrops and arches containing crevices filled with life.

1455 Green Ends Gully. NT948647. Access down a rough track to the West of the golf course. A sheltered, sandy bottom at 12m fringed with life-encrusted reefs. A natural arch is situated to the East of the large gully. Note that there is a sewage outfall in Nestends, just East of this site.

1456 Gunsgreenhill Gully. NT954641. Very similar to Green Ends Gully.

1457 Ramfauds. NT950646. A large gully leading to a complicated seabed with interconnected channels. Difficult shore access may well favour a snorkelling visit.

1458 Dulse Craig. NT948647. An easy shore entry by a large block of concrete. A bottom of green weed eventually gives way to rock. Follow the cliffs round to the West to examine interesting crevices.

1459 Eyemouth Harbour. NT947646. Cars can be parked at the eastern end of the harbour, the water can then be entered and followed round to Hettleskur. Keep well clear of the fairway.

1460 Hurker Rock. NT948649. Offshore rocks demanding boat cover as they are swept by the main tidal stream. Depths reach 16m amid scenery that is quite dramatic by the local standards and probably give the best dive in the Eyemouth area. Boat access.

1461 Hincar Rocks. NT947650. Similar to Hurker Rock.

1462 Wreck of the "Mauritania". NT947651. This steam fishing vessel lies to the North west of Buss Craig. The wreck is well broken with the boiler being notable; there is prolific fish life among the wreckage. Boat access.

1463 Buss Craig. NT947651. Good underwater scenery and life. Boat access.

1464 Luff Hard Reef. NT94650. A shallow rocky dive to 15m in places. Lots of crevices, nooks and crannies hide quantities of marine life. Boat access from Eyemouth Harbour.

1465 West of Luff Hard Reef. NT943650. Midway between Luff Hard Reef and Little Leeds, the bottom is one of rock and sand at 10-12m. Boat access. Note that there is a sewage outfall in this vicinity and the visibility is usually impaired.

1466 Little Leeds. NT941650. The large bay to the East of the caravan park gives very sheltered diving to depths of up to 12m. The bottom is a profusion of rocks, gullies and an archway, all covered by a kelp forest. Access by scrambling down the cliff.

1467 Hairy Ness Point. NT942652. The headland East of the caravan park. There are many interesting rock formations covered with a kelp forest and profuse marine life.

1468 Divers' Hole. NT941651. A dark cave with a silty bottom to the West of Hairy Ness. Leopard spotted gobies are particularly noted. Entry is made by a narrow channel at high tide from Little Leeds Bay.

1469 Blind Buss. NT941651. The small North-facing headland to the East of the caravan park. A splendid 10m-deep cliff face covered with encrusting life.

1470 Conger Reef. NT939651. Just South east of Weasel Loch is a small reef with holes containing conger eels and a famous resident wolf fish (which regularly appears in dive magazines and underwater photography competitions).

1471 Weasel Loch. NT939650. Access from the cliff-top by a new set of steps down a steep cliff to the sheltered entry point. A good training site with a depth of 9m. A rock wall with lots of small marine life is the main feature.

1472 Killydraught Bay. NT935650. Access by a long, steep path to the beach. The bay is initially solid rock, then a kelp bed to 12m followed by flat bedrock with coarse sand patches to beyond 30m.

1473 Callercove Point. NT933653. A bottom of large boulders at 10m with lots of fish life in the crevices. Boat access.

1474 Fold Buss. NT939658 (approx.). A submarine shoal, about ½ mile North of Weasel Loch, that rises from about 25m to about 13m. Fold Buss is part of a continuous reef system that extends from Hurker Rock to St. Abbs. A 20m wall can be located and this has excellent potential for further explorations. Deep water species, such as Bolocera anemones and Thiauria hydroids are found here in shallow water. Boat access.

St. Abb's Area

A few simple rules must be followed when diving from St. Abb's harbour: Do not dive in the harbour or the fairway. Do not remove any marine life. Do not dive when the Harbourmaster has said that the pier is closed due to rough weather. Pay any relevant launching fees to the Harbourmaster.

1475 Yellow Craig, Coldingham Bay, NT924662. Shore access from behind the Youth Hostel. Either side of the promontory can be dived to reach a sandy seabed at about 5m.

1476 Milldown Point, Coldingham Bay. NT919664. Similar to Yellow Craig; depths to 5m.

1477 The Kip, Coldingham Bay. NT919668. Good snorkelling and shallow diving along the North west side of Coldingham Bay. Depths reach 6m.

1478 Ebb Carrs. NT924672. The seabed is one of deep, impressive canyons with large shoals of fish in the summer months.

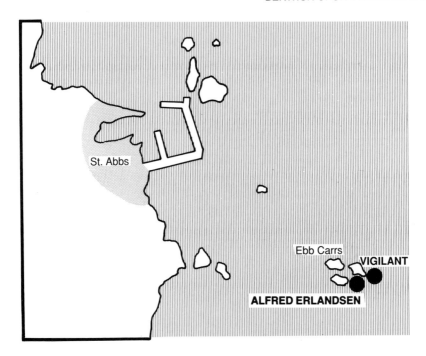

WRECKS OF THE 'VIGILANT' AND 'ALFRED ERLANDSEN'

1479 Wreck of the "Alfred Erlandsen". Ebb Carrs. NT924672. A 954-ton steamer completely wrecked in 1907 on Ebb Carrs in 12-15m. The wreck is completely broken up and the boilers, plates and spars are all kelp-covered. The wheel is displayed in the Scoutscroft Diving Centre.

1480 Wreck of the "Vigilant". NT924672. A new MFV that hit Ebb Carrs in 1976 after only one week at sea and sank in 30 seconds. She was dived 3 days later! She is smashed to pieces with only the steel wheelhouse remaining, wrapped in ropes and netting in a depth of 14m. See BSAC Wreck Register, Wreck 180.

1481 Unknown wreck, 1 mile East of Ebb Carrs. Charted at 55 54 00N 02 05 24W in about 40m of water.

1482 Thistley Briggs. NT922673. After passing through the archway at Cathedral Rock, go South west down a gully under the kelp to find more arches in a depth of 13m. Lots of life.

1483 Cathedral Rock. NT923673. As a trainee diver in Leeds I was weaned on tales of the legendary Cathedral Rock of St. Abb's. Having done a few dives since, including some in rather imposing places, I have to say that

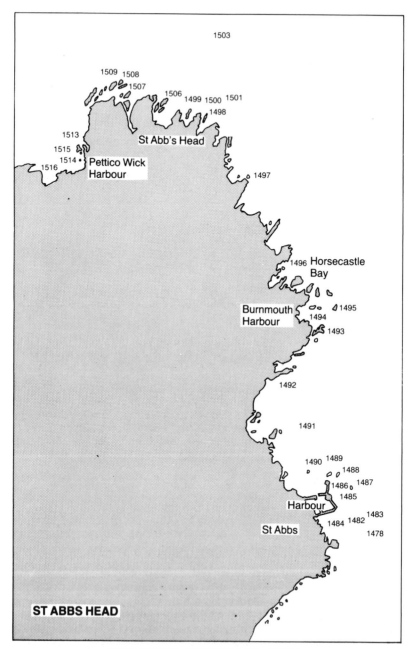

1503

1509 1508
1507
1506 1499 1500 1501
1498

1513
1515
1514
1516

St Abb's Head

Pettico Wick
Harbour

1497

1496 Horsecastle
Bay

Burnmouth
Harbour

1495
1494
1493

1492

1491

1490 1489
1488
1486 1487
1485

Harbour
1483
1484 1482
1478

St Abbs

ST ABBS HEAD

DIVE SITES AROUND ST ABBS

the site's impressiveness may have been a little overstated in the past. But remember – the upper keyhole in the Cathedral was the cradle of this four-volume work.

The rock lies in 13m of water, and just shows at low tide. This is the best way to find it, though it can also be found by swimming out about 100m from the South west channel from the harbour wall, while keeping the South wall of the harbour just "open" until you see the weed below. Location by compass is quite difficult, as there appears to be a magnetic anomaly.

The rock has an arch at the base about 5m high, 6m wide and 8m long. Above this is a small keyhole through which a diver with tank can just pass, though not in a heavy surge. All of the rock surfaces are solidly festooned with life, with a number of anemone species being predominant; fish life is notable too. If you turn left after passing through the arch you can circumnavigate the rock by turning hard left at a low but well-defined notch reached after about 50m. Highly recommended.

1484 Haven Rocks. NT922673. A deepening, kelp-filled gully running out from the corner of the South harbour wall. Profuse fish life.

1485 Scott's Rock. NT922674. This forms a pleasant gully with the South face of Broad Craig. Particularly rich in anemones.

1486 Broad Craig. NT922674. This rock faces the harbour wall in 10m of water. A swim all the way round yields a great diversity of marine life. Squat lobsters and conger eels are noted.

1487 Little Green Carr. NT923674. A little-dived rock that yields a pleasant circuit in 12m of water that can be completed in one dive. Quantities of marine life such as spider crabs, squat lobsters, sea lemons, starfish, soft coral and sponges.

1488 Big Green Carr. NT922675. This deeply-undercut rock lies North east from the North of the harbour. It has an imposing natural amphitheatre on the seaward side, with deep parallel clefts. There is also a short, almost-vertical tunnel on the shore side. A picturesque dive, normally including conger eels and wolf fish.

1489 Jonah's Rock. NT921675. Just North of the end of the North Pier. The kelp-covered rock gives a dive to 12m.

● **All the sites** from here to Pettico Wick require a boat for access. Launch at St. Abb's harbour.

1490 Maw Carr (Seagull Rock). NT915679. This lies 30m off the car park. The South side has kelp-covered rocky gullies floored with sand at 12m; the North side has a deep, dark cave almost, but not quite, running through the rock. The nearby sewage outfall attracts shoals of fish.

1491 St. Abb's Bay. NT919678. About 200m offshore the seabed is flat sand with great lengths of trawl cables, heart urchins and sea mice. Depth 13m. Further offshore the depths reach 20m and then to beyond 30m onto a shingle seabed, which can be quite dark. Tidal streams can reach 1 knot.

1492 White Heugh. NT919670. Sandy seabed at 17m after a rocky cliff with plenty of life.

1493 Wuddy Rocks. NT921682. A dramatic dive in 3 huge canyon/archway systems in 10-15m of water. The channels vary in width from a few centimetres to 5m and are covered with life – alcyonium, tubularia and nudibranchs are particularly noted.

1494 Burnmouth Harbour. NT920683. Deceivingly named, this site is actually a large, sheltered cove backed by high sea cliffs. The rock outcrops continue underwater to give impressive cliff faces and canyons with lots of life.

1495 Big Black Carrs. NT921684. A good dive can be had inside the kelp. Drop down on the outside of large boulders. Wolf fish are greatly in evidence.

1496 Horsecastle Bay . NT918686. This is surrounded on three sides by high cliffs which, in springtime, are full of breeding seabirds. The seabed consists of sand and boulders at 12m.

1497 Black Gable. NT917691. A nice underwater gully and a cave running quite far back to a hole with daylight showing through. Approach from the Cauldron Cove side.

1498 Tyes Tunnel. NT913694. A spectacular shallow tunnel underneath St. Abb's lighthouse. Depths are 6-7m with walls covered with red and yellow sponges. Dive at midday in calm weather.

1499 Cleaver Rock. NT913694. Good underwater scenery with vertical rock faces and gullies that only just allow the passage of a diver. Depths, initially 12m, rapidly reach 20m amid a seabed of huge boulders.

1500 Cruves. NT914694. A spectacular dive varying in depth from 1-12m can be had under the lighthouse round a large rock and through an extensive channel. The landward end of Cruves has a small underwater notch that allows a diver to pass through to the West and into a deep ravine formed between Cruves and Goose. Very large pollack are noted.

1501 Craig Rock. NT915694. This lies directly under the lighthouse. Good underwater scenery with vertical rock faces and gullies. Just offshore the seabed drops to 20m onto sand with rocky ridges rising up to 13m.

1502 Unknown wreck, ¾ mile East of St. Abb's Head. Charted at 55 55 00N 02 07 00W as position approximate. The seabed is at 50m and the charted clearance is 35m. This wreck could be that of the destroyer "Strathrannoch" which lies upright, broken into three parts.

1503 Wreck of the "Glanmire". NT916697 (approx.) This wreck lies in a North east – South west direction at 55 55 36N 02 08 12W in 30m of water 300m almost due North from the lighthouse. The 75m-long vessel foundered in 1912 while on passage from Amsterdam to Grangemouth with

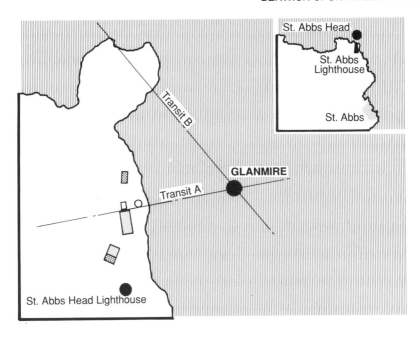

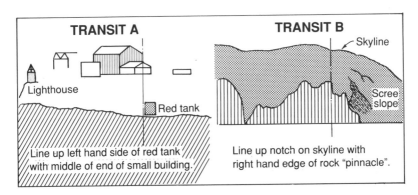

MARKS FOR THE 'GLANMIRE' (SITE 1503)

a general cargo. She is now completely broken up with the deck at seabed level. The boilers project about 5m above the shingle seabed and the four-bladed 4m iron prop and also the anchor are visible. The bows are the most substantial and spectacular portion and it is possible to enter one section. The wreckage is encrusted with Alcyonium and is the home of wolf fish, congers and other big fish, giving an excellent dive. Dive at slack water (or up to 1 hour each way at neaps) because the tidal streams are quite strong.

1504 Wreck of the "Rose of Sharon". 1 mile North north west of St. Abb's Head. A fishing vessel with nets set and holds filled, lost in 1977 at a depth of 60m; is charted at 55 56 00N 02 09 00W (3 miles out to sea) as position approximate. The depth is about 60m and the charted clearance is 28m.

1505 Wreck of the "Gasray". 2 miles from St. Abb's Head. Torpedoed in 1945 this 1406 ton merchant vessel has not been located by divers. No other positional details are known although Dunbar fishermen supposedly know the wreck's position.

1506 Foul Carr. NT912695. Good underwater scenery with vertical rock faces and gullies. Depths rapidly reach 20m on a bouldery seabed.

1507 Headland Cove. NT910694. A narrow, curving inlet with kelp-covered boulders, some rock faces and ribs of rock running out to sea. Huge plumose anemones are passed on the way to a depth of 20m followed by a brittle star bed dotted with Bolocera anemones.

1508 Skelly Rock. NT910696. A pleasant dive in a 14m deep gully, up and through a kelpy scramble and into a second channel with a sandy bottom at 10m. Large fish are noted.

1509 Floatcar Rock. NT909696. Kelp-covered boulders and ribs of rock running out to sea. About 200m North north west is a rock gallery with a row of several wolf fish at a depth of 20m.

1510 West Hurker. NT908695. Kelp-covered boulders, some rock faces and ribs of rock running out to sea.

1511 Wreck of the "Faraday". A 5533 ton, 120m long cable ship bombed and set on fire by German aircraft in 1941. She sank next day half a mile off St. Abb's Head with the loss of 16 lives. Ninety miles of her cable has been salvaged.

1512 Wreck of the SS "Bear". A 596 ton, 53m long vessel sunk by collision in 1891 with the loss of 13 lives in 50m+ deep water well offshore from St. Abb's Head. The position is known to Dunbar fishermen.

Pettico Wick

This site can be reached by boat, but the access road is now open again and it can be approached by a scramble from the shore, just as in the early days. Car parking space is available for 4 cars and entry to the private road is by permit (9am-1pm or 1pm-5pm; £3 per vehicle, £5 per vehicle and trailer). Pay the Ranger, Kevin Rideout. The access is down a steep grass slope to a recently-derelict slip which has now been renovated.

1513 Staple Rock, Pettico Wick. NT907692. Pleasant rocks leading to depth of 15m.

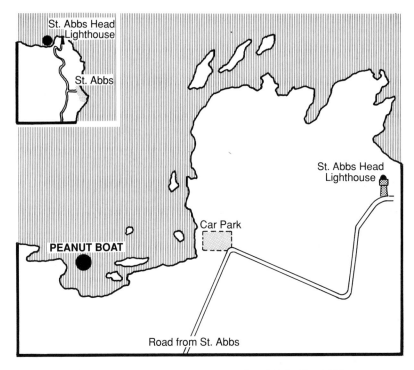

SITE 1516: THE PEANUT BOAT ('ODENSE')

1514 Pettico Wick. NT907691. The seabed slopes gently to seaward over gravel and rocks. Dragonets and blennies are noted. It is not worth the hassle, however, unless the other St. Abb's sites are inaccessible.

1515 Pettico Wick Tunnel. NT906692. In the centre of the bay there is a small tunnel in a depth of 7m in a rock called Wick Gaut.

1516 Wreck of the "Odense" (the "Peanut Boat"). NT906691. This was a 1756 ton coaster that sank in 1917 in Broadhaven Bay just West of Pettico Wick; it is an 80m snorkel directly out from Pettico Wick beach. The coaster lies in 5-12m and is completely broken up with kelp-covered plates scattered around, plus the boiler. See BSAC Wreck register, Wreck 174.

Pettico Wick to Dunbar

This whole shore is very exposed to winds from the North to East and is often subject to heavy seas.

1517 Pettico Wick to Fast Castle Head. High cliffs back the sea. The seabed slopes quite quickly to 40m and more about 400m offshore. The first part is thick kelp to 10-12m then bedrock with urchins and starfish. Below 20m is a thick brittlestar carpet, then sand and gravel patches before the sand grades into silt or mud between 30 and 40m. Boat access.

1518 Brander. NT873707. A sheer rock face to the North reaches a depth of 15m where there are arches, canyons and overhangs with a profusion of life. Boat access.

1519 Souter. NT869709. This is a prominent coastal stack 2.5 miles west of Pettico Wick. The diving is similar to Brander except that depths reach 20m. Boat access.

1520 Wheat Stack. NT862711. This stack lies just North of the cliffs of Fast Castle Head. It yields a good dive with depths to 16m. Boat access.

1521 Wreck of the SS "Nyon". Fast Castle Head. There is a tripod hoist on the cliffs which was used for rescue purposes. The wreck is surrounded by rock outcrops and lies in a line out to sea off a jagged spit of vertically-stratified rock below the hoist. The depth at low water is 3m. Some of the bow section is on the rocks and visible at low tide; the stern section was refloated and salvaged. Boat access.

1522 Fast Castle Head. NT862712. Fast Castle (the original "Wolf's Crag" of Sir Walter Scott's "Bride of Lammermuir") was a 14th century stronghold of the Homes family; it was fought over by the English and Scots in the 16th century. Underneath the castle there is a rocky shore with kelp-covered boulders leading to very nice underwater rock formations and a maximum depth of 20m. It is rumoured that there are a series of tunnels linking the sea-level cave with the remains of Fast Castle 100m above on the cliff-top. This is variously supposed to have been used for smuggling or to store a large sum in gold coin to raise a mercenary army against the English. Boat access.

1523 The Little Rooks. NT853710. This site can be identified by a bold cleft in the cliffs off which lie a small group of rocks. It may be that the wreck of the "Rose Middleton" lies hereabout; she was lost in the East Coast Fishing Fleet Disaster of 1881. Boat access.

1524 Meikle Poo Craig. NT827707. Shore access by a long steep path down the cliffs to an inlet in the shore rocks leading to a shallow reef in 8m of water followed by huge rock slabs.

1525 Unknown wreck. 1 mile North of Meikle Poo Craig. Charted at 56 56 30W 02 16 00W in about 25m of water.

1526 Cargill Rock. NT819710. A bouldery seabed at 10m with lots of crustaceans.

1527 Siccar Point. NT813710. A dramatic headland riven by a long, deep gully and featuring sheer cliff faces and large rock outcrops. Depths reach 18m close to shore and marine life is profuse. Boat access.

1528 Pease Bay. NT795710. Shore access to a shallow sandy bay suitable for snorkelling. There are rocks at each side of the bay.

1529 Wreck of the "Magicienne". This was a 116 feet long Danish auxiliary wooden schooner of 248 tons that went ashore, then slipped back into deeper water, in 1940. The quoted position is 55 56 00N 02 19 45W and this is in the shallows of Pease Bay.

1530 Little Hurker. NT790717. Just to the East of Cove Harbour there is a large submarine rock which provides many interesting crannies. Depths of 8-10m.

1531 Cove Harbour. NT788717. A tunnel to the East of the Bay leads through to a reef and a maximum depth of 10m. The North side of the harbour yields shallow reefs with gullies which are good for snorkelling. Access by a rough harbour track.

1532 Reed Point. NT780722. A very shallow rocky reef suitable for snorkelling.

1533 Bilsdean Creek. NT770727. Shallow snorkelling with shore access.

1534 The Reef. NT757744. A long spit of rock running out to sea gives a shallow dive along its sides at high tide. Lots of crustaceans.

1535 Unknown wreck. ¾ mile East north east of the Reef. Charted at 56 58N 02 22W in 13m of water.

1536 Chapel Point. NT739757. A broad shallow reef giving pleasant snorkelling.

1537 Wreck of HMS "Nymph". Reputed to be close to Chapel Point (NT740758), though there is also a report of it lying near Torness Point (NT748754).

1538 Wreck of SS "Halland". A 1264 ton, 73m long vessel bombed and sunk by aircraft in 1940 with the loss of 17 lives at 56 03N 02 17W, 6 miles North east of Chapel Point in 54m of water with a clearance of 37m.

1539 Wreck of HMS "Pallas", Barns Ness. (NT723773). This fifth rate sailing vessel is reputed to lie near the Barns Ness lighthouse, off which two large anchors lie in kelp.

1540 Ruddystone, off Barns Ness. NT722784. A submarine rock, which rises from 10m to within 5m of the surface, and is located ½ mile North of Barns Ness. Plenty of sea life. Boat access.

1541 Unknown wreck, Ruddystone. This is charted at 56 59 42N 02 26 24W immediately South east of Ruddystone.

1542 Vaultness. NT706783. Shallow reefs to 7m. Boat access.

1543 Siccar Reef. NT703800. Located at 55 56 32N 02 28 30W this rocky shoal rises to 8m from a 26m seabed. Lots of marine life because of the tidal stream. Dive at slack water unless you specifically wish to drift dive. Boat access.

1544 Meikle Spiker. NT684794. The southern headland of Dunbar Harbour. Very shallow reefs with poor marine life. Boat access.

Unknown wrecks of the South east Forth area. There are at least 7 other wrecks lying up to 6 miles offshore along the coast from Pettico Wick to Dunbar. Most are very deep but just within the range of experienced amateur divers. The positions are:

		Depth	Clear	
1545	56 01 30N 02 05 30W	62m	?	6.5 miles North of St. Abb's Head
1546	56 02N 02 12W PA	62m	?	6 miles North of Brander
1547	56 00 30N 02 13 00W PA	60m	45m	4.5 miles North of Fast Castle Head
1548	56 03 10N 02 16 45W PA	53m	?	7 miles North of Siccar point
1549	56 05 18N 02 24 54W	45m	44m	6 miles North of Barns Ness
1550	56 06 12N 02 25 18W	47m	45m	7 miles North of Barns Ness.
1551	56 03 42N 02 29 36W	37m	34m	3.5 miles North of Meikle Spiker.

Area information and services

Hydrographic charts: 160 St. Abb's Head to the Farne Islands 1:75,000; 175 Fife Ness to St. Abb's Head 1;75,000.
OS 1:50,000 maps: 67 Duns & Dunbar; 75 Berwick-upon-Tweed.
OS 1:25,000 maps: NT67/77 Dunbar; NT86/96 Eyemouth.
Local SSAC Branches: Berwickshire SSAC Branch (Lawson Wood, Northburn Caravan Park, Eyemouth 08907 50426).
Local independent dive clubs: Eyemouth & district SAC (A. Collin, Harbour Road, Eyemouth).
Air supplies: Barefoots Diving, Northburn Caravan Site (300 bar) (08907) 51050; Scoutscroft Caravan Park (200 bar).
Boat charter: MV Arctic Star (skipper: Alistair Crowe) Contact via Barefoots Diving.
Local weather: Edinburgh Weather Centre 031 246 8091.
Sea area: Forth.

Tidal constants:

	DOVER	LEITH
Eyemouth	+0334	−0029
Dunbar	+0359	+0006

Coastguard: MRSC Crail (0335) 666; CG Eyemouth (08907) 50348; Dunbar (0368) 63342.
Harbourmasters: Eyemouth (08907) 50223; Dunbar (0368) 63206.
Hospitals: Berwick Infirmary (0289) 7484.
Recompression chambers: Rosyth (038 34) 2121 ext. 3127.
Lighthouse: St. Abb's Head, Coldingham (03903) 272.
Doctor: Dr. Fenty, Coldingham (03903) 291.
Police: Eyemouth (08907) 50217; Coldingham (03903) 50217.
Garage: Coldingham (03903) 283.
Outboard repairs: Eyemouth Marine (08907) 50594.
St. Abb's Head Wildlife Reserve Ranger: Kevin Rideout Coldingham (03903) 443.
Vehicle recovery: AA – Edinburgh 031 225 8464; Galashiels (0896) 55615 (office hours only).
Local tourist informations: Eyemouth (08907) 50673; Dunbar (0386) 63353.
Accommodation: There are many hotels, guest houses and B & B establish-ments in the area. The following caravan sites are frequented by divers: Drone Hill Caravan Park, 2 miles North of St. Abb's on A1107. Scoutscroft Caravan Park, 1 mile back from St. Abb's at Coldingham. Coldingham Caravan Park. Northburn Caravan Park (Lawson Wood), on A1107 at Eyemouth.

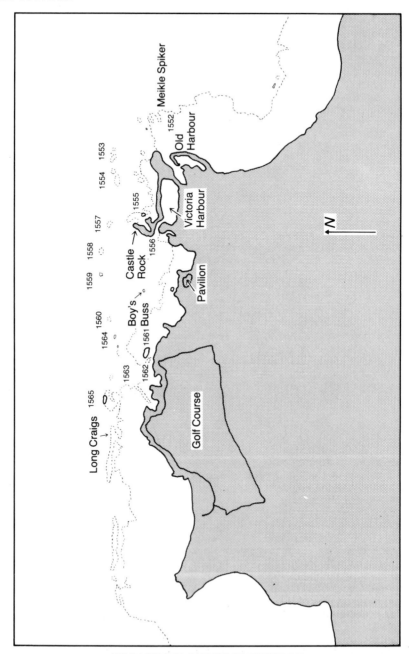

DIVE SITES AROUND DUNBAR

CHAPTER 2

Firth of Forth

FOR THE purposes of this chapter I shall define the Firth of Forth as running from Dunbar in the South via the Forth Road Bridge to Fife Ness in the North. This is a relatively popular diving area because of the concentration of local divers, both in Edinburgh and in Fife. The diving, however, is rather reminiscent of, though somewhat poorer than, the Firth of Clyde, in that the visibility can be rather poor, especially towards the head of the estuary. This diminishes the attraction of the area to visiting divers, though, like the Clyde, it has its local aficionados.

The River Forth is tidal as far as Stirling, though the Firth is normally taken as beginning at Kincardine, site of the 1936 Forth road bridge. At first the Firth broadens to 2.5 miles but 13 miles below Kincardine it narrows to 1 mile at the constriction of the dolerite sills of North and South Queensferry, the site of the 1890 railway bridge and 1963 road bridge, where the main shipping channel is almost 60m deep. Beyond these narrows the Forth gradually widen for about 40 miles before passing the Isle of May and reaching the North Sea.

The chief ports on the South are Leith, Granton, Bo'ness and Grangemouth; on the North are Methil and Burntisland, together with the naval base at Rosyth. There are numerous small fishing ports along both coasts.

The Lothian coast is generally low-lying in comparison with the West of Scotland and the Highland panoramas that form a backdrop to the Clyde estuary are absent here. Seekers of wild, dramatic places will be largely disappointed, although the area has many gentler charms. The Fifeshire scenery exhibits a remarkable diversity: its rich, rolling farmlands are interspersed with coalfield clutter. The wooded parks of the great estates, picturesque lochs and heathery hills are encircled by coastal dunes and rocky cliffs, with pretty fishing hamlets reminiscent of those of Cornwall. The soil is fertile and the climate favourable, thus Fife has the highest proportion of arable land of all the Scottish counties.

The description of the coast in detail is probably not worthwhile, though many minor features are of interest. There are many isolated shore rocks between Fife Ness and Pittenweem. Hereabouts the lowest of the old beaches has been cut away in places, giving height to the coastal cliffs. Between St. Monance and Elie there are several necks cutting through sandstone and limestones; the Ardross fault runs parallel to the coast for

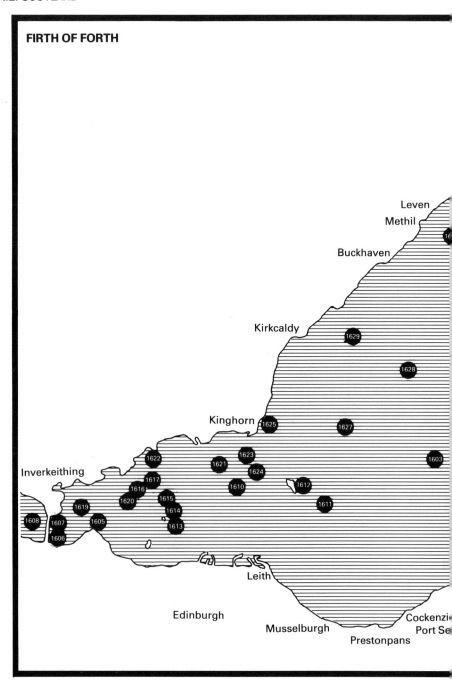

FIRTH OF FORTH

Leven
Methil
16
Buckhaven

Kirkcaldy
1629

1628

Kinghorn 1625
1627

1622
1623
1603
1621
Inverkeithing 1617
1624
1616
1610
1612
1619
1620 1615
1611
1608 1605 1614
1607 1613
1606

Leith

Edinburgh
Cockenzi
Musselburgh
Port Se
Prestonpans

Dive Sites: Chapter 2

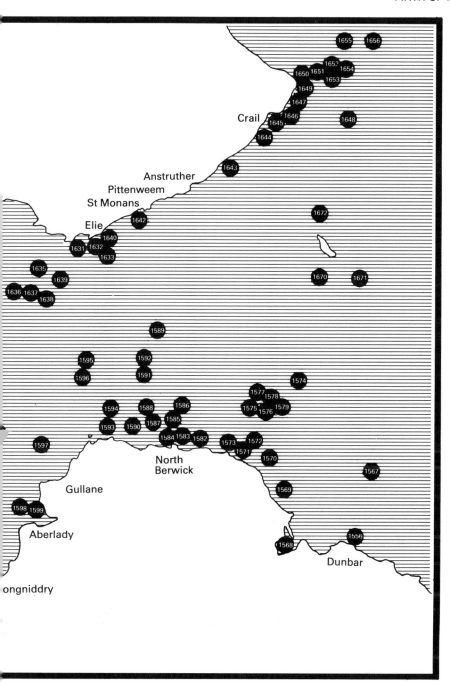

2 miles, determining the structure of the shore platform. Kincraig Point is a nearly vertical basalt precipice about 60m high, and there are several caves and chasms. Largo Bay is backed by the ancient, 290m high volcano of Largo Law. Between Leven and Kirkcaldy the coast is either built up or scarred by mining activity. The East coast coalfield is extensive although it is now being run down. At Kinghorn, Carboniferous sediments, lavas and sills reach the coast and, just North of Kinghorn, the sills run southwards out to sea for quite some distance. Moving up the Forth, the tidal water of former raised beach times reached well beyond Stirling, but the present water is so turbid that it is of virtually no interest to divers.

The small islands North and West of Edinburgh are built almost entirely of igneous rocks and represent parts of sills or dykes. Indeed the peninsula of North Queensferry is similar and is almost an island. Many of the rocks and islets are awash at high water, though Inchkeith reaches the 30m contour and has traces of the old "100 foot" raised beach. The Isle of May is one sill of dolerite which dips at a low angle to the North east. Thus the western side of the island reaches 46m and is steep, while the eastern side passes gradually below sea level.

Bass Rock is the best known landmark in the Firth of Forth. It is a volcanic plug, comparable to North Berwick Law and Taprain Law, 128m high and precipitous except to the South east. It has a long history, the first inhabitant being St. Baldred who died in 606. Bass Rock has the distinction of possessing the third biggest gannetry in the world.

Igneous structures are very important in explaining many of the minor coastal features. From Dalmeny to Prestonpans (i.e., the shoreline North of Edinburgh) has a well developed "100 foot" raised beach. From Mussel-borough to Port Seton the coast is largely built up. Aberlady Bay is a local nature reserve and has fine mudflats, sands and dunes, though of little interest to divers. Gullane Bay is also backed by dunes which give way to a rock platform leading to Eyebroughty Scar. The off-lying rocks hereabouts are all of volcanic origin, while the associated skerries are masses of volcanic ash. Basalts and agglomerates make the rock platform running to Gin Head. The coast here is composed of high cliffs of ash and breccia sometimes cut by dykes. The cliffs reach 30m at Tantallon Castle. The effects of erosion on this piece of coast depends upon the nature and resistance of the rocks; the very local complexities make for a very irregular coastline and, when combined with blown sand, this can be very attractive.

The South shores of the Firth of Forth are bordered by West Lothian, Mid Lothian and East Lothian. These are agricultural lands with an industrial overlay. The North shoreline is largely formed by the ancient Kingdom of Fife. Until the completion of the road bridges Fife was somewhat isolated from the rest of Scotland. Since then, however, its tourism has developed, aided by the beautiful coast of the East Neuk of Fife.

The wildlife of the area is not exceptional by Highland standards, and is that to be expected on northern farmland. An exception is the Bass Rock gannetry. In winter, the Firth of Forth is an important area for wintering duck and seabirds.

Access to the water is relatively easy, as much of the area is built up and quite a number of slips exist. Additionally, with the coast being relatively low-lying, shore access is straightforward, though you should not cross farm land without permission. The tidal streams outside of the Firth of Forth are weak, rarely exceeding 1 knot on springs, and variable in direction. The outer portion of the Firth also has tidal streams that rarely exceed 1 knot, though near the land they may reach 1.5 knots. On average, the ingoing stream begins −0225 Dover; the outgoing stream begins at +0345 Dover. In the inner Forth area the springs tidal streams reach 2.25 knots and can run quite strongly in the narrow channels, sometimes leading to some turbulence.

Dive shop facilities are offered by Dougie McEwan of Edinburgh Diving Centre, haven for local divers. Likewise, on the Fife coast, Les Pennington of East Coast Divers offers the services of a diving centre, complete with accommodation and hard boat hire. He specialises in diving the Island of May.

The diving is not spectacular scenically in West coast terms. Visibility is poor to extremely poor, but there are many wrecks, some of which are very deep in very dark water; they are undertakings of a most serious nature.

Thanks are due to Derek Borthwick of Edinburgh University Branch for considerable help with many of these dive sites.

South side of Firth of Forth

1552 Old Harbour, Dunbar. NT682794. Enter by the old harbour and swim past hexagonal lava columns rising from the seabed. Depths to 12m. Return to by the same route for exiting.

1553 The Yetts and Outer Perch, Dunbar. NT682796. To the North of this group of three rocks is pleasant diving at a depth of 12-14m on a bottom dissected by metres-wide canyons and interesting rock walls, encrusted with Alcyonium, anemones etc. Visibility will be, at best, 10m. Park at the harbour wall and enter water from the West side then snorkel to the rocks.

1554 Round Steeple, Dunbar. NT686791. Another rocky outcrop with a maximum depth of 18m. The tidal streams encourage the colonisation of filter feeding marine life.

1555 The Gripes and Johnston's Hole, Dunbar. NT680795. Another rocky islet giving diving to 14m. The rock can be circumnavigated, passing cliff faces and overhangs and an impressive rock amphitheatre on the seaward side. Lots of life in the deep clefts and gullies. While snorkelling out to the Gripes a sandy bottom to a depth of 7-8m is passed. It can give a useful second dive in rougher conditions. Beware of harbour boat traffic.

1556 Dunbar Harbour wall. NT678795. There is a pleasant dive along the rocky walls along the outside of the North west spur of the harbour. At 9m the rocks give way to a sandy bottom. Lots of crustaceans and fishlife are to be seen and there are reports of the occasional cannonball being found, having originated from the old battery by the harbour entrance. An exit can be made at Pebble Beach on the East side of the spur. Please note that no diving should be carried out in the harbour or its fairway.

1557 Castlefoot Rock, Dunbar. NT678797. Again an islet with depths to 14m. Plentiful life in the tides.

1558 Scart Rock, Dunbar. NT677797. A rather disappointing shallow dive requiring boat cover.

1559 Half Ebb Rock, Dunbar. NT676797. Another small islet with good underwater scenery and colourful life.

1560 Wallace's Head, Dunbar. NT674795. A rock that can be circum-navigated and which harbours a lot of life, including large crustaceans.

1561 Bathe Reef, Dunbar. NT674794. There are many large gullies that permit entry to the water, which is 8m deep and reaches 12m further offshore. The many large underwater outcrops of rock covered with life make this an interesting dive. Access from cliff top near the Bayswater Hotel, North of the harbour.

1562 Blow Hole, Dunbar. NT673794. A small crack in the Bathe Reef gives access to a perfectly round blow hole encrusted with jewel anemones. It is big enough for two divers to enter and swim to the surface.

1563 Coral Canyon, Dunbar. NT672794. This is a very distinct large canyon to the west of Bathe Reef. A very pleasant dive.

1564 Oliver's Ship, Dunbar. NT675795. Yet another small islet with lots of life on its underwater walls because of the tidal streams. Depths of 10-15m.

1565 Long Craigs, Dunbar. NT667796. The North side of the little islands give interesting diving along rock faces at depths of 7-9m in reasonable visibility. Access by a path leading down the cliffs at the end of Marine Road.

1566 Wreck of HMS "Pathfinder". This 2940 ton, 113m long scout light cruiser was the first ship to be torpedoed by a submarine, U21 in 1940. She was armed with nine 4″ guns and two torpedo tubes. The vessel sank in four minutes and most of the complement of 268 men were lost though the captain was saved. She was lost somewhere between St. Abb's and Firth of Forth and is thought to lie in the vicinity of Dunbar in a depth of 55m. The position is known to Dunbar fishermen.

1567 Unknown wreck, 3 miles North of Dunbar. Charted at 56 03 42N 02 29 36W in about 38m of water with a clearance of at least 34m.

1568 Wreck of HMS "Fox", mouth of R. Tyne. NT641798. This was an English man-o-war that was lost in a storm in 1745. It was used to provide an escape route for the English general Sir John Cape and his personal fortune after the English were routed by the forces of Bonny Prince Charlie at the Battle of Prestonpans. The vessel became a total loss and the remains can be seen (and approached in Wellington boots) protruding at very low tides. The sands cover 24 bronze cannons and supposedly also a fortune in gold belonging to the Government, along with the family treasures of Hanoverian families living in East Lothian. Plans are afoot to excavate the wreck as an archaeological project and it should not be disturbed.

1569 Beggar's Cap. NT620838. Shore access to extensive drying rock areas requiring a long snorkel. The bow section of the "Elterwater" lost in 1927 has been reported.

1570 St. Baldred's Boat. NT610850. A rocky spur that runs out to sea and gives rewarding diving among a chain of broken rocks separated by gullies full of fish and seals; the depths around extend to 7-9m. The tide can run embarassingly quickly in the very shallow water. Access from the car park (with an automatic ticket machine) at Seacliff.

1571 Tantallon Castle, West side. NT596851. Tantallon Castle was built in 1370 on the site of a former Celtic fort; in 1529 it surrendered to James V and was successfully besieged by Cromwell's General Monk in 1651. At its base there is a small natural harbour, known locally as the "midget submarine" harbour, which is connected to the sea by a 3m-wide channel. The natural "swimming pool" thus formed is 7-9m deep and gives an excellent training site with many ledges hiding crustaceans. Access by leaving vehicles in the upper car park and walking to the water.

1572 Wreck of the "Elterwater". NT603847 (approx.) A Newcastle steamer wrecked on Scoughall Rocks near Tantallon Castle in 1927. She lies in 5m of water at 56 03 06N 02 36 48W close to the shore behind Gegan Rock.

1573 Gin Head. NT594854. A bouldery slope giving way to a flat rocky seabed with little of interest. Depth 5-11m.

1574 Unknown wreck, 2.5 miles North east of Bass Rock. This is charted at 56 06 36N 02 35 12W in about 39m of water with a clearance of 33m. It is probably the wreck of the SS "Royal Fusilier", which was a 2187 ton vessel that was bombed and sunk by aircraft in 1941, 4 miles from the Isle of May.

1575 Bass Rock, East landing NT603873. Diving near to the landing steps promises so much and yields so little. The vertical rocks reach 2-3m underwater and then give way to a flat bottom of sandy shingle. Launch at North Berwick (parking congestion at height of summer) or Seacliff at high tide.

1576 Bass Rock, South end. NT602872. Bass Rock was fortified against possible attack by Napoleon. Local rumour has it that cannons from the old fort were thrown into the sea on the South side of the island but none have been located.

1577 Bass Rock Tunnel. NT602872 – NT602873. This passes right through the Rock with a length of about 120m. It is above the surface and can be negotiated in Wellington boots, though the entrance at the South east (in the back of the second cave counting from the South of the Rock) needs a swimming approach and the West exit is by a small beach well-frequented by seals. A recommended land exploration in calm conditions, torches useful.

45

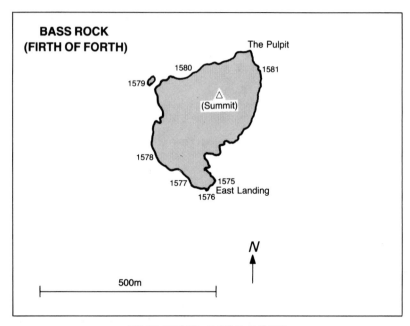

DIVE SITES, BASS ROCK

1578 Bass Rock, South west side. NT601873. Quite shallow water leads to a deeper slope with the normal marine life for the Forth.

1579 The Middens, Bass Rock. NT601875. A small islet just West of the Bass Rock. To its West there is a 42m deep hole in the seabed. The wreck reported just to the North west of the islet (at 56 04 45N 02 28 30W) has been searched for but not yet located.

1580 Bass Rock, North west side. NT603875. Spectacular surface cliffs drop sheer into the water and continue vertically to about 10m underwater, followed by a rocky slope leading to 30m and beyond. The visibility can be disappointing.

1581 Bass Rock, North east side NT604875. Spectacular surface cliffs drop sheer into the water and in places continue vertically to 20m underwater.

1582 The Leithies, North Berwick. NT571858. Enter the water from the private road to the beach. In calm weather the site gives a shallow dive over kelp with the occasional lobster. The visibility can be very poor.

1583 Old Pier, North Berwick. NT554856. Shore access to shallow water around the remaining wooden uprights.

1584 Coastguard Lookout, North Berwick. NT554857. Shallow rocks that give unimpressive diving.

1585 Craigleith island, South side. NT552869. A pleasant drift dive can be made along either the South or West faces over boulders and small cliffs. Depths reach 17m. Encrusting Alcyonium are a noted feature.

1586 Craigleith island, North side. NT552872. A shallow bottom of boulders giving way to shingle. Some tunnels are formed by the boulders.

1587 Lamb island, West side. NT534866. A boulder slope to about 8-10m. In reasonable visibility the small marine life make this an enjoyable dive.

1588 Lamb island, North Dog. NT535867. A rocky bottom with many interesting small canyons containing a good variety of marine life.

1589 Unknown wreck, 4 miles North of Lamb. Charted at 56 08 18N 02 44 48W in about 51m of water with a clearance of 48m.

1590 Wreck of the USS "Stockton", Broad Sands. NT524862 (approx,). A 94m long WW1 US Navy lend-lease destroyer of 1020 tons renamed HMS "Ludlow" by the Royal Navy. The vessel was anchored against Broad Sands near Lamb island to be used for target practice by rocket-firing aircraft, but a full salvo from the first plane hit it at the waterline and the vessel rolled over and sank. The wreckage is very broken and lies about 300m offshore in depths of 5-7m. It is weed-covered, barnacle-encrusted and sand filled but there are many interesting nooks and crannies with the occasional section just allowing the entry of a diver. Winter storms frequently shift the sand and reveal many war relics and also many pieces of brass, including some large sheets. There are large amounts of iron pigs (used for ballast) lying all around. Find the wreckage by running along the transit (there is no cross fix) until wreckage is detected with an echo sounder or proton magnetometer.

1591 Unknown wreck, 3 miles North of Broad Sands. Charted at 56 07 00N 02 45 42W in about 55m of water with a clearance of at least 28m.

1592 Unknown wreck, 3.5 miles North of Broad Sands. Charted at 56 07 20N 02 46 18W in about 56m of water with a clearance of at least 28m.

1593 Fidra island, South Dog. NT512866. A rather featureless shallow dive along slopes of small boulders.

1594 Fidra island, North Dog. NT512871. Similar to the South Dog.

1595 Unknown wreck, 3.5 miles North of Eyebroughy. Charted at 56 07 30N 02 49 06W in about 49m of water with a clearance of 36m.

1596 Unknown wreck, 33 miles North of Eyebroughy. Charted at 56 07 00N 02 49 20W in about 55m of water with a clearance of 51m.

1597 Wreck of the "Chester II", 2 miles North of Gullane Point. This wreck belongs to Edinburgh Branch. It is a virtually intact armed trawler sitting upright on the muddy seabed at 56 04 16N 02 52 12 in a depth of

29m, with its bow pointing at 45 degrees to the shore. It gives a good dive and its features are A-frames on the stern, the rudder and iron propeller, davits, winches, and hatches. It is possible to enter these hatches although there is much silt about. There are nets draped over the wheelhouse. A starboard companionway gives access to the aft of the wheelhouse and it may be possible to enter the interior of the wreck by this route. Large conger eels are reported and the whole wreck is completely encrusted with plumose anemones. Visibility is never more than 3m and can be much less. Strong tidal streams may be experienced.

1598 Unknown wrecks, Aberlady Bay. There are records of at least three wrecks in Aberlady Bay, but apparently nothing remains. No further details.

1599 Midget submarines, Aberlady Bay. NT452813. Two midget submarines lie side by side on Gullane Sands. They are exposed at low tide and can be approached by walking. From Aberlady Point (NT456805) look for a very large isolated concrete block in the middle of the Sands at low tide. The submarines were moored to this block. They can be dived at high tide should you so wish. See "Sub-Aqua Scene" magazine, February 1979, for photographs.

1600 Unknown wreck, 3.5 miles North west of Gullane Point. Charted at 56 05 15N 02 55 10W in about 36m of water with a clearance of 33m.

1601 Wreck of the "Gosford", 1.5 miles West of Craigielaw Point. This barge was wrecked in WW2 and lies in 8m of water at 56 00 42N 02 56 20W. The wreck supposedly only stands about 1m off the seabed and difficulty has been experienced in its recent location.

1602 Wreck of the "Switha", ½ mile North west of the "Gosford". This 573 ton (178 feet long) British fishery protection vessel ran aground on Herwit Rocks, a reef off Inchkeith Island, in 1980 at 56 01 11N 03 06 38W. The position lies on a transit of the radio mast North of Burntisland and the left edge of the southern building on Inchkeith. The ship's head is pointing 250 degrees magnetic. Wreckage is strewn amidst the wreckage of earlier vessels that were lost on the same rocks. In fact the reef is known locally as "the boiler" because of a large ship's boiler being stranded there still. The "Switha" is owned by S & G Underwater Services of Granton.

1603 Unknown wreck, 4.5 miles North west of Craigielaw Point. Charted at 56 03 00N 03 00 15W in about 17m of water with a clearance of 13m.

1604 Gullane Bay to Forth Road Bridge. NT450820 – NT125790. The south shoreline of the Forth is a mixture of muddy sand, mud and industrial waterfronts for a distance of about 25 miles. The coast passes Cockenzie, Musselburgh, Edinburgh and Granton. There is the occasional rocky outcrop but the depths are invariably very shallow and the visibility is appalling. Even the local divers rarely dive here and it is hardly worthwhile recording any sites. However . . .

1605 Hound Point. NT157792. Off the Scouts' sailing centre there is a totally-uninviting, almost zero-visibility dive.

1606 Port Edgar. NT120790. This is the harbour at South Queensferry. It is used by the local branches for roped diver training. The water is reported to be "liquid mud".

1607 Forth Road Bridge. NT125790. Those divers bold enough to dive here report shallow water and totally zero visibility.

1608 River Forth inland of Forth Road Bridge. a very muddy, polluted industrial river with extensive mudflats at low tide. The visibility is normally zero and there are no dives recorded.

1609 Inverkeithing Outer Buoy. A muddy bottom; some interesting debris.

1610 Unknown obstructions, 2 miles East of Inchkeith. Charted at 56 01 24N 03 04 15W and 56 01 18N 03 04 42W in about 8m of water with a clearance of 6m.

1611 Unknown Wreck, 1 mile South east of Inchkeith. A drying wreck is charted as aground on Herwit Rocks at 56 01 12N 03 06 42W.

1612 Inchkeith island. NT290830. The diving is poor and visibility is usually less than 3m.

1613 Inchmickery island. NT206806. Poor diving on a silted bottom at 6m with little life and visibility of 1m.

1614 Cow & Calves. NT206811. Poor, shallow diving on rocks and shells in polluted water of 1m visibility.

1615 Oxcars. NT203818. Poor diving in rocky shallows followed by rocky faces leading to blackness at 15m.

1616 Incholm. NT185823. Very poor shallow diving in terrible visibility.

1617 Car Craig. NT199831. As for Inchcolm.

North side of Firth of Forth

1618 Forth Road Bridge to Burntisland. Eight miles of muddy foreshore passing the bays of Inverkeithing, Dalgety, Barnhill, Aberdour and White-sands with no dive sites recorded.

1619 Unknown wrecks, 1 mile East of North Queensferry. Two wrecks are charted at 56 01 00N 03 21 12W. They have clearances of 15m and 18m in a general depth of 23m. They are probably undived and the visibility would presumably be appalling.

1620 Unknown wreck, 0.4 mile South of Middens, Inchcolm. Charted at 56 01 15N 03 18 25W, this wreck has a clearance of 21m in a general depth of 27m.

1621 Wreck of HMS "Campania", 1 mile South east of Burntisland. The Campania was an 12,884 ton (183m long) Cunard liner built in 1893. With her 30,000 horse power engines she was capable of 22 knots and had a crew of 400 and a passenger capacity of 1400. For four years she held the Blue Riband with her sister ship for the fastest North Atlantic crossing. Because of her speed she was converted into an auxiliary aircraft carrier for 10 planes. She was lost in 1918 after a collision with the battlecruiser HMS "Glorious", in very bad weather, which caused her boilers to explode. All the crew were saved. She is in two pieces; the main position is 56 02 20N 03 13 22W, with the second piece of wreckage lying 200m to the North north east. Depth to the mud seabed is 23m, charted clearance on the wreck is 13m and she is covered in Alcyonium and anemones and is well broken. The visibility is usually extremely poor. When taking into account the dangers of low or zero visibility, tidal streams, an overhanging flight deck, nets and ropes over the wreckage, and the fact that the wreck lies on the tanker route running up the Forth to Hound Point, it is easy to recognise the need for exceptional caution when diving this wreck. One visit is usually one too many, even for the most experienced of divers.

1622 Aberdour. NT201850. A shallow, sedimentary type of dive, though with a surprising number of nudibranchs.

1623 Blae Rock. NT261846 (approx.) A submarine bank running South east to North west, rising from a seabed as deep as 49m at the South east (where there is a buoy) to a depth of 4m. No sites are recorded and visibility would presumably be very poor.

1624 Unknown wreck, 0.8 mile South east of Blae Rock. A presumably small wreck charted at 56 02 11N 03 10 34W, projecting 2m clear of the seabed at 15m. Undived as far as is known.

1625 Hummel Rocks, Kinghorn. NT274869. Shore access to low reefs in 5m with reasonable life, lots of crabs, and poorish visibility.

1626 Kinghorn to Kirkcaldy. Four miles of rocky, then sandy, then industrial shoreline with no sites recorded. The diving at the South end of this strip of coastline should be similar to Hummel Rocks at Kinghorn.

1627 Wreck of the "Salvestria". A 11,938 ton (152m long) British tanker sunk by mine in 1940 with the loss of 10 lives at 56 04 05N 03 04 78W, 3 miles east of Kinghorn. The wreck projects 4m above the seabed at 18m. Well salvaged in 1972; there is a lot of debris scattered over a large area. Transits: 1) North tip of Inchkeith in line with centre gasholder and Granton; 2) centre of 3 lights of coloured block of flats in Kirkcaldy with west Lomond; 3) Fidra Light open to right of Bass Rock the same distance as sea level to the top of Fidra Light.

1628 Wreck of the SS "Royal Archer" A 2266 ton British ship carrying general cargo which sunk by mine in 1940 at 56 06 26N 02 59 56W (5 miles East of Kirkcaldy) in a depth of 24m of water with a 2m scour. The charted clearance is 14m but the wreck generally projects 3-4m above the seabed. Some salvage in 1971.

1629 Unknown wreck, 1 mile east of Dysart. The position is 56 07 23N 03 05 23W. The wreck projects less than 2m above a seabed at 1m. No other information.

1630 Kirkcaldy to Elie. Twenty miles of partly industrial, partly sandy/rocky shoreline with no recorded sites.

1631 East Vows Beacon. NT482990. Shallow diving around the beacon with a large anchor to West. Strong tidal streams. Launch at Elie Harbour.

1632 East Elie. NT484995. A shallow and kelp-dominated shore dive over interesting, very regular, basalt formations.

1633 Elie Ness. NT497993. Shore access to the shallow sandy water of Elie Bay. The rocky edges give pleasant snorkel dives.

1634 Wreck of the "Karen", 1 mile East of Methil. The position is 56 11 04N 02 58 45W. The wreck projects less than 1m above a seabed at 6m. No other information.

1635 Wreck of the MV "Arizona". A 398 ton (44m long) Dutch vessel lost with 5 crew members after striking a mine near Elie Point while bound from Methil to Holland. The position is 56 10 14N 02 52 23W, 2.4 miles and 252 degrees from Elie Ness Light. Depth is 17m and the minimum depth is 11m.

1636 Unknown obstruction, 3 miles South west of Elie Ness. Charted at 56 09 40N 03 53 18W in about 25m of water with a clearance of 23m.

1637 Unknown wreck, 3 miles South West of Elie Ness. The position is 56 09 19N 02 53 40W. Least depth is 27m in a general depth of 30m. No other information.

1638 Wreck of the SS "Rolfsborg", 3 miles South west of Elie Ness. An 1825 ton (277 feet long) British vessel (an ex-Finnish prize ship) lost in 1945 at 56 08 17N 02 51 55W in 44m of water. A large wreck that projects some 17m above the seabed. Poor visibility hinders its exploration.

1639 Wreck of the "Phaeacian", 2 miles South west of Elie Ness. The position is 56 09 24N 02 51 42W with a depth of 29m and a charted clearance of 22m. No other information.

1640 Lady's Folly, Sauchar Point, Elie. NT500995. So-named because of an old tower standing on the headland, this is a very shallow shore dive best done at high tide on a calm day. There are lots of picturesque rocky outcrops. The shallow depth gives enough light to bring out the contrast between rock, marine growth and sand. Further out there is sand, sand and more sand.

1641 Elie to Anstruther Easter. Five miles of shoreline that are still somewhat industrial; there is only one recorded diving site at Newark Castle.

1642 Newark Castle. N0517012. A very shallow site that eventually yields depths of up to 6m. There is a report of a military aircraft lost in this area. Shore access via the track to the castle.

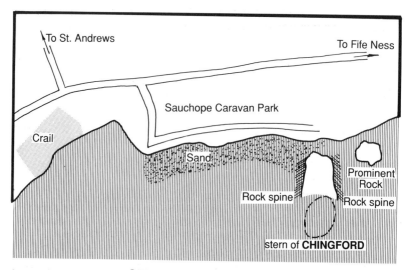

To St. Andrews

To Fife Ness

Sauchope Caravan Park

Crail

Sand

Prominent Rock

Rock spine

Rock spine

stern of **CHINGFORD**

SITE 1646: CHINGFORD

1643 The Coves. N0600058. Shallow rocky reefs separated by sand run parallel to the shore and give some interest to the dive in addition to numerous edible crabs. There is a cave on the shore which identifies the site. Launch at Celardyke Harbour at the East of Anstruther Easter.

1644 West Ness, Crail, N0613068. Pleasant diving on rocky reefs running out to depths of about 5m. Shore access.

1645 The Staples, Crail. N0623076. Pleasant diving along low rocky reefs in a depth of about 5m. Shore access.

1646 Wreck of the SS "Chingford". A 1517 ton (80m long) vessel that ran aground in 1924 at 56 15 58N 02 35 46W, just off Sauchope Caravan Site East of Crail. She was from Transgund bound for Grangemouth with a cargo of timber. The vessel lies North-south (with the stern and iron propeller inshore) in 6m of water and pieces project up 2-3m. The vessel is found by diving out to sea between two rock spines running out from the only piece of sandy beach. Access is through the caravan site, with permission.

1647 Wreck of the "Pladda", Kilminning. N0634087. This vessel was lost in 1890 and now lies to the East of a large rock in 7m. There are various piles of wreckage including a large boiler. Access from the shore after passing the old airfield buildings.

1648 Wreck of the "Lingbank", 2 miles South east of Fife Ness. This 257 ton, 132 feet long German steam trawler was lost in 1927 and is charted as position approximate at 56 15 10N 02 32 50W in 21m of water with a clearance of 15m.

1649 Coastguard station, Fife Ness. N0640097. A seabed of rocky gullies with coarse sand and kelp at a depth of 9-10m. The crevices hide lobsters and other crustaceans. There is a large boiler about 50m offshore.

1650 Lochaber Rock, Fife Ness. N0639099. Shore access down a narrow, shallow creek. Pleasant visibility among the boulders in a few metres of water with a variety of small life to examine. There is wreckage in the water immediately in front of the concrete structure. A popular training site with local divers.

1651 Wreck of "Musketeer". This was lost at Fife Ness in 1962. The wreckage is broken up and lies in 6m of water.

1652 Wreck of French fishing boat. This lies just off the rocks at Fife Ness. The boilers are still to be seen.

1653 North Carr Beacon, Fife Ness. N0647115. This is situated on a reef running out from the shore. It carries on for quite some distance underwater in depths of between 2-3m and 10-12m. There is prolific marine life including many crustaceans. Beware of the strong tidal streams.

1654 Wrecks of unknown sailing vessels, North Carr Beacon. Wreckage, including copper pins & piping, from several old sailing ships, is scattered all around the seabed in depths of 5-10m.

1655 Wreck of the "Northumbria", 1.5 miles North east of Fife Ness. A 211 ton, 42m long British commissioned trawler sunk by mine in 1917. She is charted at 56 17 31N 02 32 24W in 36m of water with a clearance of 29m. The wreckage lies 250-070 degrees.

1656 North Carr Lightship, 2 miles North east of Fife Ness. This has now been replaced with an East cardinal buoy. The depth is about 25-30m onto a bottom of mud, shingle and rock. Quite strong tidal streams run at certain states of the tide.

1657 Wreck of the destroyer HMS "Rockingham". This 1190 ton, 95m long lend-lease vessel was lost by mine in 1944 off Fife Ness. She was originally the USS "Swasey" and was capable of 35 knots and was armed with 12 torpedo tubes and four 4" guns.

Isle of May

A popular site with divers from the South east of Scotland, and with some from farther afield. Along with Fife Ness, it probably gives the best diving in the Forth, though neither area can compare in any way with the West coast of Scotland. The East face of the island is rugged and shallow with wreckage liberally strewn along it, whereas the West face is built of tumbled rocks that form stepping stones to the depths below. Access can be by means of inflatable from North Berwick (11 miles) or Anstruther (6 miles), or by means of a charter vessel.

1658 Wreck of the "Mars", North Ness. N0652002. A 600 ton Danish steamer that ran aground in 1936 and broke up. All that remains to be seen are some metal plates. These lie just offshore to the East of Mars Rock.

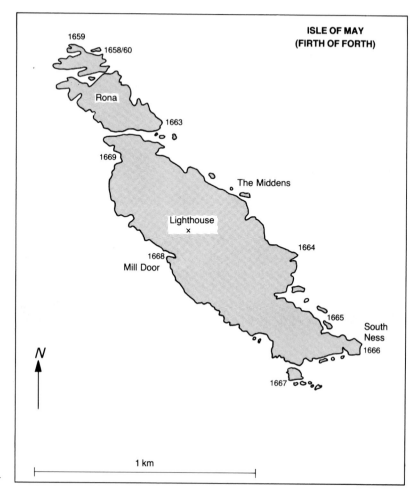

ISLE OF MAY
(FIRTH OF FORTH)

1659
1658/60
Rona
1663
1669
The Middens
Lighthouse
×
1664
1668
Mill Door
1665
South
Ness
1666
1667

N

1 km

DIVE SITES, ISLE OF MAY

1659 Wreck of the "Thomas Devlin", North Ness. A large steam trawler that was driven into the shallow reefs at the North tip of the May.

1660 Wreck of the "Ethel Crawford". An Aberdeen steam trawler lost in 1930 when she ran aground on North Ness.

1661 Wreck of the "George Aunger". An Aberdeen trawler that took off the crew of the Ethel Crawford and that was herself lost on the May later in 1930 with the loss of two lives.

Rugged and rocky, the mile-long Isle of May offers some of the best diving in the Firth of Forth.

1662 Wreck of the "Victory". Another Aberdeen steam trawler that was lost in 1934 on the May when she ran aground in calm weather.

1663 Isle of May, North east side. NT654998. This side is shallower than the South west side, with a maximum depth of 27m.

1664 Wreck of the "Island", Island Rocks. NT661993. A 1744 ton (250 feet long) steam yacht that ran aground in 1937. She lies just off the shore and is scattered about the seabed at a depth of 13m between South Ness and Island Rocks. The bows can be seen 12m up the cliffs. The wreck is owned by Perth Branch.

1665 The Pillow. NT662990. This rock formation lies at the mouth of Kirk Haven. There are quantities of interesting wreckage scattered about.

1666 South Ness. NT667988. This may be undived. It appears to give depths to 30m immediately off its rocks.

1667 Maiden Hair. NT660987. A series of shallow little channels and islets at the South of the island. Just off the rocks the depth falls to about 30m.

1668 Mill Door. NT654992. Above the surface are 30m high cliffs which continue underwater to about 12m. Then the bouldery bottom drops steeply to 30m. There are some underwater caves.

1669 Wreck of the "Ann Labbie", Altarstanes. NT6529976. A 1110 ton (231 feet long) steamer that ran aground in 1873 and is now broken up and partially buried under rocks in 20m of water. The stern and the iron propeller are still to be seen. The position is just South of Standing Head in the Bay of Altarstanes.

The outer Forth

1670 Wreck of the "Emley", 1 mile South west of the Isle of May. A 223 ton, 112 feet long British ketch sunk by mine in 1918 at approximately 56 10 30N 02 34 00w, 0.75 miles and 208 degrees from May Island Lighthouse. The depth is 44m and the charted clearance at least 20m.

1671 Wreck of the SS "Avondale Park", 1 mile South east of the Isle of May. This 2878 ton, 96m long vessel was torpedoed by a German submarine in 1945 at approximately 56 10 30N 02 31 00W in about 55m of water.

1672 Unknown wreck, 1 mile North of the Isle of May. Charted as position approximate at 56 12 18N 02 33 12W in 45m of water with a clearance of at least 28m.

1673 Unknown wrecks. Chart 175 shows at least 40 wrecks lying offshore in the outer Forth, virtually all of which are within sport diving depths. None of these has yet been located and dived to my knowledge.

1674 Submarines K4 and K17. Two of these wrecks are those of K-class submarines. They are thought to be the wrecks charted at 56 13 38N 02 24 18W and 56 13 42N 02 23 36W, about 6 miles East north east of the Isle of May. A very promising sonar target has been located at the correct position in a depth of 54m, though it has not yet been dived.

The K-class submarines were powered by steam turbines driven by oil-fired boilers. They displaced 2650 tons and had a surface speed of 23.5 knots to enable them to operate with the Grand Fleet.

A large armada of battleships, battlecruisers, cruisers and destroyers, together with two flotillas of K-class submarines, left Rosyth on January 31st, 1918, for a sweep towards the Norwegian coast. The squadrons and flotillas were in line ahead, but for an unknown reason K22 under full helm swung out of line and collided with K14. While the two submarines were locked together HMS "Inflexible" also struck K14. K17 was standing by the scene when HMS "Fearless" struck her in the darkness, cutting her in two and sending her to the bottom. To avoid the disaster K4 hauled out of line and so did K6, which was astern of K4. K4 stopped her engines, unfortunately K6 did not and collided with K4, slicing her in half and sending her to join K17. Both vessels were lost with all hands.

Area information and services

Hydrographic charts: 175 Fife Ness to St. Abbs Head 1:75,000; 734 Firth of Forth – Isle of May to Inchkeith 1:50,000; 735 Firth of Forth – North Craig to Oxcars 1:25,000; 736 Firth of Forth – Oxcars to Rosyth 1:15,000; 737

OS 1:50,000 maps: 59 St. Andrews & Kirkcaldy; 65 Falkirk & West Lothian; 66 Edinburgh; 67 Duns & Dunbar.

OS 1:25,000 maps: NT48/58/68 North Berwick; NT47/57 Haddington; NT27/37 Edinburgh; NT07/17 Linlithgow & Queensferry; NT08/18 Dunfermline; NT28 Burntisland; NT29/39 Kirkcaldy & Buckhaven; N040/50 Anstruther; N060/61 Crail.

Local BSAC Branches: Edinburgh (21); South Queensferry (1262); Heriot-Watt University, Edinburgh (507); Heriot-Watt University Technical Diving Club (1067); Edinburgh University (407); Fettes College, Edinburgh (433); Forth Valley, Alloa (81); Cupar (1094); Kirkcaldy (442); RAF Leuchars (684); HMS Caledonia, Rosyth (956); St. Andrews University (300).

Local SSAC Branches: East Lothian Divers (Haddington), Edinburgh; Edinburgh Tollcross, Midlothian (Edinburgh); Lothian Teachers (Edinburgh); Moray House College (Edinburgh); Napier College (Edinburgh).

Air supplies: Edinburgh Dive Centre, 30 West Preston Street, Edinburgh 031 667 7982; East Coast Divers, West Pitkierie Farm, Anstruther, Fife Anstruther (0333) 310768.

Outboard motor sales & service: There are many facilities in the area. Refer to the Yellow Pages for Edinburgh and for Fife.

Boat charter: Edinburgh Dive Centre 031 667 7982; East Coast Divers Anstruther (0333) 310768.

Local weather: Edinburgh Weather Centre 031 246 8091.

Sea area: Forth

Tidal constants:	DOVER	LEITH	ROSYTH
Dunbar	+0356	+0003	–
Fidra	+0546	−0007	–
Cockenzie	+0343	−0010	–
Granton (Leith)	+0353	0	−0005
Rosyth	+0358	+0005	0
Kincardine	+0349	–	−0004
Burntisland	+0350	−0003	–
Methil	+0347	−0006	–
Anstruther Easter	+0332	−0021	–
Fife Ness	+0332	−0021	–

Coastguard: MRSC Crail (03335) 666; CG Leve (0333) 23111; Dunbar (0368) 63342.

Harbourmasters: Dunbar (0368) 63206; Leith 031 554 3661; Burntisland Leven (0333) 26725; Anstruther (0333) 310836.

Hospitals: There are many in the area. The most important are: Edinburgh Royal 031 229 2477; St Andrews Memorial (0334) 72327; Dunfermline & West Fife (0383) 23131; Kirkcaldy Victoria (0592) 261156.

Recompression chambers: Rosyth (038 34) 2121 ext. 3127.

Police: Edinburgh 031 311 3131; Kirkcaldy (0592) 52611; Anstruther (0333) 310333; Burntisland (0592) 872708; Crail (03335) 215; Elie (0333) 330509; Inverkeithing Dunfermline (0383) 26711; Kincardine (0259) 30222; Kinghorn (0592) 890222; Rosyth Dunfermline (0383) 26711.

Vehicle recovery: AA – Edinburgh 031 225 8464; Kirkcaldy 62371 (office hours only).

Local tourist information: North Berwick (0620) 2197; Edinburgh 031 226 6591; Kirkcaldy (0592) 67775; Leven (0333) 29464; Anstruther (0333) 310628/310368.

Accommodation: There is a huge choice, depending on your taste and price bracket. East Coast Divers at Anstruther (0333 310768) in Fife offer simple bunkhouse accommodation aimed at divers.

Places of local nautical interest: Scottish Fisheries Museum, Anstruther (0333) 310628/310368.

The Deil's Heid, near Arbroath: sandstone cliffs with lots of guillies and caves.

CHAPTER 3

Fife Ness to Rattray Head

AN 80 MILE stretch of coast taking in well-known East coast towns such as St. Andrews, Arbroath, Montrose, Stonehaven, Aberdeen, and Peterhead. The placenames of this rich coastal lowland reveal a little of the wilder landscape of the past before the extensive marshlands were reclaimed for farming. The weather of the region is mild, and its sunshine record is among the best in Scotland.

St. Andrews lies at the North of the East Neuk of Fife with its rocky coast and picturesque fishing villages. The mouth of the River Eden is passed before reaching Tentsmuir Sands and Forest, the haunt of many water birds. Before afforestation the dunes and sands of the raised beach apparently were much clearer. The Firth of Tay with its two bridges has an industrial eastern part dominated by Dundee. Its upper reaches are quiet, reed-fringed and thus it provides shelter for many birds, especially in winter. The land backing the coast – Carse of Gowrie – is a rich and fertile farming area. Quite substantial land reclamation has been carried out around the Dundee foreshore.

Buddon Ness at the mouth of the Tay is a raised beach and this continues North to the historic town of Arbroath, where Robert the Bruce proclaimed Scotland's independence in 1320. Between Arbroath and Lunan Bay are spectacular 60m high storm-carved cliffs, at first composed of Old Red Sandstone and then much-faulted lava and conglomerates. These abound with caves and clefts and were much used by smugglers in bygone times. Lunan Bay has a 2.5 mile long sandy raised beach which gives way to cliffs of lava as far as Montrose, backed by its extensive and muddy Basin.

North of St. Cyrus Sands the coastal cliffs retreat inland and are fronted by a broad coastal platform formed by several raised beaches as far as Inverbervie. The small bays and rocky coves of the wild and rather inaccessible coast of Kincardineshire then continue past Stonehaven to Aberdeen, the granite city and centre of Britain's oil industry. The coastal rocks are a mix of sandstone conglomerates, veined and dyked metamorphics, a little granite and some boulder clay infill. At Garron Point just North of Stonehaven the Highland Boundary Fault runs out to sea.

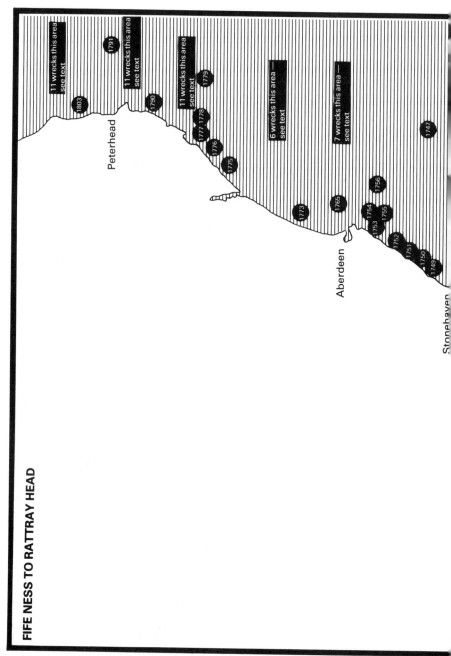

FIFE NESS TO RATTRAY HEAD

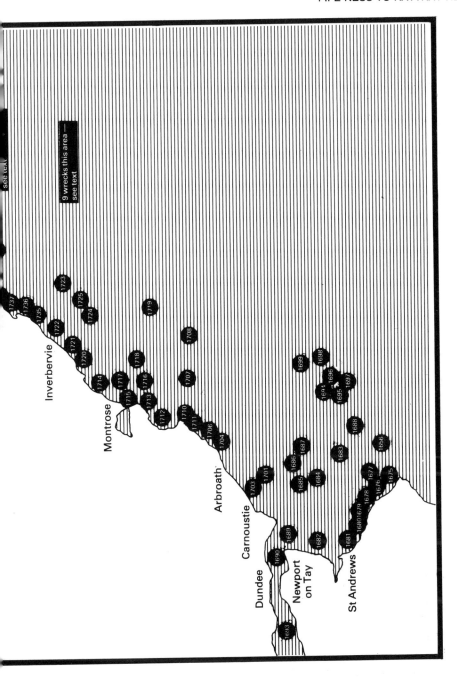

9 wrecks this area — see text

see text

Inverbervie

Montrose

Arbroath

Carnoustie

Dundee

Newport on Tay

St Andrews

1737
1736
1735
1723
1722
1725
1724
1721
1720
1719
1714
1717
1718
1708
1715
1716
1713
1707
1712
1710
1711
1706
1704
1699
1698
1696
1691
1695
1697
1688
1687
1683
1656
1703
1701
1686
1685
1684
1677
1676
1675
1678
1679
1680
1681
1689
1682
1690
1693

Montrose

North of Aberdeen a 13-mile long beach forms the shoreline at the South of the district of Buchan. When the old sea levels withdrew they left lots of sand for spasmodic formation of extensive beaches and dunes along this whole North East coastline. This is seen best at the Sands of Forvie at the North end of the 13-mile beach. Eider duck and terns breed in the almost-Saharan, 60m high dunes which are a nature reserve. The rolling farmland of Buchan ends abruptly in a series of high granite cliffs, eroded along dolerite dykes to form gullies, ravines and caves before Peterhead is reached. Peterhead is famous for its harbour and fishing fleet, and infamous for its prison. To the North of the town miles of sandy raised beaches lead on to Rattray Head and beyond. This coastline demonstrates the import-ance of glaciation in its formation.

The wildlife of the area is not particularly notable. The various wetlands and estuaries provide a haven for breeding water birds in summer and visiting Arctic geese in winter.

From a diver's point of view, the waters are generally shallow close to shore and usually rather murky. The coast is completely exposed to weather from the North north east to the South. Any wrecks anywhere near the shore are rapidly broken up by the heavy winter storms.

Diving along this coast can be very disappointing if you are especially attracted to good visibility. Average visibility is 5m. After heavy swell it needs 4-5 days of flat calm to restore the visibility to 10m. The life is nothing like as rich as that of the West coast; but lobsters, squat lobsters and edible crabs are common, and there are lots of flatfish and huge angler fish.

Spring tidal streams are generally about 1-2 knots though this can increase round headlands. Because of the linear nature of the coastline the tidal details are given here rather than repetitively in the main text.

Near Peterhead: LW slack −0450 Dover, HW slack −0110 Dover.
Girdle Ness, Aberdeen Bay: LW slack −0230 Dover, HW slack +0330 Dover, springs rate 2.5 knots.
Off Montrose Harbour: LW slack −0300 Dover, HW slack +0315 Dover, springs rate 7 knots.
Bell Rock: LW slack HW Dover, HW slack −0600 Dover, springs rate 1 knot.

1675 Englishman's Skelly, Fife Ness. N0631109. Why so-named?

1676 The Leck, Kingsbarns. N0605127. Interesting dive out from rocks past the old harbour.

1677 Wreck of destroyer "Success", Cambo Brigs. N0609123. The remains of this 305-ton, 64m long vessel (ribs and propshaft) lie close to the conspicuous post sticking out of the rocks offshore from Kingsbarns. It was lost by stranding in 1914. She was capable of 30 knots and was armed with six guns and two torpedo tubes.

1678 Babbet Ness. N0594142. Pleasant diving to 10m past rocks on to sand. Boat access from Fife Ness or St. Andrews.

1679 Craig Hartle. N0580150. An alternative site if Crail or Fife Ness are undiveable because of sea conditions. It is somewhat shallower and there is less exposed rock and therefore less marine life visible than at Crail. Shore access from track from Boarhills.

1680 Buddo Ness. N0560154. This site lies out from the wartime bunker. It is similar to Babbet Ness and Craig Hartle.

1681 Kinkell Ness. N0539159. Similar to Babbet Ness and Craig Hartle.

1682 St. Andrews to Firth of Tay. An 8-mile stretch of sandy shore with very shallow water offshore.

1683 Wreck of the "Sophren", 7 miles North of Fife Ness. This 195 ton trawler was sunk by mine in 1917 at 56 23 35N 02 35 30W. She now lies in 21m of water with a clearance of 11m.

1684 Wreck of the "Clan Shaw", 3 miles South east of the Abertay Lightvessel. A liner mined in 1917 near the Tay Fairway Buoy. At the time of the sinking the channel was farther South and so the wreck was reduced with explosives after several vessels had hit the wreckage. The wreck is located about 56 25 48N 02 36 24W in 22m of water, with a clearance of 19m. It is in two portions, one 60m long lying 37-217 degrees, the other is about 15m long and lies close to the larger piece.

1685 Wreck of the "Islandmagee", 1.5 miles South east of the Abertay Lightvessel. A Dundee sand-boat that was lost in 1953 and is thought to lie at 56 26 30N 02 38 42W in 10m of water with a charted clearance of 8m.

1686 Wreck of the coaster "Anu", St. Andrews Bay. This 1421 tons, 76m long Estonian vessel lies in 21m of water at 56 26 54N 02 35 41W, 3 miles East of Abertay Lightvessel, having been sunk by mine in 1940 with the loss of six lives. The wreck projects 1m above the seabed and there is a 2m scour. The wreckage is spread over 60m and lies 45-225 degrees.

1687 Wreck of the Submarine UC41, 5 miles East of the Abertay lightvessel. This 380-feet-long submarine was depth charged in 1917 and now lies 298-128 degrees almost buried in the sand in 24m of water at 56 27 35N 02 32 18W. The wreck has been salvaged by Alec Crawford, but sufficient remains to make an interesting dive. Near to the site there is a long low rock outcrop that gives a similar echo sounding, so be warned!

1688 Unknown wreck. This lies 8.5 miles SE of the Abertay Lightvessel at 56 23 00N 02 27 42W in 29m of water with a charted clearance of 27m.

1689 General Monck's fleet. After the sacking of Dundee in 1651, the treasure-laden fleet was lost, reputedly on Abertay Bank and presumably covered by the shifting sands.

1690 Wreck of the "Dalhousie", off Tentsmuir. Dundee-Newcastle trader which foundered with all 33 passengers and crew in a gale in 1864. The skipper tried to run the vessel aground under sail on the Tentsmuir (South) bank of the Pool. The wreck was entered by divers (from the tug "Rob Roy" owned by Mr. Cowperthwaite, whose wife and child were lost with the "Dalhousie") a fortnight after its loss, and the bodies of the passengers in the cabin were recovered.

Other wrecks of Tay approaches:
1691 The drifter "Fertile Vale", serving as an examination vessel, was sunk after collision with coaster "Empire Isle" in 1941.

1692 The coaster "Harley", foundered in 1944 with the loss of 5 lives. No further information.

1693 Firth of Tay. This is largely industrialised and no sites are recorded.

1694 Bell Rock. 56 26N 02 23W. An isolated rocky shoal marked with a famous lighthouse and lying about 12 miles East of the Tay estuary. The diving should be good, but I have no reports of the depths, which reach over 20m.

1695 Wreck of HMS "Argyll", Bell Rock. This 10,850 ton, 137m-long armoured cruiser was lost in 1915 after running into Bell Rock at 16 knots in heavy weather. The Bell Light had not been switched on as expected. She carried an armament of four 7.5″ guns, six 6″ guns, an assortment of lighter guns and 2 torpedo tubes; the guns were removed later. The wreckage lies at 56 26 00N 02 23 30W to the West of Bell Rock in shallow water (6m) and strong tidal streams (4-5 knots) and is well broken up. The propellers were recovered by the wreck's present owner, Alec Crawford, in 1970.

Other wrecks lost on Bell Rock:
1696 The trawler "Quixotic" in 1939.

1697 The "River Lossie" in 1917.
No further information.

1698 Unknown wreck, 3 miles North east of Bell Rock. Charted at 56 28 06N 02 19 12W at a depth of about 45m and with clearance of at least 40m. (This wreck may be the 575 ton SS "Bay Fisher", bombed by aircraft in 1941, 3.5 miles North east of Bell Rock.)

1699 Unknown wreck, 3 miles North west of Bell Rock. Charted at 56 29N 02 25W at a depth of about 40m.

1700 Wreck of the SS "Zealous". This Aberdeen vessel was lost in 1944 after collision "near the Bell Rock".

1701 Wreck of the SS "Hoche", 3 miles East of Carnoustie. This 2211 ton sailing vessel was lost in 1915 at 56 30 15N 02 36 30W where the depth is 19m. The vessel was supposedly holed by striking Bell Rock; she carried on only to sink some three miles to the North west. The metal wreckage is about 90m long, lying on its side, and projecting 5m off the bottom. The wreckage is well silted up though the bows are intact, clear of the seabed and covered in plumose anemones. As the wreck is followed a mast lies along the seabed but then the wreckage disappears in the sand. Poor transits, but the navigator marks are F23.3 I35.1.

1702 Carnoustie to Arbroath. A 5-mile stretch, initially rocky, then sandy. Shore access is prevented by the railway line with only one recorded site.

1703 East Haven. N0593362. A busy harbour with lobster fishermen. If you dive here please keep a low profile. The diving just offshore is shallow but picturesque. There are a lot of lobster pots and some salmon nets to steer well clear of. The harbour is the best launch for the "Hoche".

1704 The Deil's Heid. N0671419. A rather dramatic headland with 15-30m sandstone cliffs that are outstanding by East coast standards. There are lots of gullies, caves and natural arch with such names as Seamen's Grave and Dickmont's Den. No recorded sites, though the bottom looks to be rather shallow and sandy. Boat launch at Whiting Ness (N0658411).

1705 The Deil's Heid to Lunan Bay. 4 miles of jagged and interesting rocky foreshore then 2 miles of the sandy Lunan Bay with only one recorded site.

1706 Auchmithie. N0683442. Auchmithie is built on top of a cliff; a negotiable but steep and twisting track leads to the old harbour in a very shallow bay. As a dive it is shallow and unexciting, but it is a convenient launching point.

1707 Unknown wreck, 8 miles North east of Arbroath. Charted at 56 35 20N 02 21 30W at a depth of about 60m. The wreckage is 85m long, lies NNW-SSE and projects 8m off the seabed. It was sunk before 1930.

1708 Unknown wreck, 14 miles East north east of Arbroath. Charted at 56 35 54N 02 09 06W at a depth of about 52m and clearance of at least 46m.

1709 Wreck of the "Lord Beaconsfield". A Hull trawler lost "near Red Head" in 1945.

1710 Wreck of the "Fountains Abbey". A Riga-Dundee trader which grounded in fog in 1921, "within 100 yards of towering cliffs" on Red Head.

1711 Wreck of SS "Herrington". This 1258-ton British armed trawler was sunk by mine in 1917, ¾ mile East south east from Red Head (N0703474) at 56 37N 02 27W.

1712 Unknown wreck, Lunan Bay. Charted at 56 38 08N 02 27 00W at a depth of about 23m and with clearance of 16m. The steel hull of the wreckage has been damaged by explosion amidships. There is a single 4″ gun mounted forward. The wreckage contains a plate inscribed ". . . 1940".

1713 Boddin to Montrose. 3 miles of rocky shores. No recorded sites.

1714 Montrose Bay. 5 sandy miles!

1715 Wreck of the collier "Cruden". This Dundee vessel ran ashore near Scurdie Ness (N0734567) in 1930. No further information.

1716 Wreck of the SS "Clint", 1 mile East of Scurdie Ness, Montrose. This was lost in 1927 at 56 42 12N 02 24 30W at a depth of 22m and with clearance of 18m.

1717 Unknown wreck, 1 mile North east of Scurdie Ness. Charted at 56 42 36N 02 24 18W at a depth of about 19m and with clearance of 16m.

1718 Wreck of the SS "Nailsea River". This 5548-ton vessel was torpedoed by enemy aircraft in 1940 4 miles East of Montrose, where depths are about 30m.

1719 Unknown wreck, 10 miles East of Scurdie Ness. Charted at 56 41 40N 02 07 30W at a depth of about 65m and with clearance of at least 60m.

1720 Wreck of the "Petrel". This was wrecked on East Log Skelly (N0805670) near Golden Acre. No other information.

1721 Wreck of the "Speculation". This was wrecked in Haughs Bay (N0816685). No further information.

1722 Wreck of the "Caroline Agnes". This was wrecked to the South of Bervie Bay (N0835717) near Inverbervie. No further information.

1723 Wreck of the SS "Queensbury". This 3911 ton, 114m liner was bombed by German aircraft and sunk in 1941 with the loss of 11 lives at 56 50N 02 07W, 5 miles East of Inverbervie, in about 50m of water.

1724 Wreck of the "Baku Standard". This 3708 ton, 101m long tanker was torpedoed by a German U-boat in 1918 and lost 3 miles South east of Inverbervie at 56 48 30N 02 12 45W in 44m of water with a clearance of 34m and a 2m scour. The captain survived but 24 lives were lost.

1725 Wreck of the SS "Bellona II" This 840 ton vessel was bombed by aircraft in 1940, and lies 4 miles East of Gourdon at 56 50N 02 10W in 46m.

Wrecks of Inverbervie: at least 9 other wrecks charted. Positions are:

	Depth	Clear	
1726 56 47 12N 02 11 45W	52m	20m	4 miles South east of Inverbervie
1727 56 47 48N 02 10 48W	52m	50m	4 miles South east of Inverbervie
1728 56 48 12N 02 09 36W PA	52m	?	4.5 miles South east of Inverbervie
1729 56 49 24N 02 09 24W PA	50m	28m	4 miles East south east of Inverbervie
1730 56 49 30N 02 12 40W	38m	?	2 miles East south east of Inverbervie
1731 56 49 30N 02 09 00W PA	48m	?	4 miles East south east of Inverbervie
1732 56 5 00N 02 08 30W PA	43m	28m	4 miles East of Inverbervie
1733 56 51 48N 01 55 48W	75m	70m	11.5 miles East of Inverbervie
1734 56 53 06N 02 03 06W	52m	20m	8 miles East north east of Inverbervie

1735 Todhead Point. N0871770. Follow steps down the cliffs to the North of the lighthouse. The island 10m offshore has several underwater caves and lots of lobsters. The rocky bottom has lots of silt and a maximum depth of 16m.

1736 Forley Craig. N0873778. A kelpy bottom composed of conglomerate boulders, maximum depth 10m. Seals and crabs noted.

1737 Swallow Cove. N0874784. Walk past the bothy (of Montrose BSAC Branch) as far as you can along the shingle beach. Swim North to reach underwater gully in 15-20m. There are lots of undercut boulders and gullies with lobsters. The kelp finishes at 8m, which gives a pretty good indication of the average visibility.

1738 Wreck of the "Granero". This 1318 ton vessel was lost in 1933 about 600m South east of Crawton Ness (N0881799) at 56 54 28N 02 11 18W in 12m of water.

1739 Tremuda Bay to Old Hall Bay. A half-mile length of dramatic coastline just South of Dunnottar Castle, with a geo at N0882833 and seacaves at Maiden Kaim (N0882834). Undived as far as I know, though it has potential as depths appear to rapidly reach around 20m around cliffs, caves and stacks. Boat access from Cattterline or Stonehaven.

Wrecks in Stonehaven Bay. At least 3 vessels have been lost in this bay:
1740 "Dart"
1741 "Foldin"
1742 "Johanna"
No further information.

1743 Wreck of the SS "Cushendall". This 626 ton vessel was bombed by aircraft and sunk in 1941 at 56 57N 02 03W, 4.5 miles East of Bowdun Head, in about 52m of water.

Wrecks East of Stonehaven. At least 3 are charted. The positions are:

	Depth	Clear	
1744 56 57 24N 02 01 42W	55m	54m	6 miles East of Stonehaven
1745 56 57 40N 02 04 00W	52m	46m	4.5 miles East of Stonehaven
1746 56 59 24N 02 04 24W	51m	45m	4.5 miles East north east of Stonehaven

No further information.

1747 Wreck of the SS "Creemuir". This 3997-ton, 110m-long vessel was torpedoed by aircraft and sunk in 1940 with the loss of 27 lives at 57 01N 01 52W, 10 miles South east of Aberdeen, in about 60m of water. There is a "position doubtful" wreck charted in about 90m of water 2 miles South east of this position.

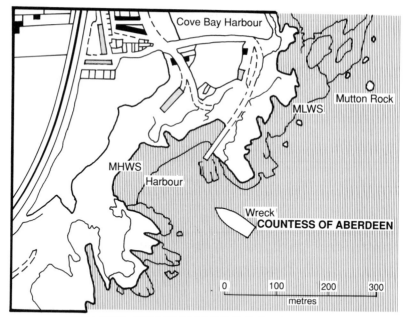

SITE 1753: THE 'COUNTESS OF ABERDEEN'

1748 Geo South of Newtonhill. N0912930. Lots of geos, chasms and gullies coated with beadlet anemones. The maximum depth is 14m, obtained by leaving the rocks and swimming over the silt. At the jetty there is a wreck, but it is totally broken up, with only the possibility of small finds.

1749 Newtonhill. N0913932. Access via East Camachmore Road and a track to the pebble beach (park here). Do not dive near the salmon nets. The dive is on to shaly rocks with a maximum depth of 14m.

1750 Downies. N0927951. Climb down 20m high cliffs and walk to end of spit of land; enter water and swim round island. Underwater are rocks as big as houses, gullies, cliff faces, and spectacular caves demanding torches. Maximum depth on rocks is 20m.

1751 Englishman's Neuks. N0932957. Why so-called?

1752 Portlethen. N0935962. At the North of the bay there is an underwater swim round to the North to an underwater arch. The bottom is solid rock, not conglomerate.

1753 Wreck of the SS "Countess of Aberdeen". NJ955005. This 575-ton vessel ran aground in fog in 1894 and lies in the Harbour South east of Cove Bay. The wreck is about 50m out from a point slightly North of the centre of the bay. It is a mass of flattened plates with lots of fish life in 6-12m of water. Avoid the salmon net set near the wreck from March to August. See BSAC Wreck Register, Wreck 19.

1754 Harbour, Cove Bay. NJ955006. Round the shoreline lobsters can be found in about 12m maximum depth. Further out 20m can be reached without going on the mud.

1755 Wreck of the "Brig". NJ957013. a trawler that was lost in Cove Bay. Only the engine block is still visible. Otherwise the bay is kelp-covered rock at a maximum depth of 10m.

1756 Wreck of the SS "Trebarthia". This 597 ton vessel was sunk by aircraft in 1940 4 miles South East of Aberdeen at 57 05 30N 02 01 00W. She lies in 42m of water with a clearance of 28m.

Wrecks East of Aberdeen.
At least 7 other wrecks are charted. The positions are:

	Depth	Clear	
1757 57 04N 01 57W PA	65m	50m	5.5 miles South east of Girdle Ness
1758 57 04N 01 54W PA	61m	50m	6.5 miles South east of Girdle Ness
1759 57 06 45N 01 57 00W PA	60m	50m	3.5 miles East south east of Girdle Ness
1760 57 07 06N 01 59 45W	48m	30m	2 miles South east of Girdle Ness
1761 57 09 40N 01 51 00W PA	70m	50m	6.5 miles East north east of Girdle Ness
1762 57 10N 01 55W PA	60m	?	5 miles East north east of Girdle Ness
1763 57 09 40N 01 51 48W PA	62m	40m	6 miles East north east of Girdle Ness

No further information.

1764 Unknown wreck, Aberdeen Bay. Charted at 57 09 42N 02 01 50W, 1 mile North east of Aberdeen Harbour, in 20m of water with a clearance of 13m.

1765 Wreck of the "Glentanar". This 817-ton vessel was lost in 1917 at 57 09 44N 02 01 40W, 1.5 miles North east of Aberdeen Harbour, in 24m of water with a clearance of 20m.

Wrecks off Balmedie.
At least 6 are charted. The positions are:

	Depth	Clear	
1766 57 13 48N 01 50 00W PA	60m	28m	7 miles East of Balmedie
1767 57 14 30N 01 40 00W PA	65m	35m	12 miles East of Balmedie
1768 57 15 00N 01 00 06W	14m	?	1 mile East of Balmedie

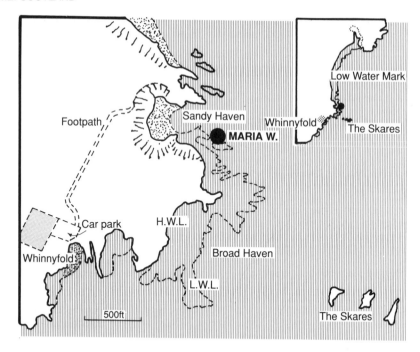

SITE 1778: THE MV 'MARIA W'

	Depth	Clear	
1769 57 15 42N 02 00 00W ED	10m	?	1 mile North east of Balmedie
1770 57 16 42N 01 41 18W	80m	60m	11.5 miles East of Balmedie
1771 57 17N 01 25W PA	85m	50m	20 miles East of Balmedie

No further information.

1772 Aberdeen to Peterhead. 25 miles of sandy shoreline with the exception of the Cruden Bay area. The diving is shallow and sandy and has little to commend it with the exception of some wrecks, some visible from the shore. Lots of flatfish.

1773 Wreck of the "Christine". This vessel was lost near Blackdog Rock (NJ965136). No other information.

1774 Unknown wreck, Aberdeen Bay area. A large steel vessel was located in 1952 and visited by divers in 8m of water.

1775 Unknown wreck. The wreck of an old steam vessel lies at the North side of a small cove, ½ mile South east of Old Slains Castle (NK054299).

1776 Wreck of HMS "Eagle", South of Cruden Bay. An 18th Century warship lost on the shoreline about 1 mile South of the Bay of Cruden.

1777 The Scares, Bay of Cruden. NJ090330. Launch from Port Errol (NJ095355) to reach the South side of the bay where there are several small wrecks amongst kelp-covered boulders at a depth of 10m maximum. Portholes have been recovered.

1778 Wreck of the MV "Maria W", North of the Scares, Bay of Cruden. This 240-ton Dutch vessel struck the Scares in dense fog and ran aground at Sandy Haven in 1966. She lies in 6m of water in a gully at 57 23 30N 01 50 29W. The wreckage is completely broken up and is generally only 1m high, though one portion projects up 4m. See BSAC Wreck Register, Wreck 139.

1779 Wreck of the SS "St. Glen". This 4647 ton vessel was bombed by aircraft in 1940 and now lies at 57 25N 01 38W, 7 miles East of the Bay of Cruden, in 65m with a clearance of 40m.

Wrecks East of Cruden Bay. At least 10 are charted. The positions are:

	Depth	Clear	
1780 57 19N 01 50W PA	46m	40m	5 miles South of Bay of Cruden
1781 57 20N 01 33W PA	76m	60m	10 miles East north east of Bay of Cruden
1782 57 21 18N 01 39 12W	66m	40m	7 miles East north east of Bay of Cruden
1783 57 23 12N 01 31 00W PA	76m	40m	11 miles East of Bay of Cruden
1784 57 23 20N 01 38 30WPA	65m	55m	7 miles East of Bay of Cruden
1785 57 28 42N 01 41 30W	60m	28m	5 miles East of Bay of Cruden
1786 57 24N 01 43W PA	60m	31m	4.5 miles East of Bay of Cruden
1787 57 24 00N 01 36 12W	64m	55m	7.5 miles East of Bay of Cruden
1788 57 24 27N 01 34 40W	65m	40m	9 miles East of Bay of Cruden
1789 57 26 00N 01 45 00W PA	51m	25m	0 miles NE of Bay of Cruden

1790 Boddam. NK137425. A good dive (by East coast standards) through an underwater arch (Transit van size) in a maximum depth of 12-15m. There is also the wreck of a small trawler; though this is well smashed boat-shaped ribs are still visible.

NB. In bad weather, the Scares and Boddam give the best visibility available in the Aberdeen area.

1791 Wreck of the SS "Port Denison". This 8043-ton, 146m-long vessel was torpedoed by German aircraft in 1940 with the loss of 16 lives (captain saved) 6 miles North east of Peterhead at 57 34N 01 39W in about 65m.

Wrecks off Peterhead. At least 10 other wrecks charted. Positions are:

	Depth	Clear	
1792 57 28 30N 01 44 30W PA	47m	28m	2 miles South east of Peterhead
1793 57 29 30N 01 32 30W PA	67m	40m	8 miles East of Peterhead
1794 57 29 48N 01 46 12W	20m	13m	0.5 mile South east of Peterhead
1795 57 30 50N 01 38 18W PA	62m	28m	4.5 miles East of Peterhead
1796 57 31 48N 01 43 00W PA	47m	20m	2.5 miles North east of Peterhead
1797 57 32 06N 01 44 07W	47m	35m	2.5 miles North east of Peterhead
1798 57 32 12N 01 43 40W	44m	41m	2.5 miles North east of Peterhead
1899 57 33N 01 46W PD	25M	?	3 miles North of Peterhead
1800 57 33N 01 41W PA	53m	28m	4 miles North east of Peterhead
1801 57 33 40N 01 43 10W PA	45m	30m	4 miles North north east of Peterhead
1802 57 34 20N 01 33 42W PA	86m	50m	8 miles North east of Peterhead

No further information

1803 Peterhead to Rattray Head. A sandy 8 mile stretch of coast. No dives recorded.

Wrecks off Rattray Head. At least 10 wrecks charted. Positions are:

	Depth	Clear	
1804 57 35 20N 01 38 50W PA	67m	40m	5.5 miles East of Rattray Head
1805 57 35 30N 01 40 42W PA	45m	25m	3.5 miles East south east of Rattray Head
1806 57 36 36N 01 43 06W	49m	48m	3 miles East of Rattray Head
1807 57 37 30N 01 38 00W	72m	50m	6 miles East of Rattray Head
1808 57 37 45N 01 43 3	51m	48m	3 miles East north east of Rattray Head
1809 57 38 10N 01 44 00W	49m	38m	3 miles North east of Rattray Head

	Depth	Clear	
1810 57 38 30N 01 44 30W PA	48m	25m	3 miles North east of Rattray Head
1811 57 38 42N 01 42 42W PD	52M	28m	4 miles North east of Rattray Head
1812 57 38 30N 01 33 24 PA	82m	40m	8.5 miles East north east of Rattray Head
1813 57 40 40N 01 34 03W PA	80m	40m	9 miles North east of Rattray Head
1814 57 42 00N 01 33 30W PA	82m	55m	10 miles North east of Rattray Head

No further information

Area information & services

Hydrographic charts: 190 Montrose to Fife Ness 1:75,000; 210 Newburgh to Montrose 1:75,000; 213 Fraserburgh to Newburgh 1:75,000; 1409 Buckie to Arbroath 1:200,000; 1481 River Tay 1:25,000.

OS 1:50,000 maps: 30 Fraserburgh & Peterhead; 38 Aberdeen; 45 Stonehaven; 54 Dundee; 59 St. Andrews & Kirkcaldy.

OS 1:25,000 maps: N060/61 Crail; N041/51 St. Andrews; N042/52 Tayport; N053/63 Carnoustie; N064 Arbroath; N065/75 Montrose; N076/86 Johnshaven; N087/88 Stonehaven; N089/99 Newtonhill; NJ80/90 Aberdeen); NJ81/91 Dyce, NJ82/92; NK02/03/13 Cruden Bay, NK04/14 Peterhead; NK05/15 Rattray Head.

Local BSAC Branches: Aberdeen (67); Aboyne (1093); Bridge of Don (906); Ellon (1193); Fraserburgh (484); Dundee (334); Montrose (500); Cupar (1094); Kirkcaldy (442); Aberdeen University (314); Dyce, Aberdeen (1329); Pedesas, Aberdeen (1087); Condor, Arbroath (1066); St. Andrews University (300); RAF Leuchars (684); Dundee University (471); Tayside Fire Brigade (936).

Local SSAC Branches: Grampian (Aberdeen); Peterhead; Aberdeen Grammer School; Ninewells Hospital (Dundee)

Air supplies: East Coast Divers, Anstruther (0333) 310768; Sub Sea Services, 21 John Street, Aberdeen (0224) 631362; Many of the local diving clubs also have their own compressors.

Outboard motor sales & services: Several, see the Yellow pages for Dundee and Aberdeen.

Boat charter: MV Hamnavoe, East Coast Divers, Anstruther (0333) 310768.

Local weather: Aberdeen Weather Centre (0224) 8091; Aberdeen Airport Meteorological Office (0224) 722334.

Sea areas: Forth, Cromarty.

Tidal constants:

	DOVER	ABERDEEN
River Tay bar	+0329	+0101
Arbroath	+0313	+0045
Montrose	+0315	+0047
Stonehaven	+0239	+0011
Aberdeen	+0228	–
Peterhead	+0149	−0039

Coastguard: MRCC: Aberdeen (0224) 52334; MRSC: Peterhead (0779) 4278, Crail (03335) 666; CG: Cruden Bay (077 981) 2680, Stonehaven (0569) 65138; Carnoustie (0241) 5221; Usan, Montrose (0674) 2101.

Harbourmasters: Dundee (0382) 24121; Arbroath (0241) 72166; Montrose (0674) 72302; Stonehaven (0569) 52571; Aberdeen (0224) 592571; Peterhead (0779) 74281/3.

Hospitals: Aberdeen Royal Infirmary (0224) 681818; Aberdeen City Hospital (0224) 633333; Aberdeen Royal Cornhill Hospital (0224) 632411; Stonehaven Arduthie Hospital (0569) 62022; Fraserburgh Hospital (03462) 3151; Arbroath Infirmary (0241) 72584; Dundee Royal Infirmary (0382) 23125; Montrose Infirmary (0674) 2020; Ninewells Hospital, Dundee (0382) 60111; Perth Royal Infirmary (0738) 23311.

Recompression chambers: Royal Infirmary, Aberdeen (0224) 681818 (or 871848 and as for the duty diving doctor); Institute of Offshore Medicine, Aberdeen (0224) 55595/55596 (after hours 671848 and ask for Medical Officer in charge of recompression facilities); MAFF Marine Laboratory, Aberdeen (0224) 876544; Comex Houlder Diving (0224) 714101; Oceaneering, Aberdeen (0224) 770444; Wharton Williams Taylor, Aberdeen (0224) 722877.

Police: Cupar (0334) 52226; St. Andrews (0334) 72222; Perth (0738) 21141; Dundee (0382) 23200; Carnoustie (0241) 52222; Arbroath (0241) 72222; Montrose (0674) 2222; Stonehaven (0569) 62806; Aberdeen (0224) 29933; Ellon (0358) 20222; Fraserburgh (03462) 3121.

Vehicle recovery: AA – Aberdeen (0224) 51231 (0700-2300), Dundee (0382) 25585 (24 hour); Perth (0738) 23551 (office hours). RAC – Aberdeen (0224) 872828 (office hours); Perth (0738) 23717 (office hours); Dundee (0382) 22543 (office hours); Edinburgh 031 229 3555 (24 hours).

Local tourist information: St. Andrews (0334) 72021; Perth (0738) 22900; Dundee (0382) 27723; Carnoustie (0241) 52258; Arbroath (0241) 72609/76680; Montrose (0674) 2000; Stonehaven (0569) 62806; Aberdeen (0224) 23456; Ellon (0358) 20730; Fraserburgh (03462) 2315.

Accommodation: Widely available to all standards.

CHAPTER 4

Rattray Head to Tarbat Ness

THE SOUTH coast of the Moray Firth is dominated by often-spectacular cliffs sprinkled with fishing villages and sandy beaches. The weather is milder than on the West coast, with much less rain. When it is raining on the West it is often only cloudy around the Firth.

Around Rattray Head lighthouse there are 20 miles of sandy beaches. In fact during a massive storm about 1720 the prosperous port of Rattray was suddenly blocked with sand and all that remains today is a ruined chapel. Fraserburgh has a big, bustling harbour and has been a centre of the herring fishing for over 300 years. Kinnairds Head at the North of Fraserburgh is made up of schists.

The coast from Pennan to Portsoy is very rugged, with caves, bird-haunted cliffs and massive headlands rising to as much as 140m above sea level. There are also ravine-like valleys, complete with fishing villages. Yet around Banff and Macduff the countryside is soft and rolling.

The Old Red conglomerate of Pennan Head has weathered into a series of narrow ridges and needles and forms one of the finest stretches of cliff in eastern Scotland. From Troup Head to Portessie the coastal rocks are a complex mixture of sandstone, conglomerate, quartzite, mica-schists, some gneiss, and grit bands. Between Rosehearty and Portgordon the old cliffs and the present cliffs are coincident. The sandy coastal features between Nairn and Burghead are a link between two areas of solid rock, as are those between Portgordon and Branderburgh.

Between Buckie and Lossiemouth lies Spey Bay with the River Spey, one of the most famous salmon-fishing rivers in the world, running into it. Passing the modern RAF base at Lossiemouth we arrive at a rugged piece of coast just East of Burghead with 30m-high, cave-studded cliffs followed by 15 miles of the afforested Culbin Sands, notable for their fossil sand dune systems.

The whole of the inner part of the Moray Firth (from Portgordon to Golspie) consists of sand and shingle spits and barriers, together with extensive sandy forelands and sandy marshes. All of these are associated with either the present beach or with the 25-ft and 15-ft raised beaches. They are often

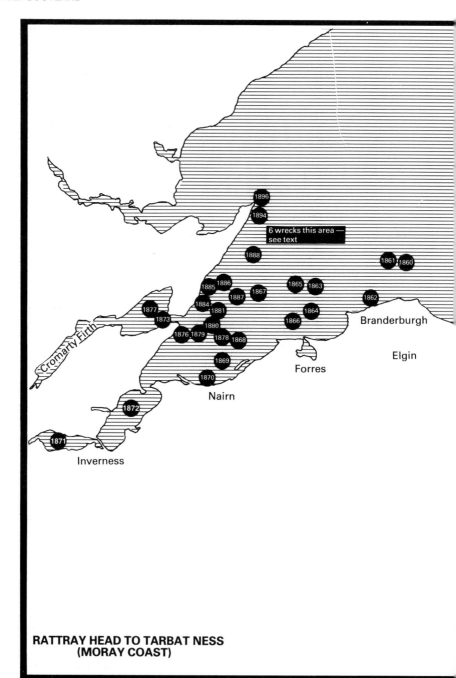

6 wrecks this area —
see text

Branderburgh

Elgin

Forres

Nairn

Inverness

Cromarty Firth

**RATTRAY HEAD TO TARBAT NESS
(MORAY COAST)**

Dive Sites: Chapter 4

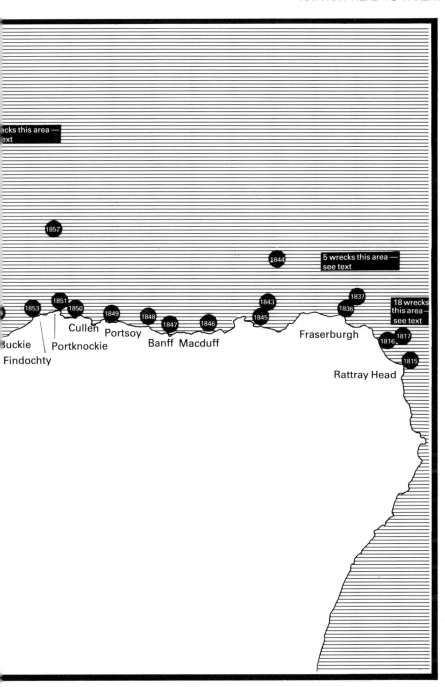

backed with substantial glacial deposits or by lines of former cliffs, sometimes cut into the shingle of former higher beaches. In raised beach times this coast was even more irregular than it is today and, in fact, the high ground between Branderburgh and Burghead was a group of islands.

Fort George 8 miles North east of Inverness is a spectacular piece of 18th century military architecture; it is now garrisoned by the Gordon Highlanders. Just East of Inverness is Culloden Moor, site of the last battle on British soil. Today the old battlefield is a peaceful place but oozing with atmosphere; a visit is still an emotive experience.

The "Capital of the Highlands", Inverness is a charming town with a slightly rural atmosphere. It is a large town (population 37,000) by the norm of northern Scotland, and offers virtually all the facilities that a visitor could wish. It is also home of the doughty Inverness branch of the BSAC.

West of Inverness lies the quiet estuary of the Beauly Firth with the flat and very fertile Black Isle to the North east. The North east coast of the Black Isle, between Rosemarkie and the Sutors of Cromarty, has 180m high steep grassy cliffs dropping to the sea. The Cromarty Firth and Nigg Bay, with its oil-related industry, has to be passed to reach the final headland of this chapter, that of Tarbat Ness. This headland has a lighthouse towering 55m above the sea and giving splendid views of the coast of Sutherland and Caithness to the North and the Grampian mountains to the South. Thousands of seabirds breed on the cliffs.

The wildlife of the area covered in this chapter is unexceptional, although the Moray Firth is a very important wintering ground for seabirds and waders. Often, large flocks of gannets may be seen in winter fishing the Moray Firth while sheltering from heavy weather. The Loch of Strathbeg just inland from Rattray Head is an RSPB reserve, and holds huge numbers of wintering waterfowl.

From a diver's point of view the 70-mile-long Moray coast gives much better sport than the Aberdeenshire coast, largely because the seabed is rocky for some distance offshore, and storms do not stir up so much muddy sediment. The visibility on occasions reaches 30m. It is considered by enthusiasts to be worth visiting from a distance. Inverness branch has located and explored many of the wrecks in the Moray Firth, and potentially the area could even begin to rival the Clyde and Forth estuaries as a wreck diving area.

The tidal streams in the Moray Firth are generally not too strong offshore, although they are somewhat stronger close to shore and around prominent headlands. The relative regularity of the shorelines allow the following figures to be extrapolated for the whole area:

Rattray Head: LW slack −0220 Dover, HW slack +0400 Dover.
Banff Bay: LW slack −0130 Dover, HW slack +0430 Dover, spring rate 0.5-0.75 knots.
Knock Head: as Banff Bay.
Knock Head to Covesea: LW slack −0200 Dover, HW slack +0420 Dover.
Tarbat Ness: LW slack −0530 Dover, HW slack +0100 Dover, spring rate 0.5-0.75 knots.

1815 Wreck of the "Repart". Lost on The Skellies (NJ109584). No other information.

Wrecks in Strathbeg Bay, NW of Rattray Head. Two wrecks recorded:
1816 "Laurel". **1817** "Grace Darling".

The Rattray Head lighthouse stands sentinel on a 20-mile stretch of sweeping sandy beaches.

Wrecks N of Rattray Head. At least 18 recorded. Positions are:

		Depth	Clear	
1818	57 41 20N 01 43 48W PA	50m	25m	5.5 miles NE of Rattray Head
1819	57 41 27N 01 46 30W	47m	28m	4 miles NNE of Rattray Head
1820	57 40 30N 01 45 38W	53m	40m	5 miles NNE Rattray Head
1821	57 41 16N 01 47 25W	44m	42m	5 miles North of Rattray Head
1822	57 41 30N 01 49 10W PA	44m	20m	5 miles North of Rattray Head
1823	57 42 18N 01 50 00W PA	48m	28m	6 miles North of Rattray Head

	Depth	Clear	
1824 57 43N 01 49W PA	52m	28m	6.5 miles North of Rattray Head
1825 57 42 50N 01 42 00W PA	71m	40m	7 miles North east of Rattray Head
1826 Position unknown	?	?	U-Boat sunk somewhere off Rattray Head by HMCS St John
1827 57N 01W	50m	?	7 miles North of Rattray Head (SS Trsat, 1369 tons, bombed by aircraft in 1941)
1828 57 44 20N 01 45 30W PA	59m	30m	8 miles North of Rattray Head
1829 57 45N 01 45W	60m	?	9 miles North of Rattray Head (SS Kildare, 3877 tons, lost 1940, bombed by aircraft
1830 57 45 10N 01 33 40W	82m	30m	12.5 miles NE of Rattray Head
1831 57 47 10N 01 34 52W PA	63m	40m	13 miles North east of Rattray Head
1832 57 47 05N 01 37 54W PA	63m	40m	12 miles North east of Rattray Head
1833 57 46 34N 01 40 30W PA	65m	30m	11 miles NNE of Rattray Head
1834 57 48 12N 01 41 00W PA	62m	35m	12.5 miles NNE of Rattray Head
1835 57N 01W PA	82m	?	12 miles N of Rattray Head (MV Cape York, 5027 tons, torpedoed 1940)

Wrecks of Kinnairds Head. Two are recorded as being lost:
1836 "Emma and Carl". **1837** "Rapid".

Wrecks off Kinnairds Head. At least 5 are recorded. The positions are:

	Depth	Clear	
1838 57 47N 01 51W PA	48m	35m	7 miles North east of Kinnairds Head
1839 57 47 00N 01 52 30W PA	56m	30m	6.5 miles NE of Kinnairds Head
1840 57 46 48N 01 53 54W PA	60m	30m	6 miles North east of Kinnairds Head
1841 57 46N 01 54W PA	60m	45m	5 miles North east of Kinnairds Head
1842 57 46 10N 01 57 42W PA	64m	46m	4.5 miles NNE of Kinnairds Head

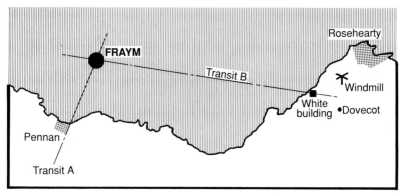

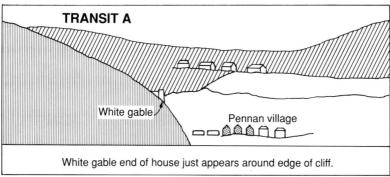

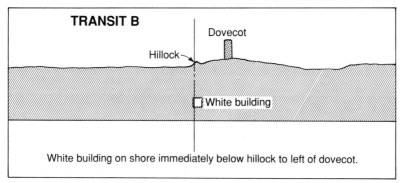

1843 Wreck of the "Fraym", off Aberdour Bay. A 2491 ton, 96m long, steamer torpedoed with the loss of 10 lives by V13 while at anchor in 1940 at 57 41 45N 02 14 42W. The wreck projects up 9m from the silty sand seabed at 45m. It is broken in half, fairly intact and lying virtually on an even keel. The bows lie some distance away in shallow water. Slack water is desirable for the dive; beware of nets and other fishing gear at the stern. Visibility can be up to 20m, but it can also be very dark because of the depth. See BSAC Wreck Register, Wreck 131.

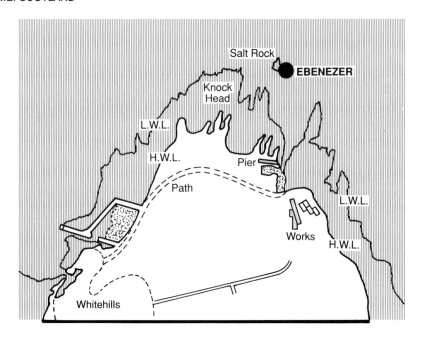

SITE 1848: THE 'EBENEZER'

1844 Unknown wreck, 5 miles North north east of Troup Head. Charted at 57 46 00N 02 13 10W in about 100m of water in the Southern Trench.

1845 Unknown wreck, 1.5 miles East of Troup Head. Charted at 57 41 43N 02 14 42W in about 20m of water.

1846 Wreck of a Heinkel dive bomber. This lies off Stocked Head in about 12m of water at approximately 57 40 30N 02 24 00W.

1847 Gun off Banff Pier. After WW1 a captured German gun was thrown into the sea off Banff Pier. It has been recovered and in the recovery a quantity of silver cutlery was found by the pier. Similar items can still be located.

1848 Wreck of the "Ebenezer". A 533-ton 40m-long, wooden three-masted barque lost in 1900 after striking Salt Rock (which is visible at low water). She lies in 9m of water, completely broken up, just off the headland to the North east of Whitehills. Boat access or very long snorkel. See BSAC Wreck Register, Wreck 106.

1849 Castle Point, Portsoy. NJ582666. Pleasantly interesting gullies lead from the shore to sand at 9m.

1850 Unknown wreck, Cullen Bay. All that remains is a large steel propeller and prop shaft in 8m of water. The position is approximately 400m off Cullen at 57 42N 02 49W.

1851 Scar Nose, Portknockie. NJ495689. Sandstone reefs, teeming with small life, running out to sand at 10m. A good dive in calm weather.

1852 Unknown wreck, 8 miles North of Portknockie. This is charted at 57 50 23N 02 53 30W in 80m of water with a clearance of at least 27m.

1853 Findochty. NJ464684. This boasts a tidal swimming pool, which certain divers have claimed to be worthwhile.

1854 Unknown wreck, 2.5 miles North west of Portgordon. Charted as position approximate at 57 42 00N 03 03 12W in about 11m of water.

Wrecks off Buckie.
At least 4 are charted. The positions are:

	Depth	Clear	
1855 57 49 51N 03 09 48W PA	70m	60m	11 miles North west of Buckie
1856 57 54 48N 03 02 48W	80m	?	14 miles North of Buckie
1857 57 57 36N 03 08 30W	49m	?	18 miles North north west of Buckie
1858 57 57 36N 03 14 24W	48m	?	20 miles North north west of Buckie

1859 U-boat wreck. A U-boat was sunk by HMS "John" in the vicinity of the last three unknown wrecks. Perhaps one of them is indeed it.

1860 Wreck of a Wellington bomber, 4 miles North north west of Stotfield Head. This is charted at 57 47 10N 03 20 00W in about 62m of water. The propeller was fouled and lifted by a fishing vessel, but was then released some distance away from the wreckage.

1861 Wreck of the MFV "Chrissie Criggle", 4.5 miles North west of Stotfield Head. This vessel was in collision with another MFV; both were substantially damaged, but only the "Chrissie Criggie" sank. She lies at 57 46 12N 03 23 45W in about 58m of water with a clearance of 50m.

1862 Hopeman. NJ142697. Similar diving to that of Scar Nose.

1863 Wreck of the "Tantivy", inner Moray Firth. This submarine was scuttled in 1950 as a sonar target. It was "lost" for some years before being re-located by Inverness Branch of the BSAC and then purchased by them. At the time of writing the ownership and control of the wreck is still to be finalised. The position is some miles North of Findhorn Bay towards the centre of the Moray Firth. The vessel is sitting upright and intact on a silty sand bottom at 40m and projects up to about 28m and gives a splendid dive. There are some nets caught on the wreck, so be cautious. Contact Inverness Branch for the more exact position and for the latest information.

1864 Wreck of the MFV "Briar", 5 miles West of Burgfield Light. Charted at 57 42 30N 03 38 54W in about 55m of water with a clearance of 53m.

1865 Unknown wreck, 6.5 miles West north west of Burghead Light. The wreck of a small wooden vessel lies in 26m of water at 57 45 30N 03 43 30W.

1866 Wreck of a Valentine tank, 2 miles North west of Findhorn Bay. This was swamped and sank in 20m of water at 57 41 18N 03 39 42W while practising amphibious tank landing in WW2 preparatory to the Normandy landings. A total of 5 tanks were lost in the exercise, although this is the only one yet located. Inverness Branch will provide exact details of the location to visiting divers.

1867 Unknown wreck, 6 miles North west of Findhorn Bay. This is charted at 57 44 20N 03 45 42W in 32m of water with a clearance of 29m.

1868 Wreck of a barge, 5 miles North of Nairn. Charted at 57 40 30N 03 50 00W in about 35m of water with a clearance of 27m. This is the wreck of a massive barge or perhaps a floating dock. It is said to be "as large as a football pitch".

1869 Wreck of the MFV "Rona", charted as 1.5 miles North of Nairn. This is charted as position approximate at 57 37N 03 51W in about 14m of water; the position is actually 57 38 30N 03 48 30W, 3.5 miles North east of Nairn in 22m of water. The craft caught fire and sank. The 4 cwt prop has been salvaged.

1870 Nairn Reef. NH874571. This lies just offshore at the West end of Nairn. A pleasant shallow dive in 6m with lots of marine life. Caution should be exercised as tangle nets are sometimes set herabouts.

1871 Beauly Firth. Flat, low and muddy, with little patches of weed. The tide goes out a long way over mud flats, which look utterly awful for diving, unless you're a shell-duck.

1872 Firth of Inverness. Similar to Beauly Firth, though not quite as bad.

1873 Cromarty Pier. NH784677. The Cromarty Firth is generally muddy and looks rather unpromising for divers. In addition, the Cromarty Firth Port Authority (whose permission is required to dive) are not very favourably disposed toward divers. Just off the pier at Cromarty, however, there is a pleasant shore dive to a depth of 6m. There is a profusion of marine life, probably due to the strong tidal streams, and octopus have been recorded.

1874 Wreck of a pinnace. This was lost in the Cromarty Firth. I have no further information.

1875 Wreck of a Sunderland seaplane. This was lost in the Cromarty Firth. I have no further information.

1876 Farquhar's Cave. NH800653. Far enough out a depth of 20m will be found on a boulder bed with occasional sandstone reefs. When the visibility is good there is a lot of life to be seen. Miller's fossil fish beds to south.

1877 Wreck of HMS "Natal". This lies South of Nigg Bay in the Cromarty Firth. Natal was a 13,500-ton, 146m-long WW1 armoured cruiser that caught fire, had her magazines explode and sank almost immediately on Christmas 1915 during a party. A total of 25 officers and 380 ratings were lost. She was blasted for clearance and is now only 2m above the seabed in a depth of 15-25m. Though the wreck is flattened (or because of it) there are lots of "goodies" to be found; though take care as there are also live shells, (and some bones). Her armaments were six 9.2" guns, four 7.5" guns, other lighter arms and three torpedo tubes. Visibility varies from zero to 10m. As the vessel lies in the fairway, SMBs are essential. Permission to dive is required from the Cromarty Firth Port Authority (Harbourmaster: Capt. D. Miller, Invergordon 852308), and, because it is a war grave, they will also direct you to the Admiralty at Invergordon.

1878 Wreck of the "Caledonia". This lies at approximately 57 38N 03 57W about 3.5 miles SSE of the entrance ot the Cromarty Firth in about 16m.

1879 Wreck of the tanker "Shell Brit 1". A 1025-ton, 70m-long vessel in ballast from Grangemouth to Inverness in 1940. She blew up, caught fire and sank with the loss of all her 21 crew. She lies in two pieces at approximately 57 40 00N 03 57 30W about 1.5 miles South east of the entrance to the Cromarty Firth in about 15m of water.

1880 Wreck of the armed trawler "Marsona". This lies in two pieces at 57 40 24N 03 55 00W about 2.5 miles East south east of the entrance to the Cromarty Firth in about 15m of water with a clearance of 14m. She is well broken up and only really the outline of the vessel is to be seen. Shells (dated 1917) can still be found in the wreckage. The wreck lies just within the limits of the Cromarty Firth Port Authority and their permission should be sought before diving as large oil rigs manoeuvre in these waters. There can be a substantial tidal stream at this site.

1881 Wreck of the liner "Durham Castle". The Durham Castle was a Union Castle liner used on the South Africa run. She had been withdrawn and was being towed to Scapa Flow for use as a blockship when she hit a mine and sank at 57 41 30N 03 54 04W, about 2.5 miles East of the entrance to the Cromarty Firth. She lies partly broken up in about 18m of water with a clearance of 14m. The visibility can be poor and this increases the sense of scale on this 600 feet long wreck.

Aeroplane wrecks off Cromarty Firth: two planes, a Wellington and a Sunderland, were lost hereabouts; it is not known which wreck is which plane.

1882 One lies at 57 41 48N 03 52 30W (about 3.5 miles East of the entrance to the Cromarty Firth) in about 24m of water with a clearance of 22m.

The often-picturesque Moray Firth coastline generally gives better diving than Aberdeenshire, with a rockier seabed and visibility reaching 30m.

1883 The other lies at 57 42 00N 03 51 06W (about 4.5 miles East of the entrance to the Cromarty Firth) in about 29m with a clearance of 27m.

1884 King's Cave. NH840711. A sandy seabed with 3m-high sandstone reefs, complete with through-holes. A good dive when the visibility improves. Best about 1-2 miles from shore, when the depth reaches 20m.

1885 Port an Righ. NH853732. Similar to King's Cave.

1886 Viking wrecks. Port an Righ means "Bay of the Kings". Legend has it that three Viking Kings were wrecked here in the Tenth Century. The legend also suggests that it was three sons of Danish kings that were drowned here while on a punitive expedition. Remains of Tenth Century Viking wrecks would be quite a find!

1887 Spoil ground North of Guillam Bank. This lies about 4 miles East of King's Cave. It is NOT a dive site and should be avoided by divers as it was used to dump cyanide waste. The seabed is laid waste and virtually devoid of marine life.

1888 Wreck of the "San Tiburcio", Moray Firth. This 5995-ton British tanker was sunk in 1940 at 57 46 33N 03 45 20W. The bottom is 24m and the least depth 18m. The vessel is virtually intact and is owned by members of Kinloss BSAC Branch.

1889 Wreck of the "Young Fox", Moray Firth. This is charted as position approximate at 57 50N 03 41W at a depth of 26m with a clearance of 15m.

Wrecks in the Moray Firth. At least 3 other wrecks charted. Positions are:

		Depth	
1890 57 49 00N 03 36 50W		27m	6 miles East south east of Tarbat Ness
1891 57 50N 03 33W		34m	7 miles East south east of Tarbat Ness
1892 57 51 42N 03 38 30W		31m	4 miles East of Tarbat Ness

I have no other information except that one of these is thought to be the "John Wackie".

1893 Balintore to Tarbat Ness. 8 miles of rocky shore that looks reasonably promising. Apparently undived.

1894 Wrecks of British destroyers. There is wreckage from either HMS "Lynx" or HMS "Exmouth" on the shore about 1 mile South of Tarbet Ness. The other vessel lies wrecked somewhere offshore, but the position is not known.

HMS Lynx, 950 tons, 81m long, 32 knots was lost in 1915 along with 70 of her crew when she struck a mine "off the Moray Firth".

HMS Exmouth, 1475 tons, 105m long, 36 knots, was lost in 1940 along with 189 of her crew when she was either mined or torpedoed "in the Moray Firth". Her armament was five 4.7" guns and eight torpedo tubes.

1895 Wreck of the "Verona". An opulent converted yacht that was lost in the Moray Firth. The position is unknown.

1896 Tarbat Ness. NH950878. A series of rocky sandstone reefs with lots of life running out to sea, reaching depths of 6-18m. In good weather the visibility can reach 15m, and this makes for good dives.

Area information and services

Hydrographic charts: 115 Moray Firth 1:200,000; 213 Fraserburgh to Newburgh 1:75,000; 222 Buckie to Fraserburgh 1:75,000; 223 Dunrobin Point to Buckie 1:75,000; 1078 Inverness Firth 1;20,000; 1462 Harbours on the North and East Coasts of Scotland; 1889 Cromarty Firth: Cromarty Bank to Invergordon 1:15,000; 1890 Cromarty Firth: Invergordon to Dingwall 1:15,000.
OS 1:50,000 maps: 21 Dornoch Firth; 26 Inverness; 27 Nairn; 28 Elgin; 29 Banff; 30 Fraserburgh & Peterhead.
OS 1:25,000 maps: MK05/15 Rattray Head, NJ96/NK06 Fraserburgh, NJ76/86 Macduff; NJ56/66 Banff & Cullen; NJ36/46 Buckie; NJ16/26 Elgin; NH96/NJ06 Findhorn & Culbin Forest; NH85/95 Nairn; NH65/75 Fortrose; NH64/74 Inverness & Culloden Moor; NH44/54 Beauly; NH45/55 Dingwall & Strathpeffer; NH46/56; NH66/76; NH67/77 Strath Rory & Nigg Bay; NH86/87; NH88/98.
Local BSAC Branches: Fraserburgh (484), Moray & Nairn (894), Inverness (346), RAF Lossiemouth. *Local SSAC Branches:* Buckie, Invergordon.
Air supplies: Sub Sea Services, 84 Telford Street, Inverness (0463) 223745.

Outboard motor sales & services: Most of the larger towns have firms specialising in outboard sales and services.
Boat charter: Vessel at Ballintore (Contact Steve Coutts, Ballintore)
Local weather: Aberdeen (0224) 8091; Kinloss Forres (0309) 72161 X673.
Sea areas: Cromarty.
Tidal constants:

	ABERDEEN	DOVER
Fraserburgh	−0059	+0129
Banff	−0122	+0106
Whitehills	−0126	+0102
Buckie	−0135	+0053
Lossiemouth	−0136	+0052
Burghead	−0131	+0057
Nairn	−0134	+0054
Fortrose	−0125	+0103
Inverness	−0126	+0102
Cromarty	−0138	+0050
Invergordon	−0134	+0054

NB. These are averaged figures and there can be variations of up to 30 minutes depending on the time of day.

Coastguard: MRCC Aberdeen (0224) 52334; MRSC Peterhead (0779) 74278; Fraserburgh (0346) 3374/4279; Lossiemouth (034381) 2009; Banff (02612) 2415.
Harbourmasters: Fraserburgh (0346) 2108; Macduff/Banff (0261) 32236; Whitehills (02617) 229; Buckie (0542) 31700; Lossiemouth (034381) 3066; Burghead (0343) 835337; Hopeman (0343) 835435; Findhorn/Nairn (0667) 54704; Inverness (0463) 233291.
Hospitals: Royal Infirmary, Aberdeen (0224) 681818; Fraserburgh (0346) 3151; Chalmers Hospital, Banff (02612) 2567; Campbell Hospital, Portsoy (0261) 2202; Seafield Hospital, Buckie (0542) 32081; Nairn (0667) 52101; Raigmore Hospital, Inverness (0463) 234151.
Recompression chambers: Royal Infirmary, Aberdeen (0224) 681818 (or 871848 and as for the duty diving doctor); Institute of Offshore Medicine, Aberdeen (0224) 55595/55596 (after hours 671848 and ask for Medical Officer in charge of recompression facilities). MAFF Marine Laboratory, Aberdeen (0224) 876544; Comex Houlder Diving (0224) 714101; Ocean-eering, Aberdeen (0224) 770444; Wharton Williams Taylor, Aberdeen (0224) 722877.
Police: Fraserburgh (0346) 3121; Macduff (0261) 32222; Banff (02612) 2555; Portsoy (0261) 2222; Buckie (0542) 32222; Lossiemouth (034381) 2022; Nairn (0667) 52222; Inverness (0463) 239191; Beauly (0463) 782222; Fortrose (0381) 20222; Cromarty (03817) 222; Alness (0349) 882222; Invergordon (0349) 852222.
Vehicle recovery: AA − Aberdeen (0224) 51231 (0700-2300); Inverness (0463) 33213 (0900-1700); Aviemore (0479) 810300 (0900-1700); Dundee (0382) 25585 (24 hrs). RAC − Edinburgh 031 229 3555 (24 hrs).
Local tourist informations: Fraserburgh (0346) 22315; Banff (02612) 2419; Cullen (0542) 40757; Elgin (0343) 3388; Forres (0309) 72938; Nairn (0667) 52753; Inverness (0463) 34353; Muir of Ord (0463) 870433/870525.
Accommodations: All grades of accommodation are available in the towns scattered along the coast.

CHAPTER 5

Tarbat Ness to Skirza Head

THIS CHAPTER covers an 50-mile stretch of coast that is far from fully explored from a diving point of view. Most divers, in fact, drive rapidly and impatiently down the twisting road that follows this coastline on their way to Scrabster and the ferry for Orkney and Scapa Flow. While no one would suggest that this coast and its wrecks rival those in Scapa Flow, it is still worthwhile to pause awhile and sample its diving on the way to greater moments farther North.

The climate of Sutherland and Caithness is actually rather mild for the latitude, though it is subject to strong winds. Temperatures in July and August can average 16° C, though rain falls on about 50% of summer days.

Around Tarbat Ness the coastline is rocky but soon this gives way to the flat sand and mud of the Dornoch Firth to the West, which is of little interest to divers; the geological importance has been briefly mentioned in the last chapter. Bonar Bridge at the head of the Firth is a small village with a large bridge designed by Thomas Telford in 1811-12. The river, the Kyle of Sutherland, is a productive salmon fishing area.

Dornoch (population 970, and county town of Sutherland) lies at the northern side of the mouth of its Firth. From here to the "top" of mainland Scotland lies one of the last true wilderness areas of Europe. It is a mixture of bleak moorlands (the "flows") backed by distant rugged mountain peaks; only 1.5% of the land is arable, the lowest proportion in Scotland. Sutherland covers 1.3 million acres, and is among the ten largest of the old counties of Britain, yet its total population is only 13,000, almost half what it was in 1801. Man has made an impression only on the coastline, evidenced by a scattering of villages; the flow country (although the subject of recent controversial afforestation) is largely left to the birds in summer and lies desolate and empty in winter. Three miles North of Dornoch, the wetlands of Loch Fleet Nature Reserve (Scottish Wildlife Trust) provide sanctuary for many water birds all year round.

The coast trends northwards to the town of Wick (population 7842) passing the villages of Golspie (population 1374), Brora (1436), Helmsdale (727), Berriedale, Dunbeath (161), Latheron, Lybster, Ulbster and

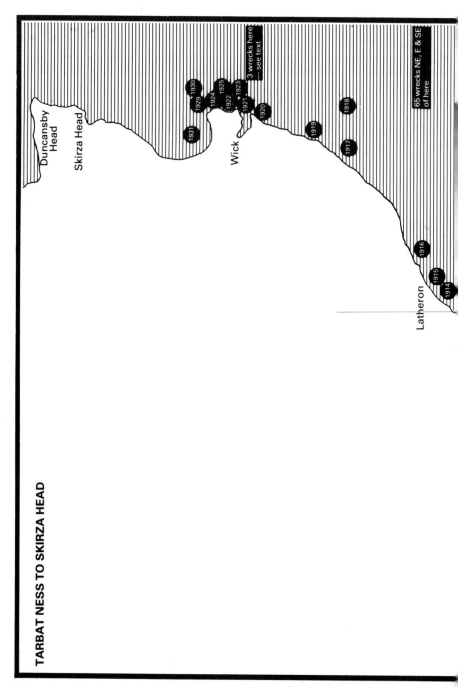

TARBAT NESS TO SKIRZA HEAD

Dive Sites: Chapter 5

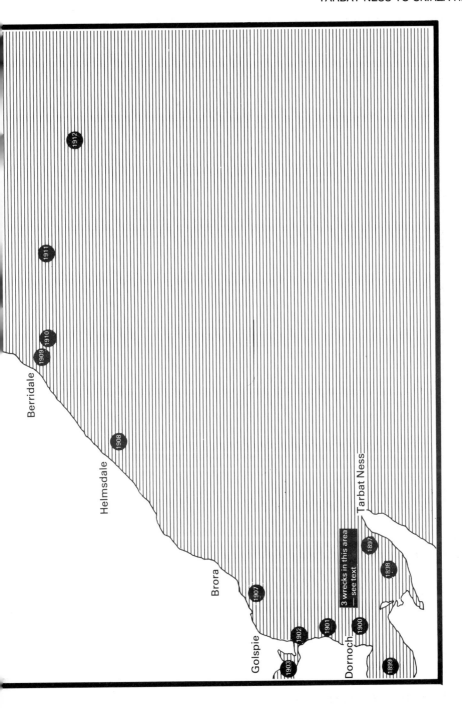

Thrumster. Places of interest include imposing Dunrobin Castle between Golspie and Brora, and Lothebeg between Brora and Helmsdale, where the last wolf in Scotland was supposedly killed about 1700. As far as Brora the beaches are sandy, but here a fault in the rocks and a band of Old Red Sandstone running out to sea change the nature of the coast. The beaches become rock and shingle farther North.

At Helmsdale, which is largely built on the old 100-ft raised beach, the coast road climbs over the 150m high Ord of Caithness (impressive views) drops steeply into the wooded valley containing Berriedale (where landslips give the impression of steps in the cliffs) and immediately climbs again before finally descending to Dunbeath and then to Latheronwheel. This 15-mile section of road is trying for vehicles pulling heavy boat trailers, and potentially quite demanding in winter conditions; occasionally drivers have died of exposure in winter blizzards on this road. The railway to Wick and Thurso makes no attempt to follow the coast and strikes well inland at Helmsdale. Caithness runs inland from Ord Point and then runs more or less North along the summits of a series of hills. The Ord itself is made of granite. The slopes facing the sea are the result of continental scarp weathering processes and only the lower parts have been modified by marine processes.

At Latheron the A895 cuts left across the moors towards Thurso (and Scapa Flow). The A9 follows the cliff-lined coast on to Wick. The villages are set in quite picturesque narrow valleys. Lybster is a model village set out by the landowner Sir John Sinclair just after 1800. He dissociated himself from the "Highland Clearances" and provided money to develop both his estates and his tenants' interests.

Wick is a grey, solid town, described by Robert Louis Stevenson as "the bleakest of God's towns". It used to be a very important fishing centre, but this has now declined. The divisional rescue headquarters of the Coastguard are sited in the town; their responsibility extends from Ullapool to Inverness and out to Iceland and Greenland – quite a patch!

Just South of Wick there is a geo (chasm or creek) and large stack – The Brough – cut into a fault; there are five other geos in the immediate vicinity. In Wick Bay there are peat patches and old tree stumps under the sand, giving evidence of changing sea levels. North of Wick lies Noss Head (made of flagstones and with numerous geos) and its lighthouse overlooking Sinclair's Bay, the longest stretch of sand in Caithness. In fact Caithness is known as the "Lowlands beyond the Highlands". A section of cliffed coast then leads North to Freswick Bay where there are traces of a 5-ft raised beach.

The flat Caithness sandstones continue under the Pentland Firth to make up the islands of Orkney. The topography of Caithness has been greatly modified by the last glaciation and most of the pre-glacial topography has been masked. Many deep river courses were filled with clay and post-glacial rock gorges have therefore been cut to give new courses. The sea cliffs are laced with dykes of igneous rock and minor faulting. The sea has worked away at these to leave spectacular clefts, stacks and geos. At Skirza Head, at the North of Freswick Bay, the link is made with volume II of this work.

The diving of this coast is not fully explored. The rock features near to shore and the wrecks further offshore offer significant potential to an exploratory diving group. Conditions are not extreme, though it should be remembered that this is a relatively quiet coast, and boat outings should be planned accordingly.

Tidal streams are generally weak in the Moray Firth, once away from Duncansby Head and the Pentland Firth. Note that there is usually a weak South-south-west-going current (as opposed to tidal stream) running from Orkney to Rattray Head. The tidal data is:

Near Freswick Bay: HW slack +0250 Dover, LW slack −0535 Dover, spring rate about 1 knot.

Near Noss Head: HW slack +0140 Dover, LW slack −0435 Dover, spring rate 1-2 knots.

Off Dunbeath Bay: HW slack +0200 Dover, LW slack −0605 Dover, spring rate less than 1 knot.

Near Berriedale: HW slack +0200 Dover, LW slack −0350 Dover, spring rate about ¾ knot.

Off Brora Point: HW slack +0410 Dove, LW slack −0320 Dover, spring rate about ½ knot.

Near Tarbat Ness: HW slack +0530 Dover, LW slack −0220 Dover, spring rate about ¼ knot.

Note that an East-going current with a rate exceeding that of the tidal stream has been reported near Tarbat Ness.

Dive Sites

1897 Wreck of a survey vessel. This was lost in about 1975 while carrying out a civil engineering survey. The position is approximately 57 52 30N 03 50 30W, 2 miles West of Tarbat Ness. The depth is about 14m.

1898 Wreck of the "Duchess", off Portmahomack. NH890844 (approx). This was lost at approximately 57 50 18N 03 50 18W in 3m of water. Only the engine remains.

1899 Dornoch Firth. Very similar to Beauly Firth – flat, shallow and muddy.

1900 Armada wreck, Dornoch Firth. An Armada vessel was reputedly lost in the Dornoch Firth, possibly on Gizzen Briggs.

1901 Embo Pier. NH822922. After a long snorkel a sandstone reef at a depth of 7m is reached. Visibility can reach 15m in good conditions.

1902 Entrance to Loch Fleet. NH815955. The flood tide can be dived at rates up to 5 knots. The bottom is sandy with mussel beds and gives a passable dive in bad weather in up to 6m depth. Visibility can reach 10m.

1903 Loch Fleet. The diving is hopeless, just like the Beauly and Dornoch Firths.

Wreck off Loch Fleet. There are at least 3 charted well out in the North Sea. The positions are:

1904 57 57 36N 03 14 24W   49m 24 miles East of Loch Fleet
1905 57 57 54N 03 29 36W   49m 16 miles East of Loch Fleet

*The rugged cliffs of
the far north-east*

1906 58 02 30N 03 24 40W   48m 20 miles East north east of Loch
                                      Fleet
I have no further information.

1907 Strathsteven. NC886016. A poor shore dive over rocks and sand.
Access is over the railway line through a gate by the house.

1908 Brora to Berriedale. A 17-mile stretch of rockyshore with no recorded
dives.

1909 Berriedale Castle. ND122224. A shore dive off a cave with gullies
and other interesting rock formations containing lots of life in a maximum
depth of 11m. Watch the tides when shore diving.

1910 Berriedale Harbour. ND122225. The flat rocks to the North give an
unexceptional dive, often in poor visibility.

1911 Unknown wreck, 7.5 miles East of Berriedale. Charted at 58 09 30N
03 15 50W in a depth of about 48m with a clearance of 35m.

1912 Smith Bank. This extensive bank lies in the North Sea about 15 miles
South east of the Caithness and Sutherland coasts. It covers an area of

about 25 miles by 15 miles and, near its centre, has depths of about 35-45m. A biological survey, carried out by dredging in 1952, revealed an unusual and interesting fauna. The Marine Conservation Society would be very interested in up-to-date biological reports from divers.

1913 Wreck of "Gretafield". This 10,190-ton, 152m-long Norwegian tanker was lost with 11 lives when she was torpedoed in 1940. She was subsequently beached and stayed ablaze for several days. The wreck lies just to the South of Dunbeath Bay and gives a pleasant dive in 10-15m of water. She has been well explored and salved by local divers.

1914 South of Latheronwheel, (Janetstown). ND190320. Shallow gullies running out from shore. Pleasant diving in good visibility.

1915 Unknown wreck, Latheronwheel. This lies 300m straight out from the green triangle of grass and is the wreck of an armed trawler with live ammunition. It is 8-10m to the sandy seabed where the boiler is still to be seen, together with various "goodies". The harbour has no slip.

1916 Invershore. ND244346. 400m to the South of the harbour there are 3 caves with depths of 10m. There are nesting cormorants and these can be seen swimming underwater. Access is via a path with 365 steps down the cliff! The geo is 20m deep and has nice life, usually in good visibility.

1917 Whaligoe. Access is via a path with 365 steps down the cliff. The rocky-bottomed geo is 20m deep and has nice life, usually in good visibility.

1918 Unknown wreck, 2 miles South east of Sarclet Haven. Charted as position approximate at 58 20 12N 03 04 18W in a depth of 54m with a clearance of 50m.

1919 Sarclet Haven. ND353433. MV "Andreas" was lifted in 1981 by Thurso BSAC Branch. She was towed to Sarclet Haven where she broke up in bad weather. Half of the vessel remains and is worth diving.

1920 Castle of Old Wick. ND370488. An interesting, sheer-walled (30m high) geo with water 10-12m deep. Access is via the steps of the pathway from the castle. The cracks in the rock are stuffed with life.

1921 Unknown wreck, just off North Head, Wick. This is charted at 58 26 24N 03 03 06W in a depth of about 20m.

1922 Broad Haven. ND380513. The South side gives a shore dive directly out from the car park for as far as you are prepared to fin. A few metres from shore the depth is 12m, and there is a natural arch 5m by 3m long.

1923 Papigoe geo. ND387516. As Broad Haven.

1924 Staxigoe geo. ND386525. Access from the track. The water is 10-15m deep and the life is interesting.

1925 Unknown wreck, off Staxigoe. This is charted at 58 27 06N 03 02 06W, about ½ mile offshore in a depth of about 30m.

Wrecks off Wick. At least 3 are charted. The positions are:

			Depth	Clear	
1926 58 25N 02 45	PA		60M	?	10 miles East of South Head, Wick
1927 58 25 54N 02 54 00W	PA		62m	44m	5 miles East of South Head
1928 58 28 30N 02 56 30W	PA		53m	?	5 miles North east of South Head

1929 Unknown wreck, Noss Head. This is charted at 58 28 36N 03 02 00W, ½ mile East of Noss Head. The depth is 20m and the clearance 11m.

1930 Noss Head. ND388551. 30m cliffs dropping into deep water. Undived.

1931 Wreck of V81, Sinclair Bay. This 1188-ton, 269-feet long, German destroyer was scuttled at Scapa Flow in 1919, raised, then foundered while on tow to Rosyth. Apparently no salvage has been attempted since. The approximate position is 58 30N 03 05W.

1932 Wrecks in the North Sea. It may interest the reader to know that chart 115 (Moray Firth) has, in addition to those detailed in this and the previous chapter, a total of at least 65 wrecks charted! Many of these are presumably U-boat losses from WW2. Their distances offshore can be up to 70 miles. Very many of these are too deep for sport divers, but there are some intriguing possibilities among the others.

Area information and services

Hydrographic charts: 115 Moray Firth 1:200,000; 223 Dunrobin Point to Buckie 1:75,000.
OS 1:50,000 maps: 21 Dornoch Firth; 17 Strath of Kildonan; 11 Thurso & Dunbeath; 12 Thurso & Wick.
OS 1:25,000 maps: NH88/98, NH68/78, NC80/90 Brora; NC81/91 Beinn Dhorain; ND01 Helmsdale; ND02/12 Berriedale; ND03/13 Latheron; ND23 Lybster; ND24/34 Thrumster; ND25/35 Wick; ND26/36 Freswick.
Local BSAC Branches: Thurso (119), Inverness (346).
Local SSAC Branches: Highland (Golspie), Invergordon.
Air supplies: Sub Sea Services, Inverness (0463) 223745; Local diving clubs.
Outboard motor sales & service: James McCaughey, Wick (0955) 2858/3701.
Local weather: Aberdeen Weatherline (0224) 8091; Aberdeen Airport Meteorological Service (0224) 722334.
Sea area: Cromarty, Fair Isle.

Tidal constants:

	ABERDEEN	LEITH
Portmahomack	−0135	+0053
Meikle Ferry	−0114	+0114
Golspie	−0148	+0040
Wick	−0211	+0027

Coastguard: MRSC Peterhead (0779) 74278; MRSC Kirkwall (0856) 3268.
Harbourmasters: Portmahomack (086287) 564; Helmsdale (04312) 347; Wick (0955) 2030.
Hospitals: Migdale Hospital, Ardgay (08632) 211; Cambusavie Hospital, Golspie (04083) 3182; Caithness Central Hospital, Wick (0955) 2261; Wick Town & County Hospital (0955) 2133; Raigmore Hospital, Inverness (0463) 234151.
Recompression chambers: Royal Infirmary, Aberdeen (0224) 681818 (or 871848 and as for the duty diving doctor); Institute of Offshore Medicine, Aberdeen (0224) 55595/55596 (after hours 671848 and ask for Medical Officer in charge of recompression facilities); MAFF Marine Laboratory, Aberdeen (0224) 876544; Comex Houlder Diving (0224) 714101; Ocean-eering, Aberdeen (0224) 770444; Wharton Williams Taylor, Aberdeen (0224) 722877.
Police: Bonar Bridge Ardgay (08632) 222; Dornoch (0862) 810222; Golspie (04083) 3222; Brora (0408) 21222; Helmsdale (04312); Dunbeath (05933) 222; Wick (0955) 3551.
Vehicle recovery: AA − Inverness (0463) 33213 (0900-1700); Aberdeen (0224) 639231 (0900-1900), RAC − Inverness (0463) 231640 (0900-1730).
Local tourist informations: Bonar Bridge Ardgay (08632) 333; Dornach (086281) 400; Helmsdale (04312) 640; Wick (0955) 2596.
Accommodation: It is possible to camp "wild" at many places on this piece of coast, although access to the water is not always easy. B & B and guest houses are available in Bonar Bridge, Dornoch, Golspie, Brora, Helmsdale, Dunbeath, Wick and in many smaller villages.

Calm seas along Orkney's rocky coastline, which has an amazing number of chasms, caves, sea stacks and arches.

CHAPTER 6

Orkney

ORKNEY IS SEPARATED from the Scottish mainland by the 6-mile-wide Pentland Firth, supposedly the wildest water around our coasts. The general appearance of Orkney is, apart from the island of Hoy, flat and mainly agricultural; there is a greenness to the land.

Depending on how an island is defined, Orkney is comprised of over 90 islands, and some 18 are inhabited. Orkney lies between 58N 41N and 59 24N latitude and 2 22W and 4 25W longitude; this is equivalent to the latitude of Leningrad, Alaska or southern Greenland. All the islands fit in a rectangle of sea 56 miles by 29 miles, with the land area totalling 376.3 square miles. The coastline length is 793km (c.f. 1450km for Shetland, 150km for Caithness), excluding holms and skerries (very small islands or reefs which may be submerged at certain times). In other words, the coastline is fairly heavily indented.

The archipelago is the product of submergence. Imagine Orkney as an undulating summit plateau, tilted to the North and east, with a major central structural depression (Scapa Flow) inland from the residual massif of Hoy. A mosaic of islands, firths (inlets) and straights has resulted. The distribution of coastal types is highly irregular. High cliffs are largely confined to the West and South east coast of mainland, West Hoy, West Westray and parts of South Ronaldsay. The cliffs at St. Johns Head are the highest perpendicular cliffs in British Isles, at 1140 feet. Sandy beaches occur most frequently in the North Isles, especially on Sanday and Stronsay.

The coastline has an amazing number of caves, sea stacks, arches and geos (chasms or creeks). The major sea stack of the Old Man of Hoy did not exist 300 years ago. It was merely a narrow, gigantic promontory jutting from the straight line of the cliffs along the coast. About 150 years ago large portions had collapsed in rockfalls leaving a great arch linking the outer end with the main cliff. About a century ago it became a stack when the remains of the arch crumbled. This process will continue, and the stack is likely to collapse in the next century or so.

Orkney is made almost entirely of relatively gently inclined sedimentary rocks of middle Old Red Sandstone age, though western Hoy consists of younger, carboniferous rocks. The crystalline basement of metamorphic rocks and granites which underlies the Old Red Sandstone throughout northern Scotland is only exposed in small inliers at Stromness and

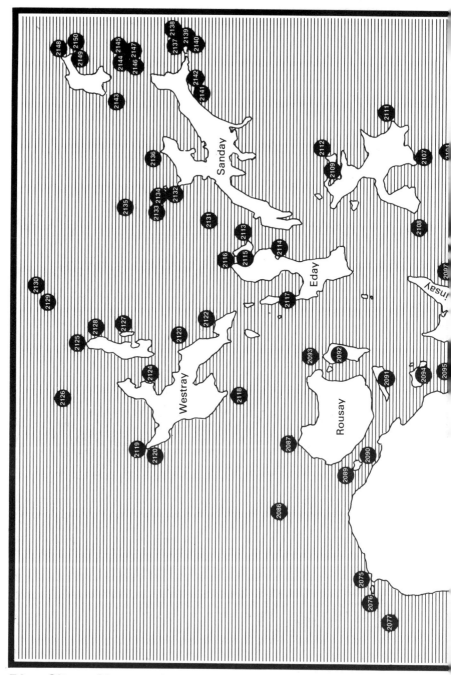

Dive Sites: Chapter 6

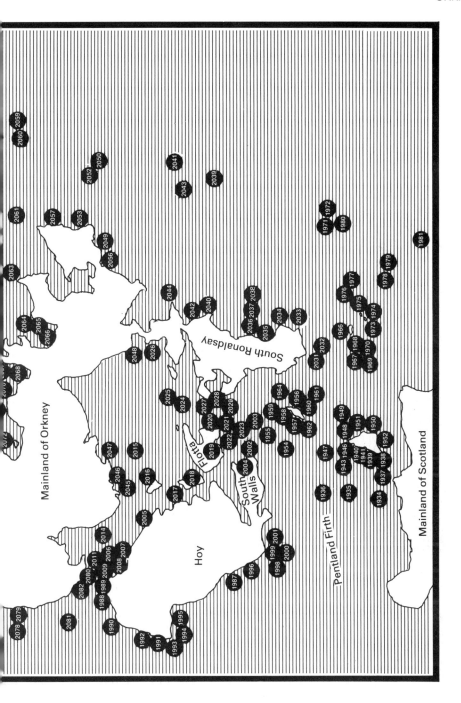

Yesnaby, and on the island of Graemsay. The prominent South east to East trending depressions now occupied by the sea and forming the straits between the main island groups, as well as the Pentland Firth, are the remnants of a South eastward trending Tertiary river system which have been submerged by the relative rise in sea level of recent times. The recent glaciations have smoothed the land somewhat and have left a covering of a fertile mantle of till on lower ground.

The weather is similar to that of Shetland, and the climate is best described as hyperoceanic, which compares to the peninsulas of the extreme West and North coasts of Scotland. Winter and summer average daily mean temperatures vary by only about 10°C. The winds are strong and frequent (24 gales annually). In fact, the archipelago is sometimes called the "islands of the grey wind". Annual rainfall is 37 inches; there are fewer frosts and less snow than on the nearby mainland of Scotland. The long summer days are a most refreshing feature, and on June 22 at Kirkwall, the sun rises at 0310 and sets at 2136, thus being above the horizon for 18 hours 16 minutes.

Orkney was the *Orcades* of ancient times; the word may be derived from the Norse for a seal. Its history has been one of Neolithic farmers, Bronze Age craftsmen, Iron Age builders, Viking warriors, Scottish adventurers, mediaeval traders, British servicemen, and many others. With the possible exception of Wessex, the Northern Isles are archaeologically the richest and most varied region in the British Isles. The islands are littered with prehistoric remains, such as underground houses (e.g. Skara Brae), brochs, circles (e.g. Stones of Stenness), tombs (e.g. Maeshowe), standing stones (e.g. the Ring of Brodgar) and earth houses. A visit to some of these should not be missed.

Unlike Shetland, Orkney was assimilated easily into the Scottish way of life. Its people became farmers first, fishermen second. The 1981 population was 19,040. Effectively, Orkney is an extension of the sandstone platform of Caithness. The isolation and exposure mean that there are fewer species of animals and plants than might be expected if the Pentland Firth did not exist. There are 90 breeding species of birds in Orkney, compared to 66 in Shetland; this is the more surprising as Orkney has virtually no trees. The presence of small mammals has led to a high concentration of raptors, such as hen harrier and short-eared owl in Orkney. The islands are the major seabird station for the British Isles because of their highly productive seas. Orkney is also internationally important for sea duck wintering in firths and on lochs of Stennes and Harray.

Marine mammals are common in Orkney waters. Grey seals have a very important population and the "common" seal is also common. One hundred pilot whales were stranded in Bay of Holland, Stronsay in April 1950 and another 67 on Westray in 1956.

In the 18th century the northern route around Britain was favoured because of its relative freedom from pirates who infested the English channel in Jacobite times, and later because of its distance from French bases. The northabout route was physically very hazardous – seas could be stormy even in summer, the coasts were unlit, and there were no charts. Ships from the South kept to the West of St. Kilda then called for water and stores at Stromness and then proceeded round the north of Shetland to minimise the chance of running ashore at night. Murdoch Mackenzie produced sets of charts for Orkney in 1757, ten years after the first survey of the North west Scottish coasts and islands by Bryce. The Lighthouse Board on Northern Shores was established in 1786. The earliest lighthouse in Orkney was lit at North Ronaldsay in 1789; Pentland Skerries and Start Point, Sanday, followed in 1794 and 1801 respectively; there are now 11 major and 11 minor lighthouses, 8 unlighted beacons and 21 buoys in Orkney. Irrespective of this, however, there have been enormous numbers of vessels lost in Orkney waters.

The tides around Orkney result from the interaction of the North Atlantic and North Sea tidal systems. Both systems rotate anti-clockwise but they reach the Orkney coastline moving in opposition, with the Atlantic peak arriving some 2-3 hours before the southward travelling North Sea wave. This produced a net West to East water flow, and produces complex and powerful tidal interactions in the Pentland Firth, among the island sounds and in Scapa Flow.

In general the diving in Orkney is very pleasant, without being sensational, though there are many exceptions to this. However, there is one especial exception – Scapa Flow – which is unique in that it contains the remains of the sunken German WW1 High Seas Fleet. In fact, the wrecks of Scapa flow are so important in diving terms that they have been allocated a chapter to themselves. The tidal streams round the headlands and in the sounds can be very strong and can form turbulent and dangerous overfalls; otherwise these very strong streams do not come too close to the coasline. Tidal stream predictions are a very important part of dive planning when diving in these waters. Water temperatures vary from 5°C in February to 13°C in July.

If sea level were lowered by 36m, the whole of Orkney would be one elliptically-shaped island, though it would not join it to Swona, Pentland Skerries or Caithness. The shore, especially on the West often falls away rapidly to 54-73m while the firths, sounds and Scapa Flow are rarely deeper than 36m.

The shallow sublittoral zone is well developed throughout Orkney. the dominant habitat is kelp-covered rocks inhabited by the animal life that is typical of such kelp forests. On level sandy bottoms there are scallops, queen scallops, brittle stars, and tunicates on solid bottoms. Bottom-dwelling and pelagic fish are common in summer. Lobsters and crabs are common. There is also the interesting brackish water environment in the lochs of Stenness and Harray, which have a complete salinity gradient making them unique. Dive sites are arranged island by island as far as possible working South to North.

Dive sites: Pentland Firth

The tidal streams of the Pentland Firth are the substance of which legends are made. They are the strongest in the British Isles and run at up to 11 knots, though locals claim there are small sections that travel at as much as 14 knots. You MUST be fully aware of the dangers of and techniques for operating in fast-moving, turbulent water before attempting to dive in this area. You should also read the five pages describing the tidal streams in the Admiralty pilot.

1933 Wreck of HMS "King Edward VII". A 16,350-ton, 138m-long, British battleship sunk in 1916 after hitting a mine at 584222N 035334W, 25 miles West of Swona. All were saved. She was armed with four 12″ guns, four 9.2″, ten 6″, 14 12-pounders, two machine guns and four torpedo tubes. The depth is 108m with a clearance of 94m, so the wreck is only of academic interest to sport divers.

1934 Shoal North of Mey Bay. This lies about 1.5 miles South of the previous shoal, about 1.5 miles North west of St. John's Point. It reaches to within 11m of the surface from a depth of 36m. Again, it is rocky and undived.

1935 Shoal under Merry Men of Mey. The Merry Men of Mey is the name given to the vast line of overfalls that appear between the Men of Mey Rocks East of Dunnet Head and Tor Ness on Hoy. The general water depth in the Pentland Firth is about 70m, but this rises quite rapidly to 21m on the shoal which is undived and presumably rocky. It lies 3 miles West of the northern tip of Stroma. Slack water is something of a joke, though you could try around LW +0100, HW −0500 Dover. This might well be the most serious drift dive in British waters.

1936 Wreck of the destroyer HMS "Immogen". This 1370 ton, 98m long vessel was cut in half by another destroyer in dense fog off Duncansby Head in 1940. She was armed with four 4.7″ guns, seven smaller guns and ten torpedo tubes. The after-part of the vessel drifted with the ebb and sank with 4 miles West north west of Stroma Light. This position is 584312N 031430W in about 82m of water. 18 lost.

1937 Mell Head, Stroma island. ND341764. This undived site looks excellent. There is a narrow geo 150m long, a narrow channel about 200m long between the island and a stack, and a natural arch. Depths appear to be about 10m.

1938 Wreck of the "Clarence G. Sinclair". A Thurso schooner that went ashore in 1898 at Mell Head, Stroma (ND339762) with a cargo of flag-stones. The vessel was badly holed and sank.

1939 Wreck of the SS "Grayson". An American collier that ran aground at Falla Geo, West Stroma (ND344767) in 1920 and was a total loss.

1940 Cave, Red Head, West Stroma. ND345775. A huge, water-filled cave which has yet to be dived. Depths reach 14m at its mouth.

1941 Wreck of the SS "North Sea". A Glasgow collier that ran aground at Broad Geo, West Stroma (ND345771) in 1898 and became a total loss.

1942 Wreck of the MV "Gannaren". A Swedish vessel lost in 1935 when she ran ashore on the West side of Stroma. After salvage attempts, the after-part of the vessel grounded again about 800m further along the island.

Wrecks on Langaton point, North west Stroma. ND348772. A PA wreck is charted.

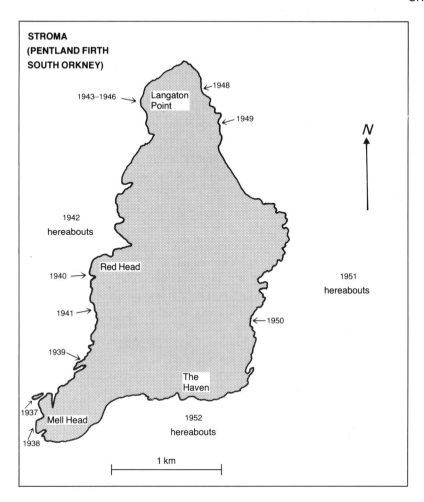

STROMA
(PENTLAND FIRTH
SOUTH ORKNEY)

1948

1943–1946

Langaton
Point

1949

N

1942
hereabouts

Red Head

1940

1951
hereabouts

1941

1950

1939

The
Haven

1937

Mell Head

1952
hereabouts

1938

1 km

DIVE SITES, STROMA

1943 Grimsby steam trawler "Hercules" became a total wreck in 1898.

1944 Peterhead steam drifter "Guide Me" ran aground in fog in 1924 and became a total wreck.

1945 Grimsby steam trawler "Mary" ran aground and was then swept off the ledge and sank in deep water in 1932.

1946 Finnish steamer "Gertrud" struck the rocks in dense fog in 1934. The vessel was pounded to pieces by heavy seas and sank in deep water.

1947 40m shoal, 0.8 mile North west from Swilkie Point, Stroma. There are depths of 57m, 59m and 84m near this 40m shoal. These, coupled with the strong tidal streams, could make for a memorable dive.

1948 Wreck of the SS "Corinthia". A Liverpool vessel loaded with wood struck the rocks at Wardie Geo, North east Stroma (ND356792) in a fog in 1903. The vessel rolled over and sank after the crew had been rescued.

1949 Geos of Bagwa, Stroma. ND357788. Very similar to the Bay of Sluggs except that depths reach 18m immediately offshore.

1950 Bay of Sluggs, Stroma. ND360770. A bedrock seabed to beyond 30m with visibility in excess of 20m reported in June. Huge shoals of saithe and lots of octopus. Please respect the ferocious tides and note that these will make for very serious diving beyond the reach of some divers. Boat access from John O'Groats (ND380735) or Burwick (ND444842) in South Ronaldsay.

1951 Wreck of the SS "Empire Parsons". A large steamer that ran ashore in darkness on the East side of Stroma in 1942 during a gale. The vessel became a total loss.

1952 Wreck of the "Anna Maria". An Orkney schooner with a cargo of coal that ran ashore on the South side of Stroma and became a total loss in 1925.

1953 Unknown wreck, 2 miles South west of Swona. This is charted as Position Approximate at 584312N 031000W right in the middle of the Pentland Firth in a depth of 69m with a clearance of 55m. Could it possibly be destroyer HMS "Immogen"?

1954 Shoal at 49m 1.5 miles West of, North Head, Swona. There is a depth of 69m immediately West of this rocky shoal. This must be an excellent dive although there are tidal streams of up to 5 knots at times.

1955 Triton Bank, 1 mile North west of Swona. A moderately extensive Bank with a least depth of 33m with surounding depths reaching 50-75m. Exposed to 7 knot tidal streams.

1956 Swona island. This lies about 3 miles West of South Ronaldsay. There are no dive sites recorded but, again, there must be great potential. There are tidal overfalls at each end of the island and the East coast drops rapidly to about 45m.

Wrecks on Swona: The owner of the island states that there have been at least 12 wreckings on the island.

1957 Grimsby trawler "Lord Percy" struck the rocks on the West side of Swona in 1930. the skipper was drowned attempting to lay out a kedge anchor. She slid off the rocks and sank in deep water.

1958 British SS "Pennsylvania" (3759 tons) struck a rock South west of the

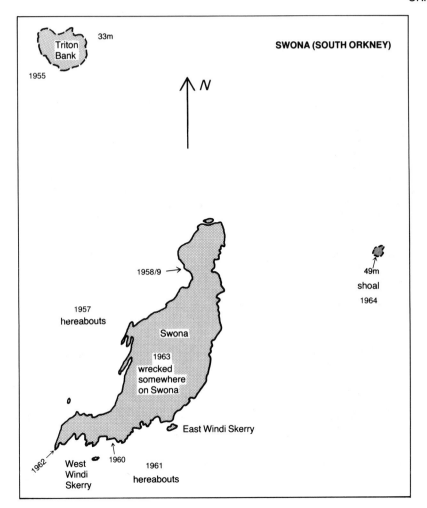

Triton Bank
33m
1955

SWONA (SOUTH ORKNEY)

N

1958/9 →

49m
shoal
1964

1957
hereabouts

Swona

1963
wrecked
somewhere
on Swona

East Windi Skerry

1962 →
West
Windi
Skerry

1960

1961
hereabouts

DIVE SITES, SWONA

Brook on the West side of Swona in fog in 1931; she became a wreck and sank at 584452N 030335W. She lies just below and to the West of a rock pinnacle which is awash at low water. The remaining wreckage (stern, prop shaft, engines and keel) lie covered with kelp at 12m at the base of the pinnacle; parts are scattered to the West down a steep rock slope to 27m.

1959 Norwegian SS "Gunnaren" (3229 tons, 108m long) ran ashore in 1035 at Swona on the same pinnacle as the Pennsylvania. She broke in half and the stern half swung round and came to rest 100m offshore at 584447N 030334W, South of the rock pinnacle. Parts of the wreck show at all states of the tide although most of the wreck has ripped away leaving only a shell.

1960 Grimsby steam trawler "Champion" struck Little Skerry and became a total loss on the South side of Swona in 1900.

1961 British steamer "Kroma" became a total loss on the South side of Swona in 1900.

1962 Schooner "Mary Grace" struck the rocks on Tarf Tail, Swona (ND378836) and sank in deep water in 1927.

1963 The "Joanna Thornden" wrecked about 1938 on Swona with a cargo that included copper ingots and barrels of paraffin wax.

1964 Shoal at 49m 0.7 mile East of, North Head, Swona. With depths of 57m between this shoal and Swona, there could be a good dive here, but the site lies under the overfalls caused by the tidal streams.

1965 Muckle Skerry, Pentland Skerries. ND464780. Pentland Skerries are a series of one island and seven small skerries. They appear to be undived by amateurs, yet must offer great potential. A fair amount of salvage diving has been carried out. Muckle Skerry is the largest; it has a series of rocky geos and immediately offshore depths reach about 15m. Slack water at neaps lasts for less than ten minutes as the tidal stream changes from more than 1 knot flowing to the East to more than one knot flowing in a westerly direction.

Wrecks on Muckle Skerry:

1966 Wreck of the MV "Kathe Niederkirchner". An 8003-ton, 142m-long, East German vessel that ran aground on North west Muckle Skerry in 1965. She rolled over after 9 hours and sank at 584131N 025557W in 16m of water with a clearance of 7m. She lies 070/250 degrees about 200m offshore from the cairn at ND466784.

1967 Stroma fishing boat "Royal Oak" was swamped near Muckle Skerry and sank in 1908.

1968 Banff fishing vessel "Strathyre" drifted onto Muckle Skerry and became a total wreck in 1909.

1969 Thurso schooner "Desdemona", carrying coal, struck the rocks on Muckle Skerry and became a total loss in 1912. Four lost.

1970 Swedish SS "Kirruna", carrying coal and contraband, struck Muckle Skerry in dense fog and became a total wreck in 1916.

1971 SS "Express" of Kirkwall sank East of Pentland Skerries in 1916. Thirteen lost.

1972 Danish SS "Christiansborg" struck a mine East of Pentland Skerries and sank in 1940.

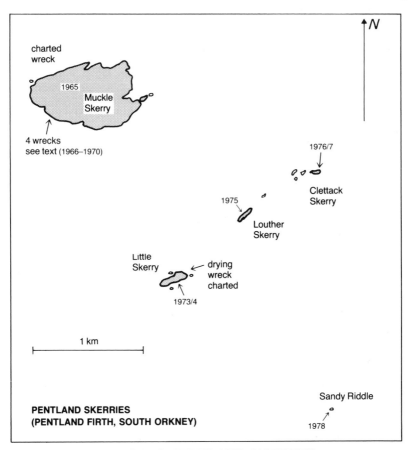

charted
wreck

1965

Muckle
Skerry

4 wrecks
see text (1966–1970)

1976/7

Clettack
Skerry

1975

Louther
Skerry

Little
Skerry

drying
wreck
charted

1973/4

1 km

Sandy Riddle

1978

PENTLAND SKERRIES
(PENTLAND FIRTH, SOUTH ORKNEY)

DIVE SITES, PENTLAND SKERRIES

1973 Little Skerry, Pentland Skerries. ND470765. This is one of seven small skerries to the South east of Muckle Skerry. They are undived and depths appear to be about 5-20m.

1974 Wreck of "Ben Barvas". A 235-ton British trawler lost on the South side of Little Skerry when she ran aground in heavy seas in 1964. In 1983, the vessel lay on its port side and was being broken up by heavy seas.

1975 Louther Skerry. ND480772. Similar to Little Skerry.

1976 Clettack Skerry. ND486776. Similar to Little Skerry.

1977 Wreck of SS "Fiona". A 1611-ton, 85m-long British armed boarding steamship that ran aground on Clettack Skerry and became a total loss in 1917. No lives were lost.

1978 Sandy Riddle, Pentland Skerries. ND487753 (approx). A shoal lying 1 mile South east of Little Skerry. It reaches to within 11m of the surface from depths of 36m to the East. This must yield a good dive.

1979 Submarine ridge, South east of Sandy Riddle. Sandy Riddle is just one high point on a submarine ridge running for 4 miles to the South east from Little Skerry. There are three other points with least depths of 14m, 11m and 31m. All are undived and have excellent potential.

Wrecks in the Pentland Firth: There have been very many vessels lost in the Pentland Firth and its environs. Some of the positions are not known and depths are sometimes too great for sport diving.

1980 Wreck of "U18". A 691-ton, 62m-long, German submarine lost in 1914 at 584209N 024800W, 3.5 miles East of Muckle Skerry. She was rammed by the trawler "Dorothy Gray", surrendered and was scuttled. The wreck lies in a trough between two sandwaves of greater height; the wreck is 4.5m high in a general depth of 70m.

1981 Unknown wreck, 6 miles South of Muckle Skerry. A 91m long vessel at 583643N 02 4740W in 65m of water. The wreckage may have sunk into the sand seabed.

1982 Unknown wreck, 7.5 miles East of Old Head. A 110m long wreck lying 150/330 degrees in 72m of water at 584415N 024037W, with a clearance of 67m.

1983 Wreck of HMS "Nessus". A 1022-ton, 83m-long British destroyer sunk at 5836N 0233W after a collision with the cruiser "Amphitrite" in dense fog in 1918. She was armed with three 4″ guns, two smaller guns and four torpedo tubes and was capable of 34 knots. The position is 16 miles East south east of Duncansby Head in 65m of water.

1984 Unknown wreck, 12.5 miles East north east of Muckle Skerry. The wreck lies at 5836N 0233W in about 60m of water with a charted clearance of 50m.

1985 Wreck of the SS "Wilston". A 2611 ton, 95m long, vessel that struck a mine at 583840N 023100W in 1916 and sank with the loss of eight lives. The position is 15 miles East of Duncansby Head in a depth of 65m, clearance 45m.

1986 Wreck of HMS "Duke of Albany". A British armed boarding steamship of 1997 tons, 101m long, that was sunk by German submarine UB27 in 1916 at 5844N 0228W, 14 miles East of Old Head, South Ronaldsay in a depth of 66m. 24 lives lost.

1987 Wreck of "X22". This 30 ton X-Craft was lost by collision in 1943 in the "Pentland Firth".

Hoy

1988 Wreck of the "Leicester City". A trawler lost at 585600N 032118W in 1953. The position is 200m East of Taing of Selwick in 2m of water.

1989 Wreck of the "Strathelliot". HY228058. This is a drying wreck lost in 1952 at 585559N 032031W on Taing of Selwick, at the North of Hoy. It dries 1m at low tide.

1990 Kame of Hoy. HY197049. A natural arch both above and below the surface with depths generally falling from 5m to 15m. Very pretty, kelp-filled, fish-frequented rock gullies descend to 25m to the West of the arch.

The major sea stack of the Old Man of Hoy is exposed to tidal streams and substantial wave action. The stack is said to be likely to collapse within the next hundred years.

1991 Old Man of Hoy. HY176009. There is a rock ridge called the toe extending out from the rock pinnacle. The North side of the toe is a cliff dropping to 15m along the full extent of the toe. Large boulders on a bedrock seabed gradually shelve away from the base of the cliff. The site is exposed to tidal streams and substantial wave action. The horizontal surfaces are covered with kelp, the vertical surfaces with alcyonium, anemones and tubularia; there is also much fish life.

1992 Cave under Old Man of Hoy. HY176009. On the North side of the toe there is a small cave at a depth of about 12m. The bottom is covered with broken weed and the cave contains many seals.

1993 Rora Head. ND173991. A pleasant dive to a bottom of kelp-covered, 3m-deep rocky gullies at a depth of 11-13m. All the varieties of life that could be expected at such an exposed site are to be seen.

1994 Wreck of the "Siberite", Rora Head. This lies at 585215N 032545W just off the rocks, 100m South of Rora Head.

1995 Too of the Head. ND186988. A shelving bottom of rock outcrops and sand. Kelp reaches 28m and the rock outcrops are covered with alcyonium, brittle and feather stars, and urchins. The site is sheltered from the North and East but is exposed to tidal streams.

1996 Wreck of the "Torsley". A Grimsby trawler that ran ashore and was totally wrecked at Berry Head, Hoy (ND235909) in dense fog in 1938.

1997 Wreck of the "Ross Puma". A 352-ton, 57m-long, British trawler that ran aground in 1968 at 584850N 032022W just South of Little Rack Wick. It is charted as a drying wreck.

1998 Tor Ness. ND255884. This is undived, although depths appear to rapidly reach beyond 30m.

Wrecks on Tor Ness:

1999 Aberdeen steam trawler "Braconmoor" was stranded on Tor Ness in a gale and became a total loss in 1929. Skipper lost.

2000 Hull steam trawler "Dorbie" ran aground on Tor Ness and became a total wreck in 1932.

2001 Grimsby trawler "Silanion" ran ashore at Tor Ness in a gale in 1933 and became a total wreck.

2002 Cantick Head. ND347996. This headland lies at the furthest South east tip of the island of South Walls, which is connected to Hoy by a causeway. A splendid drift dive can be made a long the rocky wall under the lighthouse. Depths reach about 20m and the tidal streams can flow at up to 4 knots. Maximum tidal streams at +0210 and +0545 Dover; high water slack lasts much longer than the water slack. Boat access from Osmondwall (ND333994) or from Bay of Howton (HY318039).

2003 Wreck of the SS "Dennington". A British steamer that went ashore on Switha in a blinding snowstorm in 1905. The vessel slid back and sank. Two lost.

2004 Unknown wreck, Kirk Hope. Charted at 5847139N 030859W, just East of the slip at Osmondwall, on the rocks in a depth of less than 1m.

2005 Scad Head. HY290007. A sandy seabed to beyond 20m, with scallops. Shore access.

2006 Graemsay island. It is shallow all round the island and no sites are recorded. There are very strong tides of at least 8.5 knots in Hoy Sound; heavy overfalls and standing waves form when the outgoing stream meets an Atlantic swell. Slack water at +0500 and −0110 Dover.

2007 Unknown wreck, Burra Sound. This lies at 585532N 031841W, 200m South east of Middle Skerry. It lies in 5-10m of water and shows at low tide.

2008 Wreck of the "Gobernador Bories", Burra Sound. Lost in 1914 at 585525N 031833, 500m South east of Middle Skerry. The depth is about 10m, and the tides flow at up to 6 knots.

2009 Wreck of the "Inverlane", Burra Sound. Charted at 585543N 031840W 250m East of Middle Skerry in 8m of water. This drying wreck is the conspicuous remains of a blockship sunk in WW1, although these were supposedly dispersed in 1962. It is visible at all states of the tide. Actually only the bow section of the 9100 ton tanker was used as a blockship. The stern remains near Whitburn, Sunderland where the vessel was lost by mine. The bow section was saved, sealed, towed to Scapa Flow and used for 4 years for fire fighting practice before being sunk as a blockship.

Shoals near Graemsay. There are four shoals:

2010 The Fleshes (4m), to the South.

2011 Showbelly (least depth 4m), 500m North of Hoy Sound Lighthouse. Tidal overfalls and tidal streams of up to 8.5 knots.

2012 Sand Eel (4m), to the North east.

2013 Riddock Shoal (3m) to the East.

These are all shallow and undived. They must have some potential.

2014 Anti-submarine barrier, Clestrain Sound. This was built up of railway lines in WW1. It was "crushed down" by an ice-breaker after the war. It lies immediately east of Riddock Shoal at 585555N 031445W, with a least depth of 6m in a general depth of 15m. It is 900m long.

2015 Barrel of Butter. HY325009. The drying rocks in the centre of Scapa Flow only give an average dive in poor scenery to 20m, though the site usually provides good views of seals.

2016 Cava island. No sites are recorded although the island is rocky all round and fairly quickly reaches depths of 10-20m.

2017 Rysa Little. ND313980. The site of one of the wreck salvage operations lies about half a mile to the North east of the island of Rysa Little. The rusting remains of the battleship "Seydlitz" inlcude a large mound of sizeable lumps of stoking coal. The seabed around is shingly mud at a depth of 15-20m.

2018 Fara island. Similar to Cave with no sites recorded.

2019 Flotta island. This quite large island has a number of rocky headlands and shallow bays but few sites have been recorded. Note that diving is restricted anywhere near the pipeline running from Pan Hope on Flotta to Burray.

2020 Hullderow, Flotta. ND377926. An excellent drift dive runs from here towards Stanger Head. Close inshore is a steep boulder slope with shoals of pelagic fish, cuckoo wrasse, many shellfish and octopus to be seen. By levelling out at 20m calm water will sweep you right round Stanger Head with a South-flowing tide. If you go any deeper, you may be pulled deeper still by the tidal stream and down to a bottom solidly carpetted with Alcyonium.

2021 Stanger Head. ND376924. There is a natural arch, but this is not deep enough to dive. The end of the headland is very colourful underwater, with plenty of hydroid beds and associated nudibranchs under the huge kelp fronds. Porpoises have been noticed fishing here.

2022 Wreck of the "Barbara". A schooner carry coal that was driven before a gale from the Pentland Firth. She failed to make the shelter of Longhope, went ashore on Flotta and became a total wreck in 1913.

2023 Switha, North end. ND368913. Very similar to Stanger Head.

2024 Nevi Skerry, Sound of Hoxa. ND397957. This skerry dries 2m at low water and has depths of 10m and more all round. It lies 0.6 miles East of Roan Head Light on Flotta.

2025 The Grinds, Sound of Hoxa. A shoal that is awash at low water, 0.7 mile North east of Nevi Skerry. Depths reach about 15m to the North and South of the shoal.

2026 Shoal East of Glims Holm. ND450990. At the South east of Scapa Flow this rocky shoal reaches to within 12m of the surface from depths of 27m.

South Ronaldsay

2027 Hoxa Head drift. ND403927. Another good drift dive over a steep, rocky, kelp-covered slope beyond 20m. Cup coral and cuckoo wrasse noted. Beware of strange tidal eddies.

2028 Bloie Geo, Hoxa Head. ND404926. An interesting boulder slope descends to the East of the geo. There are brass shell cases lying about.

2029 Wreck of the "James Barrie". This 666 ton, 55m long trawler was lost in 1969. She lies at 584847N 030209W, 0.5 mile South west of Hoxa Head in about 35m of water with a clearance of 22m. The seabed is of stones with brittle stars and hydroids. Often a 0.5 knot tidal stream.

2030 Unknown wreck, Widewall Bay. This drying wreck, possibly an MFV, is charted at 584833.4N 025959.5W near some ruined piers and slips. The hulk is about 35m long and is lying on the high water line.

2031 Wreck of the "Mary Roberts". A schooner carrying coal that struck Lother Rock, South Ronaldsay (ND434828) and became a total wreck in 1903.

2032 Wreck of the "Dubbleman". A steam trawler that was stranded on Lother Rock and became a total wreck in 1912.

2033 Wreck of the "Duna". A steamer carrying wood that ran ashore in fog near Old Head, South Ronaldsay (ND470834) and became a total wreck in 1912.

2034 Halcro Head. ND474856. A marvellous dive reminiscent of St. Kilda. There is an obvious cave in the middle of the East-facing cliff face. The bottom is sand at 20m with some kelp-covered rock outcrops. The cliff walls are sheer and undercut near the bottom. There are obvious signs of erosion and the bottom 5m in the cave are bare of life. The interior of the cave is lit by shafts of light coming through the upper entrance, and there is a huge buttress supporting the wall which makes the cave even more cathedral-like. The life in the cave is limited although the outside walls are covered with Alcyonium, sea squirts; hydroids and sponges. A superb dive.

2035 Unknown wreck. (ND457870 approx). This is charted at 584600N 025615W in Wind Wick as a drying wreck.

2036 Wreck of HMS "Opal". A 1000-ton, 83m-long, British destroyer lost in a violent gale and snow storm at 584615N 025548W, just South of Hesta Head (ND466880) in 1918. She was armed with three 4" guns, two smaller guns and four torpedo tubes. All lost.

2037 Wreck of HMS "Narborough". A 994-ton, 83m-long, British destroyer lost at 584615N 025548W just South of Hesta Head (ND466880) at the same time as HMS "Opal". Armaments same as "Opal". All lost. Both wrecks are lying close under cliffs immediately South of the Cleft of Crura (ND465874), heading in a northerly direction about 80m from each other. The northern vessel is a mass of broken iron work on a rock ledge. The southern vessel is less broken and in deeper water. No masts or funnels show and both wrecks are almost completely submerged at high water.

2038 Clett of Crura. ND463875. Impressive stack with a mixture of rock outcrops and sand at their bases. Lots of life in huge visibility.

2039 Wreck of SS "Giralda". A 2178-ton, 85m-long, British vessel bombed and sunk in 1940 at 584748N 024554W, 4.5 miles East of Kirkhouse Point, South Ronaldsay. Water depth in 66m, with a clearance of 40m.

2040 Grim Ness. ND494927. Several large caves are the home of seals. Rocky gullies with good fauna run to sand at 28m. The site is sheltered from the West. Launch off beach at Honeysgeo (ND488932).

2041 Wreck of the "Remus". A 1079-ton, 67m-long collier torpedoed and sunk by U-boat in 1918 at 5848N 0244W, 5 miles East of Grim Ness, in about 66m of water. Five lives lost.

2042 Wreck of the SS "Irene". This 9975-ton, 98m-long, Liberian vessel ran aground in 1969. The position quoted is 584908.4N 025348.9W, but the longitude should be 025339W. The vessel is ashore and sitting upright 18m above MHWS at the North of the Bay of Lime. She is breaking up and wreckage is scattered around.

2043 Wreck of the "Daghenstan". A 5742-ton, 61m-long, British tanker sunk in 1940 by German submarine U57 at 584945N 014230W, 4 miles East of Grim Ness. She lies 140/320 degrees in 57m of water, with a clearance of 42m.

2044 Burray Ness, Burray. ND506965. A good scenic dive with a sandy seabed at 20m with kelp and lobsters. Boat access from the fourth Chruchill barrier.

Mainland

2045 Midland Ness. HY323033. A scallop and lobster dive down a muddy sand slope. Poor.

2046 Ophir Bay. HY334043. A shallow profile shore dive; 300m out it is only 20m deep. Kelp, urchins and starfish noted.

2047 Toy Ness. HY356043. A boulder slope to 10m, then muddy sand, then a sand slope leading to 30m.

2048 Howequoy Head. HY465007. A pleasant dive in 10-15m depth with colourful life.

2049 Castle. HY564032. Rather flat, locally rugged, rocks covered with kelp and running out to sea.

2050 Copinsay island. No sites are recorded and depths are generally shallow, although at the North Nevi (HY618018) they reach 23m.

2051 Wreck of the SS "Girlanda". This collier was bombed and sunk in WW2 and now lies at 58539 0237W in 64m. The vessel is in two places. It is known locally as the "Girlanda" but may well be the "Giralda" (site 2039).

2052 Wreck of the "Navena", North Copinsay. There is a drying wreck charted at 585412N 024024W just off Kamesgeo Taing at HY613018 (approx.). The Navena was a 353 ton, 41m long, British trawler that was torpedoed in 1943. The wreck lies 600m from the base of 30m high cliffs and is very badly smashed and covered in weeds.

2053 Wreck of the "Tennesee", Tommy Tiffy, Deerness. This 5667 ton Norwegian vessel ran aground in 1940 carrying general cargo at 585552N 024225W in a depth 9m, though a drying wreck is charted at this position The wreck is completely broken and the gullies are filled with debris. The props were removed in 1972 and little remains.

2054 Unknown wreck, off Deerness. A small cargo ship left Kirkwall carrying empty shell cases for reloading. It was reputedly lost "off Deerness".

2055 Wreck of the SS "Vestfoss". A 1388 ton, 77m long, Norwegian collier bombed by German aircraft and sunk while under tow in 1940 at 5854N 0223W, 9 miles East of Copinsay Light. The depth is 80m and the charted clearance 66m. There were some survivors.

2056 Wreck of the SS "Faro". An 844 ton, 213 feet long, Norwegian steamer that was torpedoed in 1940 off Old Head, South Ronaldsay. The vessel was disabled and driven ashore in Taracliff Bay, Deerness at 585446N 024552W. Seven crew lost.

2057 Marka Ber. HY594075. This is similar to the site at Castle

2058 Wreck of the SS "Urania". A 1688-ton, 78m-long, Norwegian vessel sunk in 1917 at 585730N 022100W 10 miles East north east of Copinsay Light. Depth is 79m with a clearance of 68m.

2059 Wreck of the SS "Svinta". A 1267-ton Norwegian vessel torpedoed by submarine at 5858N 0235W, 4 miles East of Mull Head, Deerness in 1940. The general depth is 55m.

2060 Wreck of the SS "Ruby". A 234-ton, 38m-long, British vessel that struck a mine and sunk in 1917 at 585900N 023530W, 3.5 miles East of Mull Head. Six lives lost. The depth is 48m and the clearance 38m.

2061 Wreck of the "Zarefah". A 279-ton British yacht that struck a mine and sunk in 1917 at 585920N 024130W, 1 mile North north west of Mull Head. The depth is 35m and the clearance 24m.

2062 Wreck of the "Crown". This vessel was lost on 10th December 1679 whilst carrying Covenanters to exile in America. The position is near the mouth of Deer Sound to the West of Mull Head.

2063 Rerwick Point. HY542119. Access by a path past farmhouse and coastal defence buildings. A very good scenic dive with lots of gullies descending to 22m.

2064 Wreck of the MV "Danmark". A 10,517-ton, 150m-long, Danish tanker torpedoed in 1940. She sank in Inganess Bay at 585848N 025305W,

The north mainland of Orkney. The Orkney group comprises over 90 islands, of which only 18 are inhabited.

1 mile South west of Yinstay Head, 9 days after she was torpedoed. The vessel has been completely dispersed to the seabed; depth is 11m.

2065 Wreck of the SS "Loch Maddy". This 4995-ton British vessel was torpedoed and blown in two by a U-Boat to the East of Orkney. The after half was towed into Inganess Bay, East of Kirkwall, where she now lies in 12m of water at 585805N 025333W, 600m West of Weethick Head and dries 0.9m at low tide. She has been fairly well salved, though some of the cargo of Oregon pine is still left. It is reported to be possible to swim the length of the ship down the propeller shaft tube, though this is claimed to be "hairy".

2066 Wreck of the "Nana". A British tanker sunk as a blockship. The 61m long bows were refloated and towed to 585751.2N 025440.5W in the South west of Inganess Bay, where she dries at low tide 200m offshore, in about 2m of water.

2067 Wreck of "Disperser". This lies in 12m of water at 585958N 025736W, 0.7 miles North of Kirkwall Pier light.

2068 Unknown wreck, Bay of Kirkwall. This lies close inshore on South side of Crow Ness in about 1m of water at 585936N 025800W.

2069 Five Fathom Patch, Wide Firth. A small shoal at 590120N 025748W with a depth of 8m and surrounding depths of 11m.

2070 Scargun Shoal, Bay of Kirkwall. HY440144. A 2m shoal which is buoyed to the North, 1.5 miles North north west or Kirkwall, with surrounding depths of 10m.

2071 Quanterness Skerry. HY420148. A skerry North of Quanterness that dries 2m. Depths around reach 5-10m.

2072 Bay of Firth. Cannon balls have been found here while diving for scallops.

2073 Bay of Puldrite. HY422187. A sheltered, shallow site.

2074 North Mainland. I have no sites recorded for the next 14 miles of the Mainland North coast. At first this runs along Eynhallow Sound and appears rather shallow. However, the last 4 miles face North north west and appear to be rocky cliffs dropping into deep water close to shore.

2075 Skipi Geo. HY248285. A rocky dive off the North coast of Mainland with large numbers of crabs noted.

2076 Brough Head, Brough of Birsay. HY237287. Midway along the North coast of Brough are several interesting caves. These are exposed and are subject to waves and tidal streams. Close to the North side the water is shallow and the bottom is a rock slope cut with deep gullies. The evidence of surge action on the boulders ìs dramatic. The gullies run North and stop at about 15m; from there to 20m is a gentle rock slope leading to rock outcrop with a sheer South-facing cliff rising to 10m and stretching several hundred metres East-west. The wall is covered with encrusting life.

2077 Wreck of the HMS "Hampshire". A 10,850-ton, 137m-long, British armoured cruiser that struck a mine and sank in 1916 at 590730N 032300W, 1.6 miles South west from Brough Head Light (a recent report quotes the distance as "more than 1.6 miles offshore"). There was great loss of life, including Lord Kitchener and his staff, with only 12 survivors out of a total of 662 persons on board. The vessel was armed with four 7.5", six 6", two 12lb, twenty 31lb guns and two torpedo tubes.

The wreck has been dived by both German (1977 & 1979) and Swedish (1983) divers but is now designated a war grave, and should not be dived. The seabed depth is reported as 60m, with the depth to the wreck exceeding 48m.

2078 Brough of Bigging. HY217157. A rugged, weed-covered bottom, but relatively shallow close to shore. Further out good gullies descend to beyond 35m. An abundant though not very diverse sessile life; lots of fish. Excellent visibility.

2079 Stack of Yesnaby. HY219159. A superb sea stack that has not been fully explored underwater. The coastline is very rugged, with stacks, caves and geos, and must be well worth diving. Shallow near to shore, depths fall rapidly offshore to scoured and fairly lifeless bedrock beyond 40m.

2080 Wreck of submarine, 16.5 miles West of Inga Ness. A 90m-long wreck (thought to be a submarine) projecting 4m above the seabed at 81m at 590052N 035345W.

2081 Unknown wreck, 1.5 miles North west of Breck Ness. MFV "Ilene" was damaged when she struck a submerged object at 585848N 032330W. The general depth is 60m so, if this is a wreck, it must be worth diving.

2082 Wreck of the "Maranda". A 17m long British MFV lost in 1980 when it ran ashore on Kirk Rocks (HY233080).

2083 Wreck of the "Norholmen". A 141-ton, 36m-long Norwegian MFV that ran aground at 585714N 031934W on the Mainland to the East of Kirk Rocks in 1966. It is above the high water mark.

2084 Lettan Rock (West of Stromness). A vertical-walled shoal with cliffs from 8m to 25m. The walls are plastered with life.

2085 Lochs of Stenness and Harray. These large lochs are a substantial feature in West Mainland and drain an area of about 60 square miles. They are connected to the sea at the Bay of Ireland by a tidal channel called The Bush, at the South of Loch Stenness. Loch Stenness (area 2.46 square miles, maximum depth 5m) is a saltwater loch (with half to three-quarters the salinity of the sea) which receives much freshwater at its East end because it is connected by a narrow, shallow channel at Brodgar to Loch Harray (area 3.78 square miles, the 16th biggest loch in area in Scotland, maximum depth 4m), which is slightly brackish as it receives some saltwater at high tide by reverse flow through this channel. The brackish water leads to an unusual flora and fauna.

Northern Orkney Isles

The diving in the northern isles of Orkney is barely explored at all. There are many excellent scenic sites, and every expedition returns with several splendid new sites. There have been many vessels lost around these isles, although many positions are only known approximately. Those wrecks that have been located and dived are invariably well broken.

2086 Wreck of the "Tosto". A 1234 ton, 73m long Norwegian vessel sunk by mine in 1917 at 591230N 031100W, 3.5 miles West north west of Sacquoy Head, Rousay in about 60m of water.

2087 Rousay island. At large is with no sites recorded. Depths quickly reach 30m off the headlands and, in particular, the Rullard Röst off Sacquoy Head must give a good dive.

2088 Wreck of a Spanish vessel. There is legend of a gold-carrying Spanish vessel being lost off Rousay.

2089 Bowcheek, Eynhallow. HY355297. Pleasant diving at the North of the island in quite shallow water, though beware the röst (meeting of two tides) in Eynhallow Sound between Mainland and Rousay.

2090 Sheep Skerry, Eynhallow. HY362285. A superb seal dive, though beware of the röst.

2091 Wyre island. This small island lies to the South of Rousay. It appears to be surrounded by shallow water and there are no recorded sites.

2092 Egilsay island. Lying to the East of Rousay this, again, has no recorded sites.

2093 Kili Holm. HY476328. Promising diving in rather shallow water.

2094 Gairsay island. There are no sites recorded and depths appear to be shallow all round the island.

2095 Skerries and shoals South of Gairsay. Little Seal Skerry, Seal Skerry, Boray Skerries, Skertours, Taing Skerry, Broad Shoal, Skerry of Vasa, Puldrite Skerry, Linga Skerry, West Skerries. All undived?

2096 Shapinsay island. This irregularly-shaped island lies North of Kirkwall. Its headlands should yield worthwhile dives but there are no sites recorded.

2097 Bass of Linton, HY555188. A sandy shoal with a least depth of 10m with surrounding depths reaching 30m. The position is 5903189 024630W, 1 mile East of Shapinsay.

2098 Wreck of the "Swiftsure". A 823-ton British vessel lost by mine in 1917 at 590110N 024500W, 2.5 miles East of Hacksness, Shapinsay with the loss of one life. The depth is 29m and the charted clearance 15m.

2099 Unknown wreck, Elwick, Shapinsay. Charted at 590201N 025338W, this is the hulk of an MFV that is hard against the coastline.

2100 Wreck of the SS "Charkow". This Danish vessel (1026 tons, 72m long) lies somewhere to the South east of Shapinsay after being torpedoed by a U-Boat in 1940. All lost.

2101 Auskerry. A small island lying South of Stronsay. Its southern point appears to drop straight into about 35m of water but there are no sites recorded.

2102 Obstruction, South of Auskerry. This is charted at 590100N 023415W, 0.5 miles due South of Auskerry Light. It was reported in 1917.

2103 Wreck of the "Cotavia". A 4020 ton British cargo vessel lost in 1917 at 5901N 0230W, 2 miles East of Auskerry Light in about 60m of water.

2104 Wreck of the "Hastings County". A 4178-ton, 116m-long Norwegian vessel wrecked 1 mile North west of Auskerry in 1926 at 5903N 0233W in about 30m of water. The vessel broke in half and the bows sank. The wreck is spread over a wide area and only one of the two propellers have been found.

2105 Wreck of "U47". A 745-ton, 64m-long German submarine sunk by the destroyers HMS "Forester" and HMS "Fortune" in 1939 at 590012N 020842W, 13 miles East of Auskerry Light, in over 70m with a clearance of 67m. Interesting, but too deep.

2106 Wreck of "U92". A 998 ton, 66m long German submarine mined at 5900N 0130W, 33 miles East of Auskerry Light in 1918 in 100m of water. For armchair wreck detectives.

2107 Wreck of the "Ruby". A 234-ton British cargo vessel lost in 1917 at 590400N 023545W, about 400m off Tor Ness, Stronsay in about 14m of water.

2108 Wreck of the "Boy Graham". A 44-ton, 22m-long British fishing vessel lost in 1981 at 599430N 024336W, about 1 mile West of Rothiesholm Head, Stronsay in 31 metres of water with a clearance of 16m. A burst pipe in the engine room allowed the vessel to flood and sink.

2109 Concrete Barge, Papa Sound, Stronsay. HY646295. This lies on flat sand at 5m and projects out of the water at all states of the tide to the West of Stronsay Harbour. It provides an oasis for life to settle. The top couple of metres form a canopy protecting the life on the walls underneath; there are dozens of species of sponge, hydroids, squirts and anemones; pipe fish and wrasses are noted. The sand bottom around the wreck is also full of life and is worthy of investigation.

2110 Lamb Head, Stronsay. HY694213. There is an inlet with an obvious cave at its rear on the North side of the point. The gully entrance is rocky and drops to sand at 12m. The gully narrows and becomes sheer-sided as it penetrates to the South; it then becomes a cave which penetrates about another 15m or so until it is less than 1m wide. Surging water in this cave poses all the normal problems associated with such gullies. Very rich in life, both fish and sedentary.

2111 Wreck of the SS "St. Rognvald". This 486-ton vessel was lost on Burgh Head, Stronsay in 1900. Only a porthole has so far been located.

2112 Wreck of the SV "Edenmore". A full-rigged steel vessel wrecked "on Papa Stronsay". It was well-looted by the islanders and now probably only the keel and the bottom will be left. Odds and ends such as deck planking and china still come ashore.

2113 Unknown wreck, Calf of Eday. The well-broken wreck of an MFV lost while carrying scrap. The position is off Lashy Skerry, Calf of Eday. The very shallow water is only suitable for an inflatable.

2114 Wreck of the "Char". A 32m Admiralty tug lost in 1915 when she was rammed by a trawler. She was fitted with triple expansion engines and has two cast props. Depth is 14m. The position is just East of Mill Bay, Eday.

2115 Calf Sound, Eday. HY566393. A great drift dive on the flood tide. Scallops below the light.

2116 Red Head, Eday. HY570408. There is a large rock just underwater that has been the grave of at least two trawlers.

2117 Faray island. This island lies South of Westray and has no sites recorded. It appears to be shallow all round, except at the Point of Scaraber in the South.

2118 Wreck of the "Scandanavic". A 3072-ton vessel lying about 0.6 miles West of South end of Skea Skerries, Westray at 591434N 025934W. The wreck is in a depth of 13m on a reef about 200m wide with the wreck in the centre. It is well broken and is half buried in kelp-covered gullies.

2119 Noup Head, Westray. HY390503. At the North west of Noup Head are a series of skerries running North west. These are the home of large numbers of seals. There is an 8m-wide, cleft-like gully extending right to the surface and with a bottom at about 20m. The walls are solidly lined with encrusting life, and the cleft acts as a natural playground for the seals. A superb dive.

2120 Noup Head, Westray. HY392500. Just South of the previous site the seabird-covered cliff drops to 5m and a steeply shelving bottom of huge boulders. All the rocks are covered with encrusting life typical of exposed headlands.

2121 Wrecks North west of Westray. Four are recorded, but all are too deep for sport divers.

2122 Stanger Head, South east Westray. HY513429. About 200m off the shore of lowish sandstone cliffs with many caves the depth reaches 26m on sand past a bottom of boulders and slabby sandstone. A rather poor dive.

2123 Skerry Skelwick, Westray. HY502458. A steep drop-off to beyond 36m on the North east side of the skerry.

2124 Ouze Ness, Westray. HY459495. This has a sand bottom with small boulders sloping gently towards 8m.

2125 The Bore Röst, Mull Head, Papa Westray. HY500560. The high cliffs continue underwater to beyond 36m. There are both underwater caves and scallops, so everybody should be happy. The Röst can be quite dramatic with big overfalls and rather large standing waves. It would provide a most challenging drift dive, but one that might be difficult to carry out safely.

2126 Shoal 3 miles North west of Mull Head, Papa Westray. This undived shoal reaches to within 21m of the surface from general depths of 33-48m. There are tidal rips charted so presumably the shoal is an outcrop of rock. This should give an excellent though challenging dive.

2127 Wreck of the "Danzig". This was wrecked in 1811 off the Holm of Papa, Papa Westray.

2128 Wreck of the "Bella Vista". This 6299 ton vessel was carrying iron ore when she was lost on Foal Craig, Papa Westray in 1948. The wreckage is scattered over a wide area, and both propellers (cast) are still there.

2129 Wreck of the "Island Lass". A British mailboat lost in 1962 at 5926N 0243W, about 6 miles North east from Mull Head, Papa Westray in about 60m of water.

2130 Shoal 7 miles North east of Mull Head, Papa Westray. This shoal reaches to within 27m of the surface and, on the North west side, rapidly reaches depths approaching 60m. Its position is 592730N 024500W and one would expect a good dive.

2131 Cuthe Bank. A sandy shoal reaching to within 18m of the surface from general depths of about 30m at 591511N 024100W, 3 miles South west of the Holms of Ire.

2132 Holms of Ire, Sanday. HY648460 (approx). About 70m offshore this has a kelp slope from 12-18m. A 3m-high rock shelf leads to a boulder slope going beyond 28m. Shallow gullies cut back toward the shore and have much life. Elephant's ear sponge noted at depth.

2133 Wreck of the "Utrecht". This Dutch frigate was wrecked on Landward Geo, Sanday (HY650469) after a fight with a British man-o-war.

2134 Wreck of the SS "Alex Hastie". Lost near Landward Geo, Sanday in 1940.

2135 Runnabrake shoal. 592142N 023806W. This lies about 3 miles North of the Holms of Ire. It is a rocky shoal reaching to within 5m of the surface from general depths of about 20-35m. The top of the shoal is covered with kelp and there are several small gully systems. To the East, lots of little overhangs and crevices lead to splendid rocky gullies at about 10-20m. To the North west there is kelp to 20m then rocky steps and walls leading to beyond 30m. Lots of life typical of exposed shoals in tidal streams.

2136 Wreck of the "Wanja". This vessel was captured and beached by the British near the Ebb of the Riv, Sanday during WW2.

2137 Wreck of the "Aberdeen City". A 264-ton, 35m-long trawler lost on Start Point at 591648N 022200W in 1963. A drying wreck is charted.

2138 Wreck of HMS "Goldfinch". A 747-long British destroyer wrecked in dense fog in 1915 on Start Point, Sanday at 5917N 0225W. She was armed with two 4″ and other guns and two torpedo tubes; her speed was 27 knots. The vessel was holed and stranded ashore.

2139 Start Point. HY788435. A shallow dive. Lots of non-ferrous scrap litters the seabed, testifying to the number of wrecks over the years.

2140 Wreck of the "Fair Dawn". A British MFV that went ashore in 1974 at Start Point at 591600N 022230W and broke up. The position given is about 0.7 miles offshore in 30m of water, but presumably this is incorrect.

2141 Wreck of the "Strato". A trawler lost in 1934 at 5717N 0226W. This position is ashore in the Bay of Lopness, immediately South of Northwall.

2142 Wreck of the "B98". An 1843 ton, 98m long German destroyer that was seized at Scapa Flow and later wrecked at 591646N 022650W. A drying wreck is shown in the Bay of Lopness, 2 miles east of Start Point, in a depth of 1m.

2143 Masewell Rock. A shoal with a least depth of 9m rising from about 14m, 1.5 miles West of Strom Ness, North Ronaldsay at 592045N 022820W. There are tidal overfalls in the vicinity at certain states of the tide.

2144 Reef Dyke, North Ronaldsay. An area of shallow water and dangerous tides lying to the south east of North Ronaldsay. Depths fall from 4m to 20m in a short distance. It is expected to have the remains of several wrecks for the diligent searcher.

2145 Wreck of the "Mistle". A 485-ton British vessel lost in 1957 when it struck the Reefdyke at 5920N 0222W.

2146 Wreck of the MV "Mim". A 4996 ton, 126m long Norwegian merchantman that was lost on the Reef Dyke on her maiden voyage in 1939, when she was driven ashore and broke up in heavy weather at 592100N 022216W. One bronze prop was recovered, one still missing. A drying wreck is charted at this position.

2147 Wreck of the "Svecia". A 600-ton Swedish East Indiaman wrecked and broken up with the loss of about 60 lives in 1740 at 5921N 0222W on the Reefdyke. Located in 1977 by Rex Cowan in 8m of water in a deep tangle of kelp. Artefacts from the wreck together with historical documents have been displayed in the Register House, Edinburgh in 1979.

2148 Wreck of the "Kron Prinsen". A Danish ship wrecked near Versa Geo, North Ronaldsay in 1745. She was equipped with 24 carriage guns.

2149 Wreck of the "Hansi". A 4996 ton vessel lost in 1939 at 592300N 022304W, in the North of Linklet Bay, North Ronaldsay. A drying wreck is charted on the shore rocks at this position.

2150 Armada wrecks. Legend has it that two Spanish Armada vessels were lost in Dennis Roost, North Ronaldsay.

Area information and services

Hydrographic charts: 35 Scapa Flow & approaches 1:30,000; 219 Western approaches to the Orkney & Shetland islands 1:500,000; 1553 Bay of Kirkwall 1:12,500; 2162 Pentland Firth & approaches 1:50,000; 2249 Orkney islands – western sheet 1:75,000; 2250 Orkney islands – eastern sheet 1:75,000; 2568 Plans in the Orkney islands, various; 2581 Southern approaches to Scapa Flow 1:25,000; 2584 Approaches to Kirkwall 1:25,000; 2622 Plans in the Orkney & Shetland islands, various.

Ordnance Survey 1:50,000 maps: 5 Orkney islands (Northern Isles); 6 Orkney Islands (Mainland); 7 Pentland Firth.

Ordnance Survey 1:25,000 maps: HY75/85 North Ronaldsay & Fair Isle; HY45/55, HY44/54, HY64/74 Sanday (North); HY33/43, HY63/73, HY22/32 Dounby; HY42, HY52/62, HY21/31 Finstown; HY41/51 HY10/20 Stromness; HY40 Scapa Bay; HY60 Deerness; ND19/29, ND49/59, ND48, ND37/47 Duncansby Head. Maps with names are published, those unnamed are awaited.

Local BS-AC branches: Flotta; Stromness (inactive); Thurso.

Local SS-AC branches: Kirkwall.

Air supplies: Kirkwall SSAC; Scapa dive boats.

Outboard motor sales & services: Kirkwall.

Boat charterers: These are numerous in Scapa Flow (1986) – see chapter 8.

Harbourmasters: Stromness (0856) 850744; Scapa (0856) 2634; Kirkwall (0856) 2292; Stronsay 257.

Local weather: Kirkwall Airport Meteorological Office (0856) 3802 (office hours).

Sea area; Fair Isle.

Tidal constants:

	ABERDEEN	DOVER
Muckle Skerry	−0230	−0010
Burrayness	−0200	+0020
Deer Sound	−0245	−0025
Kirkwall	−0255	−0035
Otterswick	−0355	−0135
Pierowall	−0355	−0135
Eynhallow Sound	−0400	−0140
Stromness	−0405	−0145
Stronsay	−0400	−0140
Widewall Bay	−0400	−0140

Coastguards: Kirkwall MRSC (0856) 3268; Auxiliary watch and rescue equipment is maintained at North Ronaldsy, Sanday, Deerness, Brough Ness, Long Hope, Stromness, Westray, Papa Westray and Stronsay.

Lifeboats: Kirkwall, Long Hope, Stromness.

SAR helicopter: The nearest one is based at Aberdeen, and covers all of the North of Scotland and Orkney. It has a radius of action of 150 miles, a speed of 120 knots and a passenger capacity of 10. It is available at 1 hour notice during daylight hours via the Coastguard. There is also a SAR helicopter based at Sumburgh, Shetland.

Police stations: Kirkwall (0856) 2241; Stromness (0856) 850222, South Ronaldsay (085 683) 529.

Doctors: In Kirkwall, Stromness, Roussay, Shapinsay, Eday, North Ronaldsay, Stronsay, Sanday, Westray.

Hospitals: Balfour Hospital, Kirkwall (0856) 2763 (serious cases are flown to Aberdeen – 1 hour).

Recompression chambers: Nearest are at Aberdeen; there is a private chamber on Flotta but it has been stated that this is NOT available to amateurs even in an emergency. See Appendix 2.

Vehicle recovery: None available.

Ferry operators: P & O Ferries (Thurso – Scrabster, vehicular, aboard MV St. Ola) Stromness (0856) 850655 (booking almost essential in peak season); Thomas & Bews, Ferry Office, John O'Groats (passengers only, John O' Groats – Burwick, South Ronaldsay) (095581) 353; Inter-island ferries (some passenger, some vehicle) run to all of the main islands: S. Mowat, Barkland, Cairston Road, Stromness (0856) 850624 (passengers only, Stromness – Hoy); Orkney Islands Shipping Co, Ltd., 4 Ayre Road, Kirkwall (0856) 2044 (vehicles, South Orkney isles; passengers only, Kirkwall – Shapinsay; passengers only, Kirkwall and North isles); Wide Firth Ferries Ltd., "Horries", Deerness (0856 74) 351 (passengers only, Kirkwall and North isles); Flaws Ferries, Rousay (0856) 82213/82332 (passengers only, Rousay, Egilsay, Wyre); Tommy Rendall, "North Haven", Westray (085 77) 216 (passengers only, Westray – Papa Westray). There is also an Orkney-Shetland ferry run by P & O.

Air connections: Kirkwall Airport has connections to Wick, Aberdeen, Edinburgh and Glasgow. Operators: British Airways (041 887 1111 & 0856 2233); Loganair (041 889 3181 & 0856 3457).

Local tourist information: Stromness (0856) 850716; Kirkwall (0856) 2856.

Places of local marine interest: Stromness Museum (0856) 850025 (Scapa Flow wrecks, wildlife local history); Tankerness House Museum, Kirkwall (0856) 3191 (wildlife, local history).

Accommodation: There are hotels in Stromness and Kirkwall. There are many B & B establishments all over the islands.

A British boarding party alongside a sinking German destroyer.

CHAPTER 7

The Wrecks of Scapa Flow

A LEGENDARY British dive site, lying at the far North of Scotland, Scapa Flow is a destination to which many experienced divers make regular pilgrimages. Why? Because Scapa Flow's inner 32 square miles contain the greatest concentration of sunken warships anywhere in the world. Even Truk Lagoon in the Pacific Ocean (where the Americans finally got their revenge on the Japanese for the surprise attack on Pearl Harbour in WW2) cannot compete.

British divers have a reputation for being fascinated by wrecks, and yet in many parts of our waters it is difficult to understand why. In Scapa Flow lies the answer. Scapa Flow is to wreck divers what St. Kilda is to British scenic diving – the ultimate. The number of shipwrecks in Scapa Flow is quite incredible – the German WW1 High Seas Fleet consisting of 3 battleships, 4 light cruisers and 5 torpedo boats (destroyers), a WW2 German destroyer (F2), 2 German submarines, 27 large remnants of German warships or salvors equipment, 16 known British wrecks, 32 blockships, and 2 large British battleships ("Vanguard" & "Royal Oak") – a total of 92 wrecks; additionally, there are a further 54 unidentified or unknown wreck sites! And, no doubt, there are more.

The history of Scapa Flow and its development as a base for the British Fleet is well documented in many sources, in particular in Weaver's recent and detailed book "This Great Harbour – Scapa Flow". Initially used by the first Orcadians, Scapa Flow served as a refuge down the years to Vikings, Scots and then British vessels before becoming a base for the Royal Navy in 1812, with major developments during the two World Wars of the present century. The White Ensign was finally lowered at Lyness in 1957.

Scapa Flow is the most sheltered large (area about 120 square miles) anchorage in the British Isles, protected by an almost completely encircling group of islands. It lies about 15 miles North of the North east tip of Scotland, across the stormy Pentland Firth. Access is by daily car ferry from Scrabster, run by P & O Ferries, Orkney and Shetland Services (New Ferry Terminal, Pierhead, Stromness, Orkney; Tel: 0856 850655). Booking is strongly recommended. There are regular flights into Kirkwall Airport, though for many divers that could leave the problem of the equipment transportation.

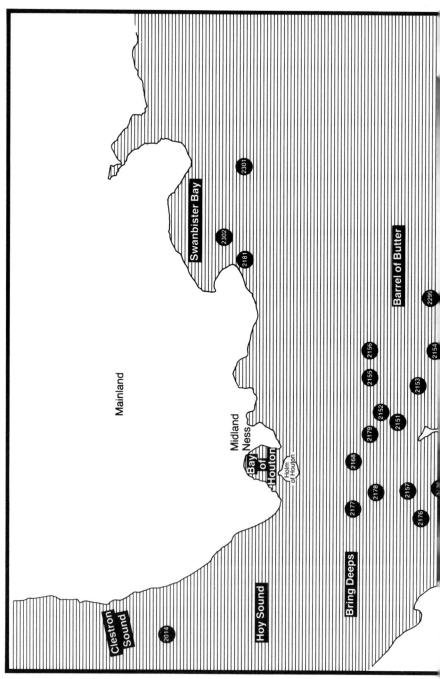

Dive Sites: Chapter 7

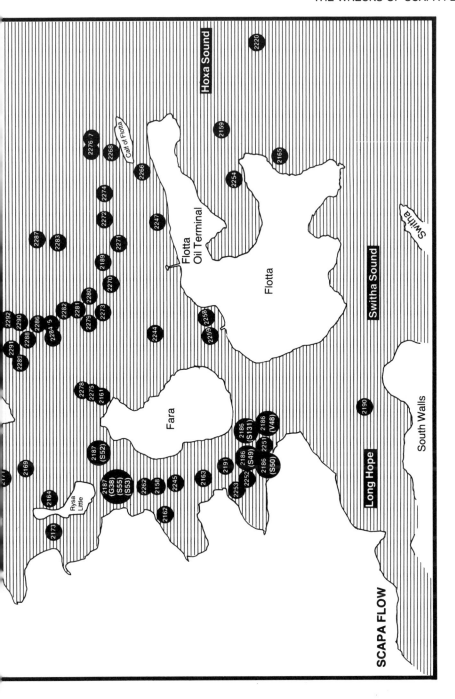

For years the number of visiting divers was small, and the wrecks were dived by camping, usually at Midland Ness, and running out to the wrecks with your own inflatable. The wrecks were sometimes buoyed by the salvors and sometimes not. Often the first two or three days of holiday were spent in locating and buoying the unbuoyed wrecks. That has all changed now, due no doubt to the large volume of divers going to Orkney over the last few years. There are now many dive charter boat operators based in Orkney, all very largely vying for the divers trade in Scapa Flow. In fact, the income from visiting divers is a relatively important source of revenue to Orkney.

Unfortunately, because all of Scapa Flow is a Harbour, regulations govern diving there. Byelaw 33 of the Orkney Harbour Areas General Byelaws 1977 states:

(1) No Person who is wearing or equipped with clothing or apparatus designed or adapted for swimming underwater or diving shall swim underwater, dive or fish in a harbour area except with the written permission of the harbour master.

(2) Without prejudice to the foregoing provisions of this byelaw no person shall swim underwater, dive or fish –

(a) within 100 metres of any of Her Majesty's ships or vessels, within a harbour area, save with the licence in writing of the Queen's Harbour-master, Rosyth and in accordance with any conditions attached thereto; nor

(b) within 30 metres of the walls, slipways or boundaries of Her Majesty's Royal Naval Oil Fuel Depot, Lyness.

Additionally, the Director of Harbours requires you to obtain a written diving permit before diving in the Orkney Harbour Areas. Naturally, the charter boat operators already have these written permissions.

The convenience of being able to travel light to Orkney, possibly even by air, is considerable. In many respects it is much better to dive the wrecks from the comfort of a hard boat. Further, the skippers can generally put you over virtually the exact spot on any wreck that you wish. However, it is still a source of regret to me that an independent dive group can apparently no longer merely turn up and dive the wrecks just as easily.

There are now numerous charter operators who offer various combinations of boat charter, equipment hire, compressed air, and accommodation. Some of them are listed at the end of this chapter. You should shop round to find the one that best suits your requirements. Some only operate in Scapa Flow, while others will go much further afield.

Most of the significant wrecks in Scapa Flow involve diving to over 30m. A single cylinder set will not usually be adequate; sets of 3000 to 4000 litres capacity are recommended. The use of a "pony" or "bale-out" cylinder is advisable on deeper dives and on dives where penetration of the insides of the wrecks is planned. An "octopus" regulator is also very worthwhile. Entering the wrecks involves elevated risks and should only be attempted by divers with the correct training and temperament. It has been my experience that to explore the deeper wrecks substantially it is necessary to indulge in dives involving stage decompression. If you plan these you should be appropriately equipped and experienced.

Diving conditions can vary substantially. Even though the Flow is almost land-locked it can be quite rough. Visibility, except in the plankton blooms, is usually good; exceptionally it can be up to 30m near the surface and often as much as 15m at depths of 36-42m. It can be quite dark at depth, particularly on overcast days, even though the visibility itself may be quite good; torches are strongly recommended. Tidal streams are not significant and do not exceed 0.5 knots, even at spring tides, except at the narrow entrances to the Flow. Most wrecks are deep and your party should consist mainly of experienced divers who are worked up for 30m+ diving; beginners are out of place and would be at risk on many of the dives.

Some concern has been expressed recently about the allegedly "different" nature of the diving in Scapa Flow and the raised incidence of decompression sickness occurring among divers in the Flow. In essence, the suggestions are that divers will normally have travelled long distances to Scapa Flow and will naturally be enthusiastic about maximising the number of wrecks they dive (and possibly the bars they frequent) in the relatively short time of their visit. It has also been suggested that divers from afar may not have the experience to dive safely to the depths at which the best wrecks lie.

Now that these worries have been subjected to sober medical and statistical analysis they have proved not to be based on reality. In fact, relative to the large numbers of divers visiting Orkney and the very large number of dives that take place in Scapa Flow the rate of decompression sickness incidences is actually somewhat lower than might be expected proportionately from figures for the whole of the British Isles. Nevertheless, this should not be taken as grounds for complacency and divers should be aware that the potential combination of tiredness, repetitive deep diving (within tables but nevertheless not allowing complete nitrogen elimination between diving days) coupled with enthusiasm, inexperience and, perhaps, an excess of alcohol, may predispose a diver to decompression sickness.

Orkney Health Board in consultation with medical personnel in Aberdeen, local boat operators and the SSAC have suggested a code of practice for Scapa Flow diving; much of this code is very sensible. The BSAC was involved in the discussions but its considered opinion is that deep diving in Scapa Flow is not significantly different from deep diving elsewhere in British waters; it also considers that its best advice on deep diving and related topics given throughout its publications is too comprehensive to be usefully summarised in a brief code of practice.

The history of the German WW1 High Seas Fleet

During the latter part of last century and the early part of the present century Germany was assembling a fleet of ocean-going warships to challenge the might of the Royal Navy, then the world's greatest sea power. The political events of the early years of this century culminated in the First World War, and Germany had then a need for her new High Seas Fleet.

The British Grand Fleet skirmished with the German High Seas Fleet on January 24th 1915, but there was relatively little damage. Then they met again at the famous Battle of Jutland May 31st 1916; losses were quite heavy on both sides and indeed both claimed a victory, although the result was inconclusive. Finally, on November 21st, 1918, the German High Seas Fleet surrendered to the Grand Fleet and was led to internment in Scapa

Salvage operations on the German battleship 'Baden'.

Flow while the Allied Powers deliberated on its fate. As far as Admiral von Reuter, the Commander of this Fleet, was concerned, Germany was still technically at war with the Allies until the final peace treaty was signed. Thus, in the event of negotiations failing, Germany would again have need of her High Seas Fleet. However, as at this stage his disarmed fleet was interned in Scapa Flow, all von Reuter would be able to do would be to prevent the ships falling into Allied hands. Consequently, when it appeared to him that the breakdown of negotiations was imminent, he gave the order to scuttle the whole fleet at 1030 hours on 21st June 1919. Vice-Admiral Ludwig von Reuter is the only man to have destroyed a whole navy with a single order; almost half a million tons of the most powerful warships ever built sank during the next few hours in the greatest act of self-immolation ever inflicted in the history of naval warfare. (For a complete discussion of the scuttling and the events preceding and following it, consult "Scapa Flow, 1919" by Ruge, and "The Grand Scuttle" by van der Vat.)

At the time of the scuttling there was a total of 74 German ships interned in Scapa Flow, comprising 11 battleships, 5 battlecruisers, 8 light cruisers, and 50 torpedo boats; a total of 488,163 tons of the latest warships which if stretched bow to stern would have formed a continuous line 5.2 miles long. Their wartime crews numbered 26,345 officers and men, although this was reduced to a skeleton of about 4,700 for internment. The German fleet was policed by British vessels, but at the time of the scuttling the majority of these were out of the Flow on exercises; those that remained were taken completely by surprise. Because the Germans had prepared thoroughly for the scuttling, most of the ships sank quite rapidly (2-6 hours) in varying depths of water, and it was only possible to beach a few of the smaller ships. In total, 20 torpedo boats were beached and three remained afloat, the battle cruiser "Baden" remained afloat in shallow water, light cruisers "Frankfurt" and "Emden" were beached in Swanbister Bay, and light cruiser "Nurnberg" broke its mooring chains and drifted ashore on Cava. Thus a total of 47 ships went to the seabed.

There was no little excitement and some panic among the remaining British guard vessels and there was some small arms fire directed at the German crews for one reason and another. Out of a total of 1774 German internees, 8 were killed and 16 more wounded by gunfire. (Note that at least 2,200 had been previously repatriated for various reasons.) One of the dead was the captain of the "Markgraf" who was shot through the head though he emerged holding a white flag. One German sailor was shot dead for disobeying a British order later that day. Surprisingly, no-one was drowned. There were no British casualties.

After the war a start was made at salvaging the sunken vessels. The small Stromness Salvage Syndicate bought destroyer G89 (beached on Cava) from the Admiralty, refloated it and brought it to Stromness for dismantling. In 1923 J.W. Robertson formed The Scapa Flow Salvage & Shipbreaking Company. This company purchased four destroyers and lifted them with huge airbags.

Then, in 1924, the legendary salvage expert, Ernest Cox, bought 26 destroyers and two battleships (followed later by others) from the British Admiralty and set about the salvage work. He successfully raised many of the ships, often using novel methods, over a period of 10 years, but he apparently made a loss of about £10,000 on the whole salvage operation. In all, he lifted 26 destroyers, 2 battleships, 4 battle cruisers, and one light cruiser. He died in 1959 at the age of 76.

In 1933 the salvage rights were bought by Metal Industries Ltd, led by their managing director and salvage expert Robert McCrone (previously Cox's customer for the scrap metal of the wrecks). Their salvage efforts continued until 1946 and they were responsible for lifting 5 battleships, 1 battlecruiser and possibly a few destroyers.

An intriguing aside to the main story is that some of the recovered armour plating was sold to Germany in the 1930s and partly used to build Hitler's new navy. And this at a time when the Royal Navy was suffering from a shortage of armour plate! Some of the metal may well have been scuttled for a second time when the seacocks of the battleship Graf Spee were opened after the Battle of the River Plate in 1939. Rumour also has it that some of the salvaged metal has left Earth as part of NASA's space probes.

The story of the salvage attempts makes fascinating reading (see "The Man Who Bought a Navy", Bowman, 1964 and "Jutland to Junkyard", George, 1973). At the end of the lifting operation in 1947 there were 7 large ships (3 battleships, 4 light cruisers) and 3 destroyers still on the bottom, because these were technically too difficult to raise. They remain there to this day.

In 1956 salvage was restarted by Arthur Nundy (of Nundy Marine Metals) an ex-diver of Metal Industries and Cox & Danks, largely for non-ferrous metals and also some armour plate. He used both hard hat and aqualung equipment, though some mystery surrounds his operations.

Salvage rights then passed in 1970 to David Nicol and Dougal Campbell of Scapa Flow Salvage, based at Lyness on Hoy. His basic procedure, having located a salvageable item, was to blast it loose, then heave it free with a large steam winch and lift it to the surface. Tidal lifts were also employed to break loose obstinate items and I well remember an epic lift as the first line of portholes submerged on his 60m lifting vessel, the ex-boom defence vessel "Barneath" before the 22-ton gun metal torpedo tube broke loose with an enormous crack, causing the whole lifting vessel to oscillate violently to and fro.

The rights were then bought by an oil company, reputedly to stop the explosions of salvage work which might interfere with their own underwater pipeline operations. They did no salvage. Then an American consortium, Underseas Associates of Aberdeen, bought the wrecks with the intention of lifting them in entirety. Fortunately this came to nought when the partnership with Scapa Salvage Company collapsed in 1979. The Orkney Islands Council then proposed to buy the wrecks in 1981 for £50,000, assisted by a donation of £2000 from the BSAC. This also bore no fruit. Later in 1981 Clark Diving Services of Lerwick bought four of the wrecks and leased the other three; salvage was their intention.

Although the German WW1 wrecks have been well blasted and extensively salvaged, they are so huge as to still be substantially whole. Compared to many wrecks that are dived on around the country, they could be described almost as "pristine". They all yield magnificent dives.

Completed in 1914, the three battleships ("Konig", "Kronprinz Wilhelm", and "Markgraf") were large ships of 25,390 tons displacement, with a complement of about 1200 men. Their dimensions were 176m × 29m × 8m. Their main armament was ten 30cm guns mounted on five twin turrets. Additionally, they had fourteen 15cm and eight 9cm guns, together with five 50cm torpedo tubes (one bow, four beam). Their armour plate was 13.75" thick in places and their maximum speed was 22 knots.

The light cruisers were much lighter than the battleships. The "Brummer" (completed 1916) had a displacement of 4400 tons with a top speed of 34 knots and a main armament of four 15cm guns and two 50cm torpedo tubes; she also carried 400 mines. Her dimensions were 140m × 13m × 6m. The "Karlsruhe" (completed 1916), "Dresden" and "Koln" (completed 1918) all had displacements of 5600 tons ("Karlsruhe" 5440 tons) with a top speed of 28 knots and a main armament of eight 15cm guns and four 60cm torpedo tubes; they carried 200 mines. Dimensions were 156m × 14m × 7m; the length of the "Karlsruhe" was 151m.

The torpedo boats varied in size from 802 tons to 1374 tons. Speeds ranged from 33 to 37 knots. Guns varied from three 12-pounders to four 10cm, and their torpedo tubes from three 45cm to six 50cm; they all carried 24 mines.

More details of the ships (eg. their scuttled positions, sinking and raising history, and current remains) are given in the tables later in this chapter.

The wrecks are grouped into categories – German wrecks, German salvage sites, British wrecks, blockships, other wrecks and, finally, unknown wrecks – and described in an approximate order of importance.

The German Wrecks

2151 Markgraf 58 53 31N 03 09 55W. The Markgraf was hit five times at Jutland on 31st may 1916, and was repaired during June/July 1916. She is the deepest of the German wrecks and is lying near the "Kronprinz", almost upside down on the seabed, 42m under water. One's first impression on reaching the hull is that it is the seabed itself, so huge is the ship.

It is possible to get under the ship on the starboard side, but this cannot be recommended to the faint-hearted. Recently a diver got lost underneath the vessel and only found his way out by pure luck – be warned. The armaments are not accessible. Starting at the stern one passes two large propeller shafts and two large rudders, then the blasted engine room area; another blasted area lies forward of this and finally the bows are reached. These are very sharp and impressive, and rise vertically away from the seabed, which can be as deep as 50m, when tidal scour and tide range are taken into account.

I find hovering in front of the bows a most awe-inspiring situation, with a 25000 ton battleship "aimed" straight at you! There are a line of huge portholes just above the seabed. The armour plate has been removed from one side of the ship. See BSAC Wreck Register, Wreck 170.

2152 Kronprinz Wilhelm 58 53 ·39N 03 09 46W. The "Kronprinz" was undamaged at the Battle of Jutland, but was torpedoed by the British submarine "J.1" off Horns Reef on 5th November 1916. She was repaired by early December 1916 and renamed the "Kronprinz Wilhelm" on 27th January 1918. Now she lies on her starboard side in 35m of water, a little over half a mile North east of Cava beacon. Although well heeled over, the deck is quite accessible, and many of the huge 30cm guns can be inspected. The forward part of the wreck is more vertical than the stern, and gives easy access. There has been extensive blasting near the bullbous stern. The vastness of the upturned keel area is very impressive. See BSAC Wreck Register, Wreck 169.

The 'Kronprinz Wilhelm' settles into the waters of Scapa Flow with other warships of the German High Seas fleet.

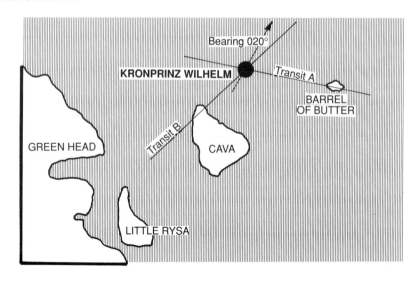

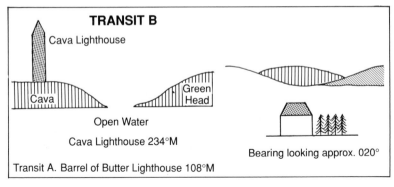

TRANSIT B

Cava Lighthouse

Open Water

Cava Lighthouse 234°M

Bearing looking approx. 020°

Transit A. Barrel of Butter Lighthouse 108°M

SITE 2152: THE 'KRONPRINZ WILHELM'

2153 Konig 58 53 13N 03 09 07W. The "Konig" was hit ten times at Jutland, and also saw action in the Baltic against the Russian ship "Slava" in October 1917. She is now in 39m of water a little South east of the "Markgraf" and "Kronprinz". She has been little blasted, and the huge barndoor rudders, 1.3m diameter prop shafts, and angled bows are all of note. Many sharp edges. See BSAC Wreck Register, Wreck 168.

2154 Dresden 58 52 58N 03 08 21W. This lies in 30m of water South of the "Konig", midway between the South east tip of Cava and the Barrel of Butter. In my opinion, it gives the most enjoyable dive of all the German WW1 wrecks. The wreck lies on its side giving access to all the deck area, including the 600-ton bridge made of solid brass! The plumose anemone-encrusted bows with their twin anchor chains curving away to the seabed are an unforgettable sight. Swimming underneath these bows has been known to excite some divers! See BSAC Wreck Register, Wreck 105.

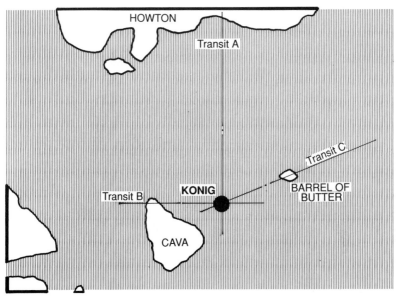

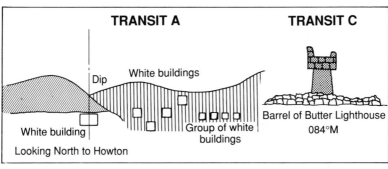

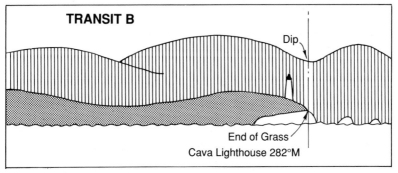

SITE 2153: THE 'KONIG'

2155 Brummer 58 53 50N 03 09 07W. The masts and crow's nest run out along the seabed as the wreck yet again lies on its side (starboard) in 33m of water. The magnificant curved bows with both anchor chains running out are very memorable. The main deck gun at the bows is in good condition. The engine room has been blasted and blast damage to the stern allows access to the interior of the wreck. The bridge still contains charts. Appears more silty than other wrecks.

Dougal Campbell of the Scapa Flow Salvage Company with a lamp from the 'Brummer', salvaged from Scapa Flow in 1973.

2156 Koln 58 53 52N 03 08 27W. The "Koln" lies on her starboard side in a depth of 35m with her deck almost vertical. She has been well-blasted around the engine room but is otherwise almost completely intact. The port propeller shaft is visible (with no prop), but the other is in the mud; the rudders are impressive. A mast lies along the seabed, and all the super-structure is exposed to view. Suprisingly, the occasional porthole is still to be seen. There is a heavy machine gun mounted near the bridge, and the heavy guns in their turrets are accessible. See BSAC Wreck Register, Wreck 167.

2157 Karlsruhe 58 53 23N 03 11 18W. The shallowest of the German WW1 wrecks, lying in only 24m of water, half a mile North west of Cava beacon. (See maps below and overleaf.) She is healed about 60 degrees on her starboard side with the starboard anchor chain run out. The engine room, by the stern, has been heavily blasted, and this is the most salvaged of all the German wrecks – the decks have been ripped off and the huge metal reefs hold many fish and much encrusting life. All the guns are accessible and are elevated 45 degrees. The bridge is accessible and still has moving hinged windows! See BSAC Wreck Register, Wreck 166.

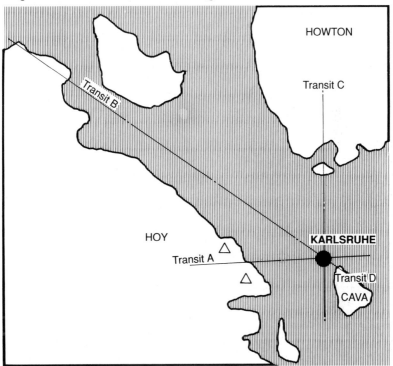

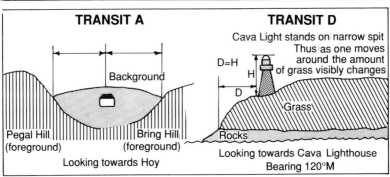

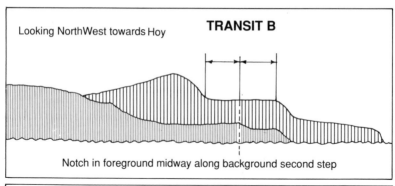

TRANSIT B

Looking NorthWest towards Hoy

Notch in foreground midway along background second step

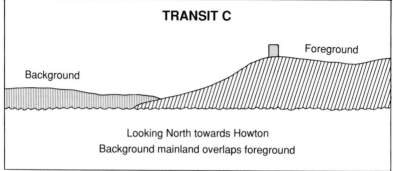

TRANSIT C

Foreground

Background

Looking North towards Howton
Background mainland overlaps foreground

SITE 2157: THE 'KARLSRUHE'

2158 F2, WW2 German destroyer, Gutter Sound. A 1065-ton 80m-long vessel allocated to Britain after WW2. She is now thought to have been a fleet sloop of 1768 tons. She was lost at her moorings and now lies just East of the wreck buoy (see maps opposite and on page 144) and rests on her port side in 15m of water with her bows intact. The stern is heavily blasted, and the propeller shaft and bearings are visible. There is a single gun in a turret near the bows; its controls are accessible and are noticeably more sophisticated than those of the WW1 wrecks. See BSAC Wreck Register, Wreck 160.

2159 German Submarine UB116 585007N 030406W. This 650-ton, 55m WW1 submarine penetrated the Flow through Hoxa Sound. British listening equipment located the vessel, and a barrage of observation mines were destonated to destroy the submarine and her crew of 36. Her remains lie off Pan Hope, ENE of Quoy Ness in 26m. After her sinking in 1918 she was raised in 1919 and resunk in her present position. She stood 5m above the seabed before she was blown to pieces in 1975 when the warhead of a live torpedo detonated while being removed. She is now well broken and totally unrecognisable, standing only 3m above the seabed. Large sections of the vessel are sunk in the soft sand.

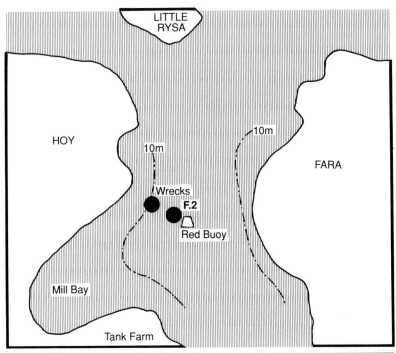

LITTLE RYSA

HOY

10m

10m

FARA

Wrecks

F.2

Red Buoy

Mill Bay

Tank Farm

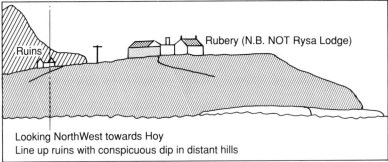

Ruins

Rubery (N.B. NOT Rysa Lodge)

Looking NorthWest towards Hoy
Line up ruins with conspicuous dip in distant hills

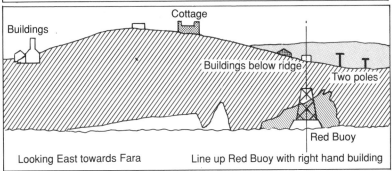

Cottage

Buildings

Buildings below ridge

Two poles

Red Buoy

Looking East towards Fara   Line up Red Buoy with right hand building

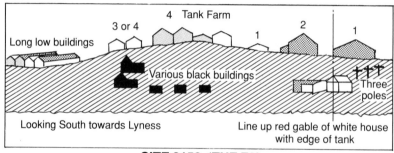

Looking South towards Lyness

Line up red gable of white house
with edge of tank

SITE 2158: 'THE F2'

2160 German Submarine U18. Local rumour has it that there is another submarine somewhat in the vicinity of Scapa Flow. In fact, the vessel was U18, which was lost in 1914. She penetrated the Flow via Hoxa Sound and found no capital ships to attack. On her return her hydroplane and periscope were damaged after being rammed by a British trawler. She collided with the Pentland Skerries and was forced to surface; her crew scuttled her and were picked up by a British destroyer.

2161 German E-boat 585130N 030935W. This MTB lies off the North end of Fara. All that remains is the very broken hull in 10m of water.

2162 Torpedo Boat V70. This was the first vessel to be lifted by Cox & Danks (in 1924) who used a tidal lift together with wire ropes around vessel. She was fitted out as a floating workshop and the stern now lies in the shallows off Mill Bay.

2163 Torpedo Boat B109 585018.0N 031120.0W. The B109 was raised in 1926 and partially scrapped. Her remains lie 4.3 cables South of the buoy marking the wreck of the "F2" in 15m of water. There is no superstructure and the 14m-long wreckage lies on its port side and stands 6m clear of the seabed. Originally this wreckage was thought to be either the "B109", "S69" or "G69"; she was identified in 1982 as B109 by her hull markings.

2164 Torpedo Boat V83 585158N 031147W. Cox & Dank stripped this vessel where she was beached on the East side of Rysa Little. She has been untouched since 1927, and now lies upright but in poor condition, broken in half and surrounded by wreckage in the shallows, with the bows in 8m and the intact stern in 20m. There is a gun on the port side.

2165 Torpedo Boat S54. While being towed South, "S54" was driven ashore on Flotta and became a total loss 0.75 miles South of Quoy Ness. The hull now lies in 16m of water after being blown open by later salvage operations.

2166 Torpedo Boat S36 585108N 031056W. After being raised "S36" was gutted and then used in the lifting of the "Hindenburg". She was then beached on the West side of Cava adjacent to North House (ND323997), where the bows now lie in poor condition in shallow water.

2167 Torpedo Boat V82. Parts of this vessel reputedly lie in the shallows off Mill Bay.

The final plunge of the German battleship 'Bayern'.

The German High Seas Fleet at scuttling

Site	Name	Class	Tonnage	Length (m)	Horse power	Props	Speed (knots)	Armour (max.) (cm)	Guns (max.) (cm)	Crew	E… b…
	BATTLESHIPS:										
2174	Kaiser	Kaiser	24380	172	35000	3	23	35	10 × 30	1088	K
2175	Prinzregent Luitpold	Kaiser	24380	172	35000	3	23	35	10 × 30	1088	G
2176	Kaiserin	Kaiser	24380	172	35000	3	23	35	10 × 30	1088	H
2177	Konig Albert	Kaiser	24380	172	35000	3	23	35	10 × 30	1088	S
2178	Friedrich der Grosse	Kaiser	24380	172	35000	3	23	35	10 × 30	1088	V
2168	Bayern	Baden	28075	190	52000	3	23	35	8 × 38	1200	H
2179	Grosser Kurfurst	Konig	25390	177	35000	3	23	35	10 × 30	1150	V
2152	Kronprinz Wilhelm	Konig	25390	177	35000	3	23	35	10 × 30	1150	G
2151	Markgraf	Konig	25390	177	35000	3	23	35	10 × 30	1150	W
2153	Konig	Konig	25390	177	35000	3	23	35	10 × 30	1150	W
	BATTLE CRUISERS:										
2169	Seydlitz	Seydlitz	24610	185	89700	4	30	28	10 × 28	1108	B
2171	Moltke	Moltke	22640	186	80000	4	28	28	10 × 28	1107	B
2172	Von der Tann	Von der Tann	19400	172	80000	4	28	24	8 × 28	910	B
2170	Hinderburg	Derfflinger	26180	210	85000	4	28	30	8 × 30	1215	V
2173	Derfflinger	Derfflinger	26180	210	85000	4	28	30	8 × 30	1215	B
2180	Baden	Baden	28075	190	52000	3	22	35	8 × 38	1200	S
	LIGHT CRUISERS:										
2181	Bremse	Bremse	4400	140	47000	2	28	4	4 × 15	309	V
2154	Dresden	Dresden II	5600	156	49000	2	29	6	8 × 15	559	H
2156	Koln	Dresden II	5600	156	49000	2	29	6	8 × 15	559	B
2157	Karlsruhe	Konigsberg II	5440	151	31000	2	28	6	8 × 15	475	V
2155	Brummer	Bremse	4400	140	47000	2	28	4	4 × 15	309	V
2183	Emden	Konigsberg II	5440	151	31000	2	28	6	8 × 15	475	W
2184	Frankfurt	Frankfurt	5200	145	31000	2	27	6	8 × 15	474	K
2182	Nurnberg	Konigsberg II	5440	151	31000	2	28	6	8 × 15	475	H
	TORPEDO BOATS:										
	No. 1 Flotilla:										
	G40	G37	822	80	25000	2	34		3 × 8.5	83	G
	G86	G85	960	83	26500	2	34		3 × 8.5	87	G
2187	G39	G37	822	80	25000	2	34		3 × 8.5	83	G
2187	G38	G37	822	80	25000	2	34		3 × 8.5	83	G
	V129	V125	924	82	25150	2	35		3 × 10.5	105	V
2187	S32	S31	802	80	25000	2	36		3 × 8.5	83	S
	No.2 Flotilla:										
	3rd Division:										
	G101	G101	1116	95	29500	2	33		4 × 8.5	104	G
	G102	G101	1116	95	29500	2	33		4 × 8.5	104	G
	G103	G101	1116	95	29500	2	33		4 × 8.5	104	G
	G104	G101	1116	95	29500	2	33		4 × 8.5	104	G
	V100	V99	1350	99	42000	2	37		3 × 10.5	114	V
	4th Division:										
2163	B109	B109	1374	98	40700	2	37		4 × 8.5	114	B
	B110	B109	1374	98	40700	2	37		4 × 8.5	114	B
	B111	B109	1374	98	40700	2	37		4 × 8.5	114	B
	B112	B109	1374	98	40700	2	37		4 × 8.5	114	B

Launched	Sank (time)	Position	Raised by	Date raised	Remains & Comments
22.3.11	1325	585257.0N 031111.0W	C&D	20.3.29	
17.2.12	1330	585303.0N 031127.0W	C&D	9.7.31	
21.6.09	1400	585320.0N 031148.0W	MI	11.5.36	Superstructure, funnels, gun turrets
27.4.12	1254	585354.0N 031135.0W	MI	31.7.35	Funnels, bridge, superstructure
10.6.11	1216	585352.0N 031103.0W	MI	29.4.37	Superstructure
18.2.15	1430	585356.0N 031048.0W	MI	1.9.34	Gun turrets, see text
5.5.13	1330	585352.0N 031006.0W	MI	29.4.38	
21.2.14	1315	585339.0N 030946.0W	Left		See main text
4.6.13	1645	585331.0N 030955.0W	Left		See main text
1.3.13	1400	585313.0N 030907.0W	Left		See main text
30.3.12	1350	585212.0N 031053.0W	C&D	2.11.28	Bridge, derricks, other superstructure parts; see text
4.7.10	1310	585223.0N 031108.0W	C&D	10.6.27	One gun
20.3.09	1415	585240.0N 031120.0W	C&D	7.12.30	
1.8.15	1700	585238.0N 031107.0W	C&D	22.7.30	Guns, 2 large concrete blocks, see text
12.7.13	1445		MI	1939	Loose parts of superstructure
0.10.15	Beached in sinking condition, Swanbister Bay				In English Channel
11.3.16	1430		C&D	27.11.29	Bridge, superstructure, ? gun
25.4.17	1330	585258.8N 030821.8W	Left		See main text
5.10.16	1350	585352.0N 030827.0W	Left		See main text
31.1.16	1550	585323.0N 031118.0W	Left		See main text
1.12.15	1305	585350.0N 030907.0W	Left		See main text
1.2.16	Beached				von Reuter's flagship
20.3.15	Beached, sunk off USA in aerial bombing expts.				
14.4.16	Drifted ashore when mooring chains broke				Broken bow section
27.2.15	Sunk	585127N 031058W	C&D	29.7.25	
24.8.15	Sunk	585120N 031104W	C&D	14.7.25	Was under G39; removed to Mill Bay
16.1.15	Sunk	585120N 031104W	C&D	3.7.25	Removed to Mill Bay
3.12.14	Sunk	585113N 031120W	C&D	27.9.24	Used in Seydlitz salvage
21.6.19	Sunk	585127N 031057W	C&D	11.8.25	Removed to Mill Bay
28.2.14	Sunk	585108N 031100W	C&D	19.6.25	Removed to Mill Bay
12.8.14	Sunk	585158N 031120W	C&D	13.4.26	Removed to Mill Bay
16.9.14	Salvaged in floating condition				
4.11.14	Sunk	585155N 031109W	C&D	30.9.25	Taken to Mill Bay, went ashore in Moray Firth during tow
3.11.14	Sunk	585157N 031120W	C&D	30.4.26	Removed to Mill Bay
8.3.15	Beached				
11.3.15	Sunk	585018N 031120W	C&D	27.3.26	Part remains on bottom, see text
31.3.15	Sunk	585131N 031052W	C&D	11.12.25	Friedrich Ruge's boat
8.6.15	Sunk		C&D	8.3.26	
11.2.15	1300	585131N 031052W	C&D	11.2.26	First Torpedo Boat to sink, removed to Mill Bay

The German High Seas Fleet at scuttling (continued)

Site	Name	Class	Tonnage	Length (m)	Horse power	Props	Speed (knots)	Armour (max.) (cm)	Guns (max.) (cm)	Crew
	No. 3 Flotilla:									
2187	S53	S53	919	83	25000	2	36		3 × 8.5	87
2165	S54	S53	919	83	25000	2	36		3 × 8.5	87
2187	S55	S53	919	83	25000	2	36		3 × 8.5	87
	G91	G85	960	83	26500	2	34		3 × 8.5	87
2162	V70	V67	924	82	24400	2	36		3 × 8.5	87
	V72	V67	924	82	24400	2	36		3 × 8.5	87
	V81	V67	924	82	24400	2	36		3 × 8.5	87
2167	V82	V67	924	82	24400	2	36		3 × 8.5	87
	No. 6 Flotilla:									
	11th Division:									
	V125	V125	924	82	25150	2	35		3 × 10.5	105
	V126	V125	924	82	25150	2	35		3 × 10.5	105
	V127	V125	924	82	25150	2	35		3 × 10.5	105
	V128	V125	924	82	25150	2	35		3 × 10.5	105
2186	S131	S131	919	83	24000	2	34		3 × 10.5	105
	S132	S131	919	83	24000	2	34		3 × 10.5	105
	12th Division:									
	V43	V43	852	80	24700	2	36		3 × 8.5	87
	V44	V43	852	80	24700	2	36		3 × 8.5	87
2186	V45	V43	852	80	24700	2	36		3 × 8.5	87
	V46	V43	852	80	24700	2	36		3 × 8.5	87
2186	S49	S49	802	80	25000	2	36		3 × 8.5	83
2186	S50	S49	802	80	25000	2	36		3 × 8.5	83
	No. 7 Flotilla:									
	13th Division:									
	S56	S53	919	83	425000	2	36		3 × 8.5	87
	S65	S53	919	83	25000	2	36		3 × 8.5	87
	V78	V67	924	82	24400	2	36		3 × 8.5	87
2164	V83	V67	924	82	24400	2	36		3 × 8.5	87
	G92	G85	960	83	26500	2	34		3 × 8.5	87
	14th Division:									
	S136	S131	919	83	24000	2	34		3 × 10.5	105
	S137	S131	919	83	24000	2	34		3 × 10.5	105
	S138	S131	919	83	24000	2	34		3 × 10.5	105
	H145	H145	990	84	24000	2	34		3 × 10.5	105
2185	G89	G85	960	83	26500	2	34		3 × 8.5	87
	No. 9 Flotilla:									
	17th Division:									
2166	S36	S31	802	80	25000	2	36		3 × 8.5	83
	S51	S49	802	80	25000	2	36		3 × 8.5	83
2187	S52	S49	802	80	25000	2	36		3 × 8.5	83
	S60	S53	919	83	25000	2	36		3 × 8.5	87
	V80	V67	924	82	24400	2	36		3 × 8.5	87
	Total tonnage:		488163		8325					26345

Abbreviations:

K	Kiel D Y	W	Wilhelmshaven D Y
G	Germaniawerft, Kiel	B	Blohm & Voss, Hamburg
H	Howaldtswerke, Kiel	C&D	Cox & Danks
S	Schickau, Danzig	MI	Metal Industries
V	A G Vulcan, Hamburg	SFSS	Scapa Flow Salvage & Ship Breaking Co
WB	A G Weser, Bremen		

Launched	Sank (time)	Position	Raised by	Date raised	Remains & Comments
18.9.15	Sunk	585059N 031122W	C&D	13.8.24	
11.10.15	Beached	584934N 030440W	C&D	5.6.25	Lost on Flotta while under tow, hull remains
6.11.15	Sunk	585105N 031122W	C&D	29.8.24	
16.11.15	Sunk	585105N 031122W	C&D	12.9.24	Removed to Mill Bay, stern remains
14.10.15	Sunk	585053N 031126W	C&D	1.8.24	
24.9.15	Beached				
27.5.16	Sunk				Parts lie off Mill Bay
27.5.16	Beached				
18.5.17	Beached				
30.6.17	Beached				
28.7.17	Beached				
11.8.17	Beached				To Italy
3.3.17	Sunk	584943N 031031W	SFSS	29.8.24	Beached in Ore Bay
19.5.17	Salvaged in floating condition				
27.1.15	Beached				
24.2.15	Beached				
29.3.15	Sunk	584940N 031022W			Later beached on South shore of Ore Bay
23.12.14	Beached				To France
10.4.15	Sunk	584948N 031100W			Removed to Ore Bay
24.4.15	Sunk	584948N 031100W			Removed to Ore Bay
11.12.15	Sunk	585135N 031026W	C&D	5.6.25	Taken to Lyness
14.10.16	Sunk	585125N 031039W	C&D	16.5.25	Removed to Mill Bay
19.2.16	Sunk	585127N 030956W	C&D	7.9.25	Removed to Mill Bay
5.7.16	Sunk	585158N 031147W			Broken hull remains: see text
15.2.16	Sunk				S C George states this boat was saved
1.12.17	Sunk	58120N 031033W	C&D	3.4.25	Used in Seydlitz salvage
9.3.18	Beached				
22.4.18	Sunk	585125N 031040W	C&D	1.5.25	Taken to Lyness Pier (Leader of Torpedo Boats)
14.3.25	Sunk	585120N 031033W	C&D	14.3.25	Removed to Mill Bay
11.12.15	Beached	585105N 031040W			
7.10.14	Sunk	585108N 031056W	C&D	18.4.25	Removed to Mill Bay, bows remain
29.4.15	Beached				
14.6.15	Sunk	585109N 031056W	C&D	13.10.24	Removed to Mill Bay
3.4.16	Beached				
28.4.16	Beached				

The German salvage sites

QUITE recently the interests of regular visitors to the Flow have moved from the seven main wrecks to exploring the sites from where wrecks were lifted. This programme is now bearing fruit.

2168 Bayern guns 58 53 56N 03 10 48W. The battleship "Bayern" was the first to be salvaged by Metal Industries (in 1933) rather than Cox & Danks. She was 28,075 tons, 185m long, and was fitted with eight 38cm (15") main guns in four turrets. She lay bottom-up in 37m with a starboard list of 9 degrees. During the lift with compressed air all four gun turrets (weighing about 2500 tons in total) fell off. She was beached in shallow water less than one mile from Lyness, then at Lyness. Two of the gun turrets and barbettes have now been located within 10m of each other, about one mile South of the Holm of Howton. They lie upside down rising about 10m above the silty seabed, in about 35m of water. Presumably the other two turrets are nearby. The area is littered with scrap and chain.

2169 Seydlitz wreckage 585212N 031053W. This lies midway between Rysa Little and Cava. The derrick post, bridge and other parts of super-structure were blasted away by divers during original salvage in 1928. They now lie on their starboard side in 17m along with various pieces of salvors' equipment. There is also a large mound of stoking coal from her bunkers estimated at 4000 tons.

2170 Hindenburg 585238N 031107W. This battlecruiser was Cox's first (unsuccessful) salvage attempt in 1926; he succeeded in 1930, at which time the "Hindenburg" was the largest ship ever lifted using compressed air. She lay upright on the seabed in 22m, with superstructure 24m out of

The German battleship 'Bayern', seen here with the massive rear gun turrets about to disappear under the water.

the water. She was beached in shallow water in Mill Bay. The superstructure was partially removed before the lift, and the guns now lie directly South of the "Karlsruhe," and West of Cava. They are undived as far as is known.

2171 Moltke 585223N 031108W. This lay bottom-up in 24m. The bridge, masts, funnels, derrick posts, ventilators etc were blasted off while the wreck floated upside down full of air. One of the 11" guns fouled the bottom while being towed to Lyness; it was blasted away and remains on the seabed, unlocated, to this day. The "Moltke" was the first of the many great capital ships to be towed hazardously upside down to the Firth of Forth for breaking.

2172 Von der Tann 585240N 031120W. This lay with a starboard list of 17.5 degrees in 27m of water. She was lifted, beached on Cava, then towed to Lyness in 1930.

2173 Derfflinger. She lay upside down with a 20 degree list with 33m of water over her North west of Cava. She was salvaged in 1938; all loose parts of her superstructure that were dragging on the bottom were blasted away. Towed inshore and moored in 18m, she was then towed behind Rysa Little and left for the duration of WW2 before finally being towed to Rosyth in 1949. She was the last ship to be raised, and holds the world record for the ship afloat upside down for the longest time.

The German battle cruiser 'Derfflinger' moments before sinking.

2174 Kaiser 585257N 031111W. After salvage in 1928/29 from lying bottom-up in 24m, she was beached on Cava. A gun turret was beached at Lyness after dropping from the wreck during the salvage.

2175 Prinzregent Luitpold 585303N 031127W. She was raised with compressed air in 1931 after she lay bottom-up in 33m with a port list of 17 degrees, then towed to Lyness and beached alongside the "Von der Tann". The seabed around the lifting site is marked as foul, though there is no report from divers yet.

2176 Kaiserin 585320N 031148W. Lay bottom-up with starboard list of 11 degrees in 42m about 0.75 mile from Cava and 3.5 miles from Lyness. She was salvaged with compressed air in 1935; after being grounded in 22m, the superstructure, funnels and gun turrets were blasted away before she was towed to Lyness. Her lift site is listed as a foul anchorage. Undived?

2177 Konig Albert 585354N 031135W. Lying in 42m upside down with port list of 9 degrees, all her turrets and superstructure were buried in mud. She was salvaged with compressed air in 1934/5; she was towed 2 miles and then beached where her funnels, bridge and superstructure were blasted away. Lift site listed as a foul anchorage.

2178 Friedrich der Grosse 58532N 031103W. Lying upside down with a heavy port list of 16 degrees, she was salvaged with compressed air in 1936/7. She was towed to shallow water off Rysa Little where her super-structure was blasted away. Lift site listed as foul anchorage.

2179 Grosser Kurfurst 585352N 031006W. She was refloated using compressed air in 1938. Lift site listed as foul anchorage. Several steel plates used in Queen Mary were forged from the metal salvaged from the Grosser Kurfurst.

2180 Baden. The "Baden" was the only capital ship not to sink. She was beached in a sinking condition in Swanbister Bay, having been towed there by the "Flying Kestrel", an Admiralty tender that had been taking local children on a site-seeing tour of the German fleet. Baden was then used for gunnery practice and sunk in the English Channel off Portsmouth in 1921. I am not aware if her present exact position is known or if she has been dived.

2181 Bremse. The British only just failed to beach the light cruiser "Bremse" at Toy Ness (HY356043) on the North side of Flow when she capsized with her stern in 20m as the fore end touched the shore. She was salvaged in 1929 by filling with air then blasting away bridge and other parts of superstructure. The anchor cable now remains, running ashore with assorted wreckage on the seabed just offshore.

2182 Nurnberg 585245N 031030W. After scuttling, her anchor-chain was explosively cut by the crew of a British destroyer, and she drifted ashore on the West coast of Cava. She was refloated by the Royal Navy in 1920 and towed to the Forth. The broken-up bows section of the light cruiser still lies in the shallows off Cava.

2183 Emden. This light cruiser was used as a flagship by von Reuter. The act of scuttling was delayed by the presence of two British drifters and she was subsequently beached without sinking.

2184 Frankfurt. This light cruiser was beached as she became awash. She subsequently turned turtle, was refloated by the Royal Navy, taken to the USA and sunk off Cape Henry while being used as a target for aerial bombing experiments.

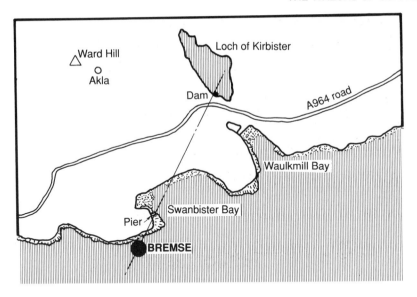

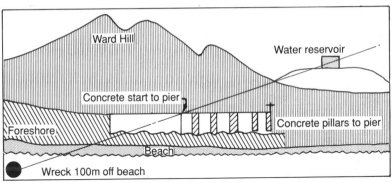

SITE 2181: THE 'BREMSE'

2185 Torpedo Boat G89. Salvaged in 1922 by the Stromness Salvage Syndicate, G89 was stripped then used by Cox & Danks in an attempt to stabilize the list of the "Seydlitz" while she was lifted with compressed air.

2186 Parts of 6th Flotilla of Torpedo Boats S49, S50, S131, V45. These were beached in Ore Bay, South of Lyness, and subsequently refloated and towed South. There are lots of bits still marked as "foul ground".

2187 Parts of the 1st, 3rd & 9th Flotillas of Torpedo Boats S52, S55, S53, G39, G38. These were raised to the North west of Fara. Again marked as foul ground, and again very much worth investigative dives.

The German cruiser 'Nurnburg' immediately after being refloated by Royal Navy salvage crews.

The British naval wrecks

THESE are not as numerous as the German wrecks. However, there are the remains of two magnificent battleships, both lost in tragic circumstances. The other British wrecks are largely a collection of small vessels.

2188 Royal Oak, Scapa Bay 58 55 50N 02 58 58W. This is the best dive in Scapa Flow, but is, unfortunately, totally out of bounds to unauthorised amateur divers as it has been declared an official war grave. DO NOT ATTEMPT TO DIVE IT.

Because of the importance of the wreck and, because the ban may not last forever, the wreck is described. This information was gained by diving in 1973, before the ban existed. The only exception ever made to this ban was for a large BSAC group to film the wreck in 1979. The wreck is "surveyed" annually by a diving team from HMS "Cochrane" and a White Ensign is fastened to the ensign mast to be "flown" for another year.

The battleship Royal Oak displaced 29,150 tons and was 188m long (× 27m × 8.5m). She was fitted with anti-torpedo blisters which increased her beam to 31m. Her armament consisted of eight 15″ guns (in four turrets of two), twelve 6″ guns, eight 4″ and 16 21lb anti-aircraft guns, and four 21″ torpedo tubes; she also carried one aircraft.

The official story of the sinking is that during the night of 13/14 October 1939 the Royal Oak was sunk at anchor by three torpedoes from "U47" commanded by Lieutenant Prien. Of the complement of 1146 men and some guests over 800 were lost; there were 424 survivors. "Black Saturday" by Alexander McKee is an account of the sinking, though apparently somewhat embellished in places. During the six years of WW2 divers from Metal Industries brought up the remains of electrically driven torpedoes from near the wreck, thus adding to the official evidence. After the sinking

HMS 'Royal Oak' is potentially the best dive in Scapa Flow, but is out of bounds to sport divers, having been designated as an official war grave.

the Admiralty decided to fully block the eastern entrances to the Flow, and thus the Churchill barriers were built by Italian prisoners of war.

The wreck lies about 3 miles South of Kirkwall at the eastern end of the Scapa Flow in 29m of water. She is marked with a prominent wreck buoy, itself marked "Unauthorised diving prohibited". When you are over the wreck, the brown weed on the hull is visible 6m under the surface. Additionally, the full oil bunkers stream an oil slick.

The ship is lying on her starboard side but nearly upside down with the deck at about 110 degrees to the vertical. A powerful torch is needed to explore the deck fully due to the angle of the keel. The greatest impression is made by the massive 15" guns mounted in pairs in huge turrets, but to see these properly one has to go under the deck of the keel of the ship. There is a line of 4" guns mounted along the port side of the ship. The props were salvaged just after the sinking, but the large prop shafts and rudder remain. Lying upright on the seabed alongside the bridge area is the captain's pinnace, which is about 8m long. On the port side of the ship is a double row of portholes, but only about one third of these were in place in 1973. The port bow has been blasted inwards by the torpedo explosion, leaving perhaps 6m of crumpled and torn iron plates, otherwise the vessel is intact.

In 1983 the wreck was reported to be still complete except for the spotting top which has now collapsed alongside the wreck. The boats are still in their davits.

2189 HMS Vanguard, North of Flotta 58 51 27N 03 06 20W. HMS "Vanguard" was a British battleship of 19,250 tons and was 172m long with a final main armament of twenty 12" guns. She was lost in 1917 after a massive internal explosion which tore her to pieces. The wreck lies about 0.75 mile North of the Flotta Oil Terminal and is marked by an East cardinal buoy. She is now spread all over the silty seabed, with her bows pointing directly at the surface; the seabed depth is 25m and depth at the bows is 8m. The stern section with the torpedo room is still largely intact. There are still live 46cm torpedo warheads, 30cm shells, and cordite sticks around, so caution is required. There is a second caution – parts of the wreck lie very near to an oil pipeline and the oil company may not like diving thereabouts, check first. The story of HMS "Vanguard" is told in "They called it an accident" by Hampshire. The site is a war grave. The wreck was sporadically salvaged by both Nundy Marine Metals and Scapa Flow Salvage.

2190 HMS Roedean 584836N 030948W. A 1094-ton, 85m-long fleet minesweeper that sank at the entrance to Longhope in 15m of water after dragging her anchor in 1915 and fouling the ram of HMS "Imperieuse". She was armed with twin 12-pound guns. Explosive dispersal was carried out in 1953 and 1956 but the starboard side, boilers and timber decking are recognisable under a thick covering of silt.

2191 HM Drifter Imbat 585000N 031100W. This 92-ton vessel was lost by collision in 1941. Her remains now lie 300m East of Lyness Pier. No diving information.

2192 HM Tug Oceana. Lost by collision "at Scapa" in 1918, she was 337 tons and 43m long.

2193 HM Trawler Strathgarry. Listed as "sunk off Scapa" after a collision in 1915. She was 202 tons and 34m long.

2194 HM Tug Alexandra II. Wrecked in 1915 in Hoxa Sound, she was 168 tons and 28m long.

2195 HM Drifter Dewey Eve. A 109-ton vessel lost by collision 304 degrees from No 6 buoy at a distance of 1 cable in 1940.

2196 HM Drifter Token. An 89-ton vessel that was grounded and wrecked in 1941 in Skerry Sound.

2197 HM Drifter Catherine. A 78-ton vessel foundered in 1942 "in Scapa Flow".

2198 HM Drifter Ruby. A 46-ton vessel wrecked in a gale in 1942 at Lamb Holm.

2199 HM Drifter Legend. Wrecked on Flotta in 1942.

2200 Unknown boom defence drifter 58 49 43N 03 02 56W. Lost with 14 crew, this lies in Hoxa Sound and was first located by the Admiralty in 1974 from HMS "Herald". She has been swept to 33m, and the least depth over the wreck is 49m; general seabed depth 55m. Another, smaller, object was detected 120m South of the main wreck. Undived as far as is known, she is, no doubt, one of the vessels listed above.

The Blockships

SINCE the early years of this century the British Admiralty had worried about the security of Scapa Flow as a fleet anchorage. In the early part of WW1 21 ships were sunk in the channels to the East of the Flow and in Burra Sound to the West. A further 22 were added to the early part of WW2, but without total success, as Prien still managed to get his U-boat in to sink the "Royal Oak". Finally, the narrow eastern channels were completely blocked by Italian POWs who built four causeways out of thousands of huge concrete blocks.

Of the 43 blockships (total tonnage 101,516) some 11 were later removed, leaving 32 which now provide shallow diving for those who wish to explore beyond the confines of the large wrecks in the centre of the Flow. Water depth is usually very shallow – about 5m. Consequently, these wrecks are heavily overgrown with weed, but there are still "goodies" for the persistent. Amazingly, portholes are still being found. The blockships are useful dives for beginners or in very rough weather, but most experienced divers will find them rather boring, especially when there is such a glut of superb diving nearby and time is generally so short.

I have listed all the details of the blockships that are known to me in the following table (overleaf). Only a few of the more interesting remains are briefly described below. Blockships in Burra Sound include the Inverlane

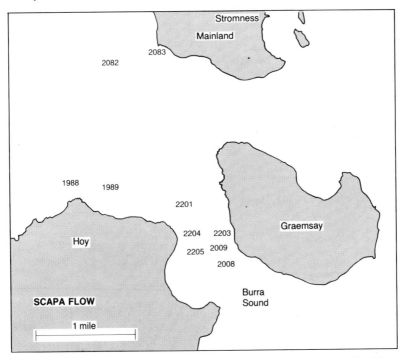

DIVE SITES, INCLUDING BLOCKSHIPS, IN BURRA SOUND

Scapa Flow blockships

Site	Name	Sunk	Tonnage	Type	Built
	Burra Sound:				
2201	Ronda	1915	1941	Steel, single screw steamer	1889
2202	Budrie	1915	2252	Steel, single screw steamer	1882
2203	Rotherfield	1914	2831	Steel, single screw steamer	1889
2204	Urmstom Grange	1914	3423	Steel, single screw steamer	1894
2009	Inverlane	1944	8900	Steel single screw motor tanker	1938
2205	Moyle	1940	1761	Steel, single screw steamer	1907
2008	Gobernador Bories	1915	2332	Iron, single screw steamer	1882
	Water Sound:				
2206	Collingdoc	1942	1780	Steel, single screw steamer	1925
2207	Gondolier	1940	173	Iron paddle steamer	1866
2208	Clio	1914	2733	Steel, single screw steamer	1889
2209	Pontos	1914	2265	Steel, single screw steamer	1891
2210	Carolina Thornden	1942	3645	Steel single screw motor tanker	1938
2211	Lorne	1915	1186	Iron, single screw steamer	1873
2212	Juniata	1940	1139	Steel twin-screw motor tanker	1918
2213	Carran	1940	1017	Steel, single screw steamer	1894
2214	Nana	1939	–	Concrete barge	
	East Weddel Sound:				
2215	Martis	1940	2483	Steel single screw steamer	1894
2216	Reginald	1915	930	Iron 3-master motor schooner	1878
2217	Empire Seaman	1940	1921	Steel single screw steamer	1922
2218	Gartmore	1915	1564	Iron, single screw steamer	1880
2219	Lapland	1915	1234	Steel, single screw steamer	1890
2220	Unknown				
	Skerry Sound:				
2221	AC6 barge	1941	–	Barge, ex-Metal Industries	
2222	Emerald Wings	1940	2139	Steel, single screw steamer	1920
2223	Argyll	1914	1185	Iron, single screw steamer	1872
2224	Elton	1915	2461	Steel, single screw steamer	1880
2225	Reinfield	1914	3634	Steel, single screw steamer	1893
2226	F/C pontoon	1941	–	Pontoon, ex-Metal Industries	
2227	Cape Ortegal	1939	4896	Steel, single screw steamer	1911
2228	Ilsenstein	1940	1508	Steel, single screw steamer	1898
2229	Teeswood	1914	1589		1882
2230	Lycia	1940	2338	Steel, single screw motorship	1924
2231	Rosewood	1915	1757	Steel, single screw steamer	1889
2232	Almeria	1915	2418	Steel, single screw steamer	1888
	Kirk Sound:				
2233	Tabarka	1941	2624	Steel, single screw steamer	1909
2234	Busk	1940	367	Steel, single screw steamer	1906
2235	Lake Neuchatte	1939	3859	Steel, single screw steamer	1907
2236	Aorangi	WW1	4268	Steel, single screw steamer	1883
2237	Thames	1914	1327	Steel, single screw steamer	1887
2238	Minieh	1915	2890	Iron, single screw steamer	1876
2239	Redstone	1940	3110	Steel, single screw steamer	1918
2240	Ghambira	1939	5257	Steel, single screw steamer	1910
2241	Soriano	1939	3543	Steel, single screw steamer	1917
2242	Numidian	WW1	4836	Steel, single screw steamer	1891
2243	Unknown		101516		

Total gross tonnage:

Registered	Position	Condition
Hull	585540.0N 031838.0W	Blown up & dispersed 1962
India	585540.0N 031838.0W	
London	585540.0N 031838.0W	Blown up & dispersed 1962
London	585540.0N 031838.0W	Blown up & dispersed 1962
Dublin	585533.0N 031841.0W	Dries 15m. Midships & bow left
Belfast		
Chile	585525.0N 031833.0W	Hull broken up, stern intact
Canada	585023.1N 025408.3W	Great Lakes steamer
Glasgow	585020.0N 025357.0W	Capsized & sank in deep water
Hull		Boilers & engines exposed
Greece	585024.1N 025405.0W	85m portion of hull dries
Finland	585030.0N 025404.0W	Bombed Faroes. Mostly removed
S'hampton	585030.0N 025404.0W	Partially blown up, but parts dry
London	585029.0N 025356.0W	11m section of hull remains
Grangemouth	585033.3N 025402.0W	Mast collapsed across intact 70m hull
Stromness	585029.1N 025359.4W	35m of bows left
London	585215.5N 025449.2W	Stern & bows removed
Glasgow	585217.0N 025448.0W	Schooner stern section on side
London	585217.4N 025433.1W	Bow, stern & engines removed. Midships broken
S Shields	585217.0N 025447.0W	No trace left
Liverpool	585217.0N 025447.0W	Totally collapsed. Beneath Barrier
	585214.4N 025440.4W	35m length of blockship stern
Britain	585252.0N 025400.0W	Only plates, girders and debris left
London	585254.5N 025353.2W	Very broken up, most of hull shows
Hull	585253.0N 025402.6W	Very broken up, large drying piece of hull
W Hartlepool	585258.5N 025352.0W	Midships & engine left
Germany	585257.0N 025356.0W	Very broken up, mostly dries
Britain		
Glasgow		Rolled over & broke up in gale
Germany	585258.5N 025352.0W	Replaced Cape Ortegal
Britain	585302.5N 025350.0W	Only engines left
Glasgow	585303.0N 025357.0W	Hull removed down to engine room, shows at LW
S Shields	585311.0N 025419.0W	Almost completely dispersed
Cardiff	585257.0N 025351.0W	
France	585320.0N 025350.0W	Raised 1944, removed to Burra Sound
Whitehaven	585321.0N 025348.0W	Broke up in gale, hull lifted
London	585324.0N 025354.0W	Salvaged 1948, Metal Industries
N Zealand	585326.0N 025142.0W	Raised 1920 & resunk off Holm Kirkyard
Grangemouth	585330.0N 025400.0W	Stern removed, hull cut down to main deck
London	585327.0N 025350.0W	Hull removed
London	585334.0N 025400.0W	Removed
London		Raised 1943, sunk off Llandudno
Uruguay	585339.0N 025401.0W	Removed
Glasgow	585342.5N 025353.5W	Salvaged 1924, East Coast Salvage Co
	585342.5N 025405.0W	Hull under 1m (not Ghambira)

and the Gobernador Bories. These are dealt with in the previous chapter (sites 2108 and 2109).

2206 Collindoc. A Great Lake steamer with typical long, narrow hull, forward bridge and aft funnel; the most accessible of the blockships. The bridge area still exhibits a crude protection of concrete slabs. She lies at the South Ronaldsay end of No. 4 Barrier (Water Sound). The gunwhale dries and the wreckage is about 75m long and oriented 34-216 degrees.

2209 Pontos. The entire hull is intact in Water Sound with the bows toward the beach. All the ship shows at low water, but at high water only the top 2m and the aft davit shows. The bridge has collapsed and two masts are intact. The stern runs into the "Cleo".

2211 Carran. This lies North-South at the Burray end of No. 4 Barrier. A mast lies collapsed across the intact 70m-long hull. Little superstructure remains.

2216 Reginald. This is the most prominent of the blockships in East Weddel Sound. It is a mass of steel debris partially covered by sand and weed. The typical schooner stern lies on its starboard side.

2217 Empire Seaman. This is a war prize – the renamed German steamer "Morea" – seized while blockade running by the Royal Navy in 1940. The broken midships section remains in East Weddel Sound as two rectangular blocks of wreckage about 10m × 60m oriented 111-291 degrees and separated by about 50m. Shows above low water.

2236 F/C pontoon. A crane barge used by Metal Industries for their salvage work and sunk in 1941 in Skerry Sound. A large "box" of steel and mooring winches still remain.

2237 Thames. Many of the blockships in Kirk Sound have been removed. However, the wreck of the "Thames" remains in a position stated as 318.5 degree 2300 feet from Lamb Holm trig station. The wreck stands upright about 3.5m high and with 9m of water over it. The hull is intact to the gunwhale but with the stern missing.

Other wrecks

THERE are still more wrecks in the Flow.

2244 Prudentia 585051.8N 030751.6W. A 2731-ton, 95m-long British tanker lost in 1918 when she collided with SS "Hermoine" and sank in 23m. Another report states that she dragged her mooring in bad weather, fouled HMS "Iron Duke's" buoy and sank. The position is 0.5 mile West of No. 1 Jetty, Flotta and the wreck is easy to locate as she still trails an oil slick. She lies on her port side and stands up to 14m above the seabed of muddy sand. Her hull is now severely corroded and may be considered a danger to divers. Steel prop.

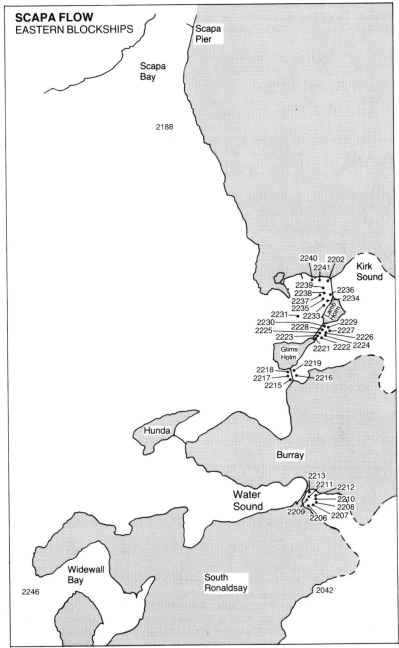

SCAPA FLOW
EASTERN BLOCKSHIPS

Scapa
Pier

Scapa
Bay

2188

2240 2202
2241
Kirk
Sound

2239
2238   2236
2237   2234
2235
2231   2233
2230   2228   2229
2225   2227
2223   2226
Glims   2221 2222 2224
Holm
2218   2219
2217   2216
2215

Lamb Holm

Hunda

Burray

2213
2211 2212
Water   2210
Sound   2208
2209   2207
2206

Widewall
Bay

South
Ronaldsay

2246   2042

POSITION OF BLOCKSHIPS AND OTHER WRECKS

161

2245 YC21 lifting barge. This is a 550 ton salvor's barge that lies near the wreck of the "F2". It is connected to it by a long hawser. The barge was lost in 1968 when moored over the destroyer; at a particularly low tide the destroyer's mast holed the barge and it sank. Not a terribly exciting dive, but a sure way of finding the "F2"!

2246 Trawler James Barrie. A 666-ton, 55m-long vessel lost in 1969 at 584847N 03029W, 5.5 cables South of Hoxa Head on a bearing of 186 degrees. Depth is 38m. She actually went aground on Louther Skerry, drifted off after the crew had been rescued, was taken in tow by the Kirkwall lifeboat, but suddenly sank off Widewall Bay. No diving information.

2247 Concrete Barge. This lies in 16m of water 0.75 mile East of No. 1 Jetty, Flotta. Possibly French in origin.

2248 Lancaster plane, Weddel Sound. Rumoured to be hereabouts. I have no further information.

2249 Unknown wreck, Toy Ness. A well smashed wreck, with the gun and mast still recognisable, lying in 15m. This may well be from the Bremse. Ask the local farmer's permission for access.

Unknown wrecks

YET more wrecks and wreckages litter the Flow. The data for these wrecks (sites 2250 to 2305) is best presented as a table (see pages 164 and 165).

A number of these unknown sites undoubtedly mark the positions from which some of the German ships were raised or where salvors left equipment. However, it should be noted that the sites of all the German scuttlings are detailed separately by the Wreck Section of the Hydrographer to the Navy.

References

Diving: The following three articles contain detailed underwater wreck descriptions:
Davidson, "Wrecks, rocks and rösts of Orkney", Scottish Diver, July-August 1983.
Ridley, "The wrecks of Scapa Flow", Benthos, 1, 1974.
Winfield, "Close encounters at Scapa Flow", The Diver's Yearbook, 1982-1983.
BSAC Wreck Register, 1981 onwards.
Graham, "The Wrecks of Scapa Flow", 1985, Orkney Press.
Hydrographer to the Navy, Wreck Section, computer printouts of wreck data for Orkney.

The vessels, scuttling, & salvage:
Bowman, "The man who bought a navy", 1964, Harrap.
Brown & Meehan, "Scapa Flow", 1968, Allen Lane.
Cousins, "The story of Scapa Flow", 1965, Muller.
Davis, "Deep diving and submarine operations", 8th edition, 1981, Siebe Gorman.

George, "Jutland to Junkyard", 1973, Patrick Stephens.
Gores, "Marine Salvage", 1971, David & Charles.
Hampshire, "They called it an Accident".
Herwig, "Luxury fleet, the Imperial German Navy 1888-1918", 1980, Allen & Unwin.
Hewison, "This great harbour Scapa Flow", 1985, Orkney Press.
Macintyre, "Jutland", 1957, Evans.
McKee, "Black Saturday", 1966, Souvenir.
McKenzie, "Marine Salvage in Peace and War", Institute of Engineers and Shipbuilders in Scotland, Vol 93 Paper 1122.
North Coast of Scotland pilot, 1975, Hydrographer of the Navy.
Parkes, "British Battleships 1860-1950", 1973, Seeley Service.
Pottinger, "The salving of the German Fleet", 1975, Stromness Museum.
Ruge, "Scapa Flow 1919", 1969, Ian Allan.
Snyder, "The Royal Oak disaster", 1976, William Kimber.
Taylor, "German warships of World War One", 1971, Ian Allan.
van der Vat, "The Grand Scuttle", 1986, Waterfront
von der Porten, The German Navy in World War Two, 1969, Pan.
von Reuter, "Scapa Flow: the account of the greatest scuttling of all time", 1940, Hurst & Blackett.
Weaver, "Nightmare at Scapa Flow", 1980, Cressrelles
Williams, Diving for Treasure, 1926, Faber & Gwyer.

General Orkney books: Large numbers of books have been written about all aspects of Orkney. Many of these contain references to Scapa Flow. Some of the best are:
Bailey, "Orkney", 1971, David & Charles.
Berry, "The natural history of Orkney", 1985, Collins.
Berry & Firth, "The people of Orkney", 1986, Orkney Press.
Buckley & Harvie-Brown, "A vertebrate fauna of the Orkney Islands", 1891, Douglas.
Gunn, "Orkney: the magnetic North", 1932, Nelson.
Gunn, "The Orkney book", 1909, Nelson.
Laing, "Orkney & Shetland: an archaeological guide", 1974, David & Charles.
Linklater, "Orkney and Shetland", 1965, Hale.
Schei & Moberg, "The Orkney story", 1985, Batsford.
Shearer et al, "The new Orkney book", 1966, Nelson.

Area services

THESE are covered in the previous chapter on Orkney. Some of the local charter operators are listed below:
Orkneyinga Charters, Walliwall Cottage, St. Ola, Kirkwall, Orkney (0856) 5489.
George Litts, Braehead Cottage, Stromness, Orkney (0856) 850434.
John Thornton, The Manse, Palace Road, Kirkwall, Orkney (0856) 4761.
Anthony Duncan, Scapa Flow Diving Centre, Karinya, Burray, Orkney (085673) 225/253.
Robert Swanney, Ayre Mills, Kirkwall, Orkney (0856) 3974.
Steve Mowat, Stromness Diving Centre, Barkland, Cairston Road, Stromness, Orkney (0856) 850624; or Don Temple (0343) 830034.

Unknown wrecks in Scapa Flow

Site	Name	Type	Position
2250	Unknown	? MFV	584833.4N 025959.5W
2251	Unknown	Steam pinnacle	584944.0N 031050.0W
2252	Unknown	Obstruction	584956.0N 031114.0W
2253	Unknown	German ship	584958.0N 031119.0W
2254	Unknown	Small wreck	584958.5N 030506.0W
2255	Unknown	German ship	584959.0N 031119.0W
2256	Unknown	German ship	585002.0N 031114.0W
2257	Unknown	Foul anchorage	585006.0N 031054.0W
2258	Unknown	Wreckage	585019.0N 030754.5W
2259	Unknown	Wreckage	585021.9N 030757.3W
2260	Unknown	Wreckage	585028.0N 025402.0W
2261	Unknown	Wreckage	585034.3N 030630.7W
2262	Unknown	Wreck	585047.0N 031142.0W
2263	Unknown	Wreck	585051.0N 030544.0W
2264	Unknown	Wreckage	585054.0N 030729.3W
2265	Unknown	Wreckage	585055.6N 030731.8W
2266	Unknown	Barges Etc	585100.0N 030500.0W
2267	Unknown	Foul anchorage	585118.0N 031042.0W
2268	Unknown	Wreckage	585119.5N 030439.0W
2269	Unknown	Wreckage	585122.5N 030655.7W
2270	Unknown	Wreckage	585122.7N 030626.2W
2271	Unknown	Wreckage	585122.8N 030602.5W
2272	Unknown	Wreckage	585126.6N 030536.2W
2273	Unknown	Wreck	585128.0N 030725.0W
2274	Unknown	Wreck	585129.6N 030512.2W
2275	Unknown	Foul	585129.6N 030918.4W
2276	Unknown	Wreckage	585134.4N 030435.2W
2277	Unknown	Wreckage	585135.7N 030433.0W
2278	Unknown	Foul	585138.8N 030910.3N
2279	Unknown	Foul	585143.0N 030737.0W
2280	Unknown	Foul	585145.7N 030711.9W
2281	Unknown	Wreckage	585151.3N 030731.3W
2282	Unknown	Foul	585157.5N 030728.2W
2283	Unknown	Wreck	585204.1N 030615.5W
2284	Unknown	Wreckage	585209.8N 030746.5W
2285	Unknown	Wreckage	585210.0N 030753.0W
2286	Unknown	Foul	585217.9N 030746.8W
2287	Unknown	Wreck	585220.3N 030615.5W
2288	Unknown	Foul	585223.4N 030801.0W
2289	Unknown	Wreckage	585224.7N 030837.7W
2290	Unknown	Foul	585226.4N 030745.8W
2291	Unknown	Wreck	585228.0N 030827.1W
2292	Unknown	Foul	585233.0N 030740.8W
2293	Unknown	Wreck	585236.5N 030745.8W
2294	Unknown	Wreckage	585238.7N 030732.7W
2295	Unknown	Foul	585243.8N 030739.1W
2296	Unknown	Wreck	585246.0N 030744.0W
2297	Unknown	Wreckage	585246.5N 030744.9W
2298	Unknown	Wreckage	585251.5N 030749.7W
2299	Unknown	Foul	585256.3N 030732.5W
2300	Unknown	Wreck	585257.8N 030630.5W
2301	Unknown	Foul	585518.0N 030454.0W
2302	Unknown	Gun turret	585518.0N 030630.0W
2303	Unknown	A/S barrier	585549.0N 031506.0W
2304	Unknown	A/S barrier	585555.0N 031445.0W

Depth	Details
0	35m drying hul in Widewall Bay
5	15m weed-covered government wreck, S side of Ore Bay
11	158 deg 820 ft from SE corner Lyness Wharf
11	Foul 172 deg 0.72 cables from SE corner Lyness Wharf
0	20 deg 260 ft from head of Pan Hope Pier, dries
10	Foul 165 deg 0.47 cables from SE corner Lyness Wharf
12	Foul 109 deg 0.5 cables from SE corner Lyness Wharf
14	Gutter Sound
5	West Weddel Sound
7	West Weddel Sound
0	Two small pieces of drying wreckage, Water Sound, ? blockship
?	Small, plots inland of Flotta Oil Terminal!
10	112 deg 2.6 cables from Rysa Lodge, 5m clearance
21	0.1 mile N of N Flotta
25	0.3 mile WNW Flotta Jetty No 1
25	0.3 mile WNW Flotta Jetty No 1
15	Barges & contractors' plant sunk W of Calf Sound by buoy, 1976
10	Five German destroyers raised from SE Gutter Sound
10	Just off NW of Calf of Flotta
32	Scattered wreckage 80m square, 0.6 mile N of Flotta No 1 Jetty
25	Immediately W of Vanguard wreck site
30	0.1 mile E of Vanguard
30	0.3 mile E of Vanguard
31	0.5 mile E of Vanguard, clearance 28m
36	0.6 mile E of Vanguard, clearance 20m
22	0.25 mile NE of Whiting Point, Fara
30	Marked foul 0.3 mile N of Calf of Flotta
30	Marked foul 0.3 mile N of Calf of Flotta
30	0.4 mile NE of Whiting Point
30	Area 30m in radius appox, 1.1 mile ENE of Whiting Point
20	1 mile N of No 1 Jetty, Flotta
21	Marked foul 1.1 mile N of No 1 Jetty, Flotta
22	0.2 mile S of SPM No 1, clearance 15m
31	0.3 mile SW of SPM No 2, clearance 20m
30	0.2 mile W of SPM No 1
31	Small, marked foul, 0.3 mile W of SPM No 1
31	0.25 mile NW of SPM No 1
28	0.25 mile W of SPM No 2
34	0.4 mile NW of SPM No 1
38	Small, 0.4 mile SE of Tuberry Point, Cava
35	0.35 mile NW of SPM No 1
40	0.45 mile ESE of Tuberry Point, clearance 28m
33	0.4 mile NNW of SPM No 1
37	0.8 mile E of Tuberry Point, clearance 28m
36	0.9 mile E of Tuberry Point
37	0.85 mile E of Tuberry Point
41	0.6 mile NNW of SPM No 1, clearance 28m
41	0.6 mile NNW of SPM No 1
37	Small, 0.7 mile NNW of SPM No 1
36	0.5 mile S of Barrel of Butter
30	0.7 mile SE of Barrel of Butter, clearance 20m
25	1.1 mile E of Toy Ness
10	Salvor's dumping ground; 5.9″ gun turret & barbette, wreckage
3	Girders forming anti-submarine barrier in Clestron Sound
6	Railway lines forming anti-submarine barrier in Clestron Sound

Sunrise Charters, 22 Slater Street, Kirkwall, Orkney (0856) 3953/78393.
Sands Motel, Burray, Orkney (085673) 298.
Smith Foubister, St. Ola Hotel, Harbour Street, Kirkwall (0856) 5090.
E Jeffrey, 8 Dundas Street, Stromness, Orkney (0856) 850489.
Thomson & Dickie, Roadside, Widewall, South Ronaldsay, Orkney (0856) 83372.
Dive Scapa Flow, Howton Ray (Tel: 0856 2872).
Ferry Inn, Stromness, Orkney (Tel: 0856 850 280).
Taversoe Hotel, Rousay, Orkney (Tel: 0856 82 375).

CHAPTER 8

Islands off Shetland

Fair Isle

ONE of an exciting pair of islands (at 59339 0138W) that provide challenging diving. By their very exposure they are often put out of reach by the weather.

Access for divers is difficult as it is not practical to take diving equipment there by either air or on the passenger ferry. The formation of a larger party and the hiring of a larger vessel is one effective way of exploring both Fair Isle and Foula. There are a couple of local divers on Fair Isle, and it is possible to arrange a short diving stay with them via Skolla Dive Centre in Shetland.

Fair Isle is a magnificent island (population 79), set midway between Orkney and Shetland, about 25 miles South of Sumburgh Head. It is difficult of access, due to heavy weather; as far as is known, the West coast has virtually never been dived because of these heavy seas.

The island is made up of Old Red Sandstone and is 3.5 miles long and 1.5 miles wide. The southern half of the island is quite fertile, although the northern half is moorland and Ward Hill (217m) is the highest point. The western and northern coasts are fine cliffs, reaching 183m high at one point. There are numerous caverns, geos, stacks and arches.

The island is a most important landfall for migratory birds and over 300 species have been recorded. The important bird observatory was established at North Haven in 1948. In bird watchers' eyes, Fair Isle ranks second only to St. Kilda in importance.

There is a fascinating booklet – "The Shipwrecks of Fair Isle" by Jerry Eunson – which may still be available from W.S.Wilson, Stackhoull Stores, Fair Isle. This details 85 different shipwreck incidents between 900 and 1945. Many of the sites are only approximate, but quite a number of very specific sites are quoted. I have noted six of these below, though none have been located or dived as far as I know. Nowaday, with the existence of two lighthouses, there should be much less chance of modern shipwrecks.

The diving is excellent and in first class visibility. The West coast has yet to be explored but promises many exciting sites.

The tidal streams run quite strongly and, in view of the island's remote-

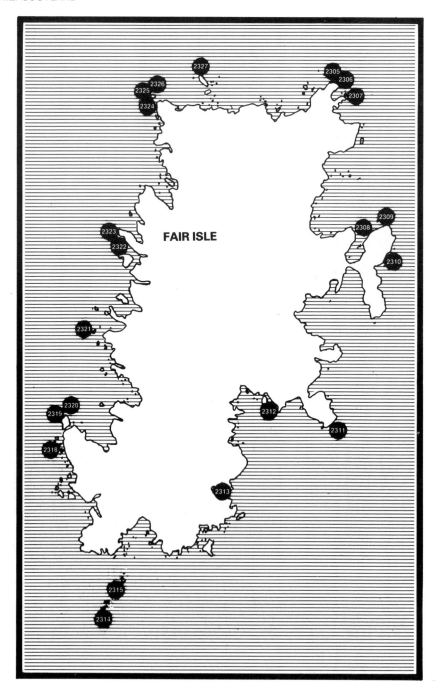

ness, due care should be taken in dive planning. Races form off both ends of Fair Isle during the height of the tidal movement. The following table summarises the tidal streams:

−0430 Dover − South east going stream begins and gradually moves clockwise.

HW Dover − stream running South south west.

+0100 Dover − stream running South south west off the East side of the islands, and West south west off the West side.

Maximum Spring rate 4 knots.

+0200 Dover 8 North west going stream begins, initially flowing West north west.

+0600 Dover − direction changes gradually clockwise.

Maximum Spring rate 5 knots.

2305 Skerry of Grindoline, the Nizz. HZ743223. Undived headland and skerry, depth appears to be about 10-15m, initially.

2306 Wreck of the "Norseman's Bride". An Orkney MFV lost in 1975 just below the North light at 5933109 013624W. The ship was holed and making water; she was later abandoned ashore. She provides an easy dive in 7m. Prolific kelp growth obscures much of what remains. The prop was recovered by Alex Crawford and Simon Martin. The maker's name plate is in the Fair Isle Museum.

2307 Cristal Kame. HZ224744. Gullies and rocks lead on to vertical, richly encrusted rock walls with sandy beds at 15m in between. Seals and cormorants noted underwater.

Fair Isle is one of an exciting pair of islands (the other is Foula) which provide challenging diving, often from specially-equipped charter boats.

2308 North Haven, West entrance. HZ225728. A seabed of large boulders at 25m with numbers of ling skulking in the channels around the rocks.

2309 Wreck of the "Joanna En Pietrenella". This Dutch two-masted fishing vessel went ashore at the mouth of North Haven, slid off the rocks and went aground again on the Stack. Only the cabin boy was saved.

2310 Bu Ness. HZ228725. This headland drops into 20+m depths and provides an excellent and spectacular dive. Lobster noted.

2311 The Ruff. HZ222708. Undived headland that appears to drop into about 15-20m.

2312 Wreck of the "Lessing". HZ216711. An 1800-ton barque lost in 1868 with 465 emigrants aboard. She was driven by a gale and in thick mist ran across the mouth of Clavers Geo, completely blocking the entrance with her bowsprit wedged in the cliff face. All the passengers and crew were saved by the Fair Isle men with their boats. Artefacts from the wreck are in the Fair Isle Museum.

2313 Wreck of the "El Gran Griffon", Stromshellier. HZ210703 (approx). This flagship of 23 hired Armada transports was lost in 1588. The crew and soldiers, some 300 people, climbed the masts and escaped up the cliffs. They spent several weeks of Fair Isle, nearly causing a famine before they were transported in Mainland. Two brass cannons were recovered in 1728 and a further two together with several lead ingots were raised by Colin Martin in 1970. All there is to be seen now is the eroded iron cannon, some rather small pieces of wood and occasional lead shot; the anchor still lies in 23m.

2314 The Skerry. HZ198690. An undived rock that drops into about 15m.

2315 Wreck of the "Maverick". This 48-ton, 70-feet-long British MFV ran ashore at the Skerry in 1980 despite the modern lighthouse. She later floated of and sank in a depth of 20m. The position is between The Keels and The Skerry at 593030N 013900W. Strong tidal streams effectively limit diving to slack water. The maker's plate is in the Fair Isle Museum.

2316 Wreck of the SS "Duncan". Built of iron in 1874, the "Duncan" was lost when she hit the Head o' the Baa in thick fog in 1877. The crew were saved then the vessel sank close inshore. The iron prop is a prominent feature, together with brass bits and pieces encrusted in concretion. A heavy swell usually restricts diving.

2317 Wreck of the "Canadia". A 5000-ton Danish steamer went ashore at Heely Stark. The crew were saved by breeches buoy and much of the cargo of cotton and flour was salved by the islanders. The iron propeller is to be seen at 10m; there is still much brass in evidence. The builder's plate is at the Fair Isle Post Office.

2318 Malcolm's Head. HZ194707. The gullies between the islets give splendid dives. However, even in quite calm conditions, the Atlantic swell causes divers to be swept to and fro by up to 10m; consequently the dive is best just outside them. Underwater cliff faces drop to 20m all round. The rock is covered in sponges and hydroids with Alcyonium and tubularia in less exposed corners.

2319 Rocks North west of Fogli Stack. HZ193711. These appear to fall away as a fairly steep slope to about 27m.

2320 Wreck of the "Carl Constantine". A brig with a cargo of coal lost in 1876 when run ashore at Fogli (or Fugli) Stack after she sprang a bad leak. The master and carpenter were lost; the crew of 6 and the cabin boy were saved.

2321 Kista. HZ198717. An undived stack right on the exposed west coast of Fair Isle. It may have walls dropping vertically to 18m.

2322 Wreck of the "Caroline". A sailing vessel that struck the shore at South Naversgill in 1773 in a thick fog. All the crew were saved, though one died ashore.

2323 Burrista. HZ200728. A finger-like headland with a depth of 15m off its seaward extremity.

2324 Dronger. HZ204741. An exposed site with plenty of swell, particularly on the rocky point. A steep rock slope leads to 30m, then a gradual slope leads downwards past huge boulders. The rocks are covered with Alcyonium and Lithothamnion.

2325 The Fless. HZ204742. The stack at the North west tip of Fair Isle has a depth of 30m+ right alongside and provides an interesting dive.

2326 Wreck of the "Strathbeg". A trawler lost before WW1 at the Fless. The prop and engine are still to be seen at 27m.

2327 Stacks of Skroo. HZ209744. These lie off the north coast and have depths of 17m immediately to their North.

Foula

ANOTHER dramatic island (at 6008N 0205W), although it lies right out in the Atlantic, 24 miles West of West Burra in Shetland. It is 3.5 miles long by 2.5 miles wide, but looks bigger because of the hills rising to 418m. The 1983 book, "Foula, Island West off the Sun" by Shiela Gear (Hale, London), is an excellent source of backgroud information. The name "Foula" is a corruption of "Fugloy", which is Norse for "island of birds".

The East side of the island consists of low broken cliffs, with a few small indentations. The North and South ends are low lying. The West coast consists of precipitous cliffs, varying in height between 150m and 365m. These cliffs are the highest *sheer* cliffs in Britain, St. Kilda included.

Most of the coast is Old Red Sandstone, though there is a narrow strip

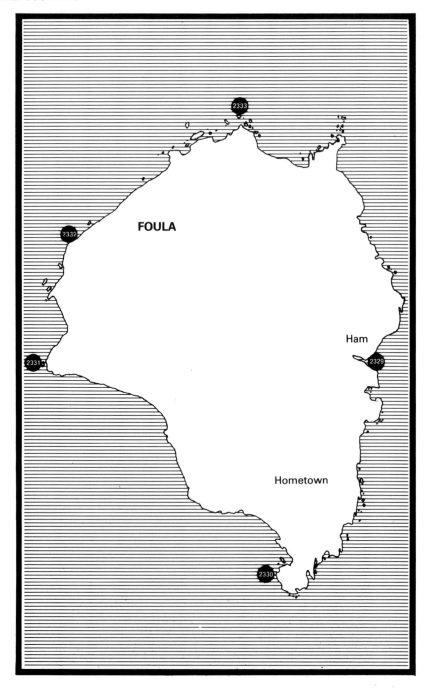

of igneous and metamorphic rocks along the East coast. The South west coastline is first dominated by the 213m high Noup. The North west coast is high and spectacular, usually exceeding 150m. The cliffs must only be receding very slowly, despite their height, as there is only a moderate amount of material accumulated at their foot.

The western portion of the North coast has many caves, arches and stacks; the eastern portion is the lowest, and has a boulder beach forming. The high cliffs are the breeding site for myriads of seabirds, typical of the northerly position of Foula. The population is about 37 people.

The gales at Foula are infamous and are probably some of the strongest in the British Isles. The island may be cut off for periods of up to one month in winter. There is no harbour, otherwise the island would be an excellent fishing base. The only landing place is at Ham Voe, a small inlet with a tiny sandy beach, above which boats can be hauled.

There are few wrecks recorded, although some might be expected. Foula is well away from modern shipping lanes.

The diving is excellent with oceanic blue water (like St. Kilda) rather than green coastal water. Its remoteness must be borne in mind when planning dives.

2328 Wreck of the "Oceanic". A 17,274-ton, 686-feet-long British armed merchant cruiser, lost in 1914 when she ran onto the North Hoevdi ground in dense fog, 2 miles East of Foula at 600703N 015818W. She became a total loss though the crew were saved. "The Other Titanic" by Simon Martin tells the story of the vessel and the salvage of 250 tons of non-ferrous metal in arduous conditions. She lies well broken-up, about 600m North East of Hoevdi Rock, at right angles to a sandstone rock in the middle of a fierce tidal race. The depth is 9-15m and one davit approaches to within 3m of the surface.

2329 Ham Voe. HT975387. The sheltered harbour on the east side of Foula. It appears to only give shallow diving.

2330 Doalie. HT965361. The southern point of Foula. It appears to be initially shallow.

2331 Wester Haevdi. HT936388. The most westerly point of Foula. There appears to be a steep drop out to sea.

2332 The Kame. HT938420. Probably the most dramatic sea-cliff in Britain. Conachair on St. Kilda is higher though not as uniformly steep. At its base a cliff runs to about 15m before depths reach 34m on a bottom of large sandstone boulders. Seals and nudibranchs were noted, along with fish life, crustaceans, sponges etc. There are probably underwater caves corresponding to faults in the cliff, but these have not been explored.

2333 Sheepie. HT960417. Sheepie is a sea-stack lying off the most northerly point of Foula. Depths at its base appear to be only about 5m.

2334 Wreck of the "Lord Kitchener". A 158-ton British trawler lost in 1917 at 600735N 022158W in 112m of water, with a clearance of 107m. She was captured by a U-boat and sunk with explosives. This wreck is included for general interest only.

Area information & services

Hydrographic charts: 219 Western approaches to the Orkney & Shetland islands, 1:500,000; 2622 Plans in the Orkney & Shetland islands, various; 3283 Shetland islands – South sheet, 1:75,000.

Ordnance Survey 1:50,000 maps: 4 Shetland – South Mainland.

Ordnance Survey 1:25,000 maps: HT93/94 Foula, HY75/85 North Ronaldsay & Fair Isle.

Dive Centre: Skolla Diving Centre, Gulberwick, Lerwick, Shetland, ZE2 9JX; Lerwick (0595) 4175.

Air supplies: Possibly from two Fair Isle divers – Neil Thompson (Fair Isle 228) and Stuart Thompson (Fair Isle 241).

Local weather: Lerwick Meteorological Office, Lerwick 2239; Sullom Voe Meteorological Office, Sullom Voe 2069.

Sea area: Fair Isle.

Tidal constants:

	LERWICK	DOVER
Fair Isle	−0025	−0033
Foula	−0135	−0143

Coastguard: Lerwick (Shetland) RHQ, Lerwick 2976/4600. Auxiliary watch and rescue equipment is maintained at Fair Isle.

Lifeboats: Kirkwall (Orkney); Lerwick (Shetland); Aith (Shetland).

SAR helicopter: The nearest is one based at Sumburgh in Shetland.

Police stations: Lerwick, 2110.

Hospitals: Gilbert Bain Hospital, Lerwick 5678.

Recompression chambers: Nearest are at Aberdeen. See Appendix 2.

Ferry operators: P & O Ferries (Aberdeen – Lerwick, vehicular, aboard MV St. Clair and St. Sunniva) (booking almost essential in peak season), Aberdeen (0224) 29111 or Lerwick (0595) 4848.

There is now a new P & O service between Orkney and Shetland. Inter-island passenger ferries run to both of the islands: Sumburgh – Fair Isle; Walls – Foula. A timetable is available from the Shetland Tourist Organisation, Information Centre, Lerwick. The ferry charges are extremely reasonable.

Air connections: Sumburgh Airport has connections to Wick, Aberdeen, Edinburgh and Glasgow; Lerwick (Tingwall) Airport has a connection with Edinburgh and also operates inter-island flights to Fair Isle and Foula.

Operators: British Airways (041 887 1111 & 0856 2233), Loganair (041 889 3181 & 0856 3457).

Local tourist information: Lerwick (0595) 3434.

Accommodation: Accomodation is available on both Fair Isle and Foula; contact Shetland Tourist Office at Lerwick in the first instance. There is a hostel for the bird obervatory, but this is for visiting ornithologists.

CHAPTER 9

Shetland

A SUPERB collection of over 100 islands, some 20 of which are inhabited. The latitudes and longitudes are 605145N to 595056N and 014030W to 004020W. The islands lie 50 miles North of Orkney, and Lerwick, the capital, is further north than the southern tip of Greenland. Sumburgh Head is 170 miles from Buchan Ness, and Out Skerries are only 204 miles from Bergen in Norway. Out Stack, the rocks to the North of Muckle Flugga, are the most northerly point of the British Isles; they lie about 648 miles to the North of London and fully 789 miles from Bishop Rock in the Isles of Scilly.

The name "Shetland" is a modernised version of "Hjaltland", meaning "Highland". The population is almost 21000, about one third of whom live in Lerwick. Scalloway (population about 900) is the only other town; it lies on the West coast, opposite Lerwick.

On the longest day, the sun rises at 0238 and sets at 2133, although while the sun is below the horizon the sky is a bright glow of delicate tints of violet, yellow and green, and it is possible for about a month to read small print through the "night". The total summer daylight of the high Arctic is not quite reached at Shetland, unfortunately, but this experience of the "simmer dim" is unusual nonetheless. Coversely, at the shortest day, sunrise is 0912 and sunset 1459, a day of just over 5.5 hours, but the long nights are often lit by the brilliant displays of the Aurora Borealis.

Shetland has a very equable temperature throughout the year. The total average range of temperature is 9°C, whereas Thurso is 11°C, Edinburgh is 12°C and London is 14°C. Summer temperatures rarely exceed 15°C. The mean annual rainfall is 1250mm, which makes the climate rather damp for most of the year. The prevailing winds range from the North west to South west, and these are quite frequent and often outside of the high summer. The highest recorded wind-speed in Britain – 177 mph – was measured at Saxa Vord on Unst in 1962.

The surface is irregular and generally rises higher than in Orkney. About half of the islands are more than 75m above sea level, although only in a few places does the altitude exceed 150m. The highest point is Ronas Hill at 450m, in the North west of Mainland. There are 2500 fresh water lochs in Shetland, but most of these are small and shallow. None are of interest to human divers, though red-throated divers like breeding on them.

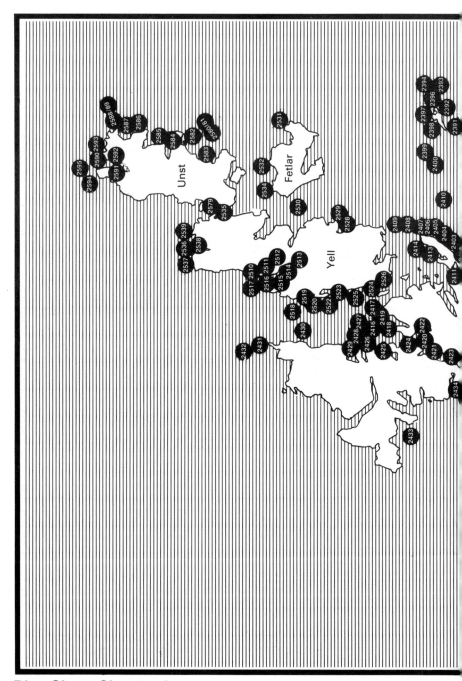

Dive Sites: Chapter 9

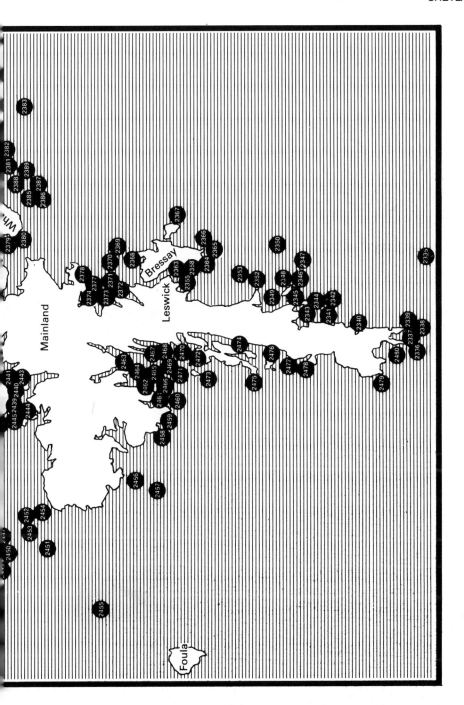

The principal island is Mainland, which has more than half of the area and four fifths of the population of the whole of Shetland. It is 54 miles long and its extreme breadth is nearly 22 miles, though no part is reckoned to be more than 3 miles from the sea. In fact, Shetland is an archipelago with a huge coastline and no inland: Mainland is very nearly divided into two islands at Mavis Grind. This is a 100m-wide neck of land at the North of Mainland that almost separates the large district of Northmavine from the rest of Mainland.

Yell is the second largest island, covering 83 square miles and having a population of about 1200. Two thirds of the surface is covered by peat, making the island rather barren. It is estimated that Yell contains 16 million tons of peat solids. Fetler is about 17 square miles in area, but it only has a population of about 100. With its fertile soils, it is known as the "garden of Shetland", but the people have continued to leave, in the 19th century because of the Clearances but nowadays presumably because they were disenchanted with the rigours of island life. Unst is the most northerly island in Britain. It has an area of 47 square miles and a population of a little over 1000.

The coastline of Shetland is 1450km in length; the land area is 1426sq km, which means that the coastline is highly indented. The rock architecture that makes up the Shetland coastline is rather special. If the 1:25,000 maps are carefully scrutinised, the following named features will be found – 246 wicks and voes, 190 stacks, 351 caves, 405 geos, 7 subterranean passages, 205 skerries, and 158 natural arches (a "voe" is a fiord; a "geo", a rocky creek with precipitous sides; a "wick" is a broad, open bay). Many more no doubt exist but are unnamed and unmapped. It that doesn't whet anyone's appetite, what will?

There is a general relation between many of the voes and the structure of the land, and almost all the larger islands are separated from their neighbours by North-South channels. The nature of the cliffs varies from the typical sandstone of Walls, Bressay and Noss to the lower flags and conglomerates between Lerwick and Sumburgh head. There are granite cliffs in South eastern Walls, Muckle Roe, Brae Wick and Ronas Voe. Andesites and basalts make up the cliffs of Esha Ness and the jagged islets, stacks and intricate coast along the Vullians of Ure. The Yell cliffs are almost entirely gneiss and are typical of similar areas off North west Scotland. The West coast and the northern half of the North coast of Unst are faced by steep cliffs. Tipta Skerry and Muckle Flugga are gneissic.

The winter gales are capable of moving huge masses of rock, sometimes of up to 8.5 tons, up to 20m above the high water mark. On the West side of Shetland the winter fury of the Atlantic Ocean has produced scenes of devastation which are difficult to describe without appearing to exaggerate. The result of this constant erosion has been to mould the outer coasts of Shetland into the most rugged and fantastic cliffs and pierce them with long, twilight caves such as those at Scraada, where they run 75m into the land with the sea reaching to the far end. In many places, the erosion has left stacks at a distance from the cliffs, such as the tower-like pinnacles of the Drongs which, from a distance, look like a fleet of sailing vessels.

The slope of the seabed around Shetland is rapid to 75m but then becomes more gradual except to the East and South east of Sumburgh Head, where the rapid slope continues to 150m. However, the main islands are all part of one bank.

Shetland is best thought of as a flooded landscape. It is estimated that a submergence of 90m has occurred since the last glaciation. This explains the existence of the deep submarine cliffs at the outer edges of islands. The seabed is stepped, with underwater platforms at 24m, 46m and 82m being widespread around the islands; these levels can be regarded as indicating erosion surfaces formed by the sea in front of retreating cliffs during previous sea levels. The present sea cliffs usually descend below sea level to considerable depths and are still in active retreat at exposed places. Thus Sumburgh Head has been cut back about half a mile from its formation as a sea cliff; other cliffs have cut back as much as one mile.

Raised beaches are absent, though there are other shoreline features of interest. There are numerous examples of tombolos (a bar of sand or gravel connecting an isalnd with another or with the mainland), and spits at both the head and middle of numerous bays. There are 40 tombolos, 5 double tombolos, 15 bay-head barriers, 21 mid-bay spits, 6 bay-mouth spits, 10 looped barriers, and 43 bars which completely cut off the voe or bay behind them from the sea. These features are all associated with a drowned landscape and the availability of glacial drift, but a detailed explanation is more difficult.

The wildlife includes stray specimens of walrus that have wandered as far South as Shetland, but this is most unusual. The common and grey seals are numerous, especially now the cull has been stopped. Schools of pilot whales are quite common, and other whales and dolphins are frequently sighted. The slaughter of pilot whales, as carried on to this day in Faroe, has thankfully now been abandoned in Shetland. The terrestrial wildlife is no less spectacular. Otters are relatively common. The breeding seabirds are almost without number, and in recent years even include an albatross that strayed North and thought it was a gannet. Rare birds of prey, such as the snowy owl, occur as stragglers from Arctic lands. Other Arctic landbirds reach Shetland as the most southerly point in their range. The sea eagle bred until late last century, and now that releases of birds bred in captivity on Rum are being made, who knows that it will not recolonise? The dominant environment is one of moorland and there are no trees.

Diving around Shetland has almost everything to offer the diver, especially if he likes exploring huge cliffs and other submarine rock scenery in crystal clear water. I don't doubt that the diving of Shetland, when more fully explored, may well come to rival that of St. Kilda. There are also over 1000 wrecks recorded in Shetland waters, although only 190 are mentioned in this chapter. This is a consequence of the fact that the amount of shipping used to be much heavier than it is today; many smaller vessels engaged in local trade between small ports, but now road transport has replaced much of this shipping. Of course, the coast of Shetland was unlit until relatively recently, and this further contributed to the wreckings. Note that permission is needed to dive on several of the wrecks.

The diving demands that you pay attention to the relative remoteness of Shetland and the ready accessibility of considerable depths coupled with clear water. There is no recompression chamber; the closest are those at Aberdeen, 60 minutes' flying away. The weather can worsen fairly suddenly, particularly at the North of the islands, and this should be allowed for when planning longer boat journeys. The strong tidal streams also require careful dive planning.

When flooding, the tidal streams run North to South. In fact, the tidal streams have a field day around Shetland, and rush through all the narrow sounds and channels at great speed, sometimes reaching 8 knots. When a South easterly gale is blowing against the run of a flood tide, Sumburgh Röst is said to be possibly the wildest portion of sea around the British Isles.

Access is varied. Generally, wherever a road reaches the sea there is no difficulty about access. However, there are great tracts of coastline where this is not possible, so these must be approached from distant launch sites.

In 1985, one of the leading local divers, Andy Carter set up the Skolla Dive Centre at Gulberwick, near Lerwick. He runs this from his house and can supply compressed air and hire equipment. He can also arrange accommodation and hard boat hire locally. He is extremely knowledgeable about Shetland diving and is most helpful to visiting divers. If planning a visit to Shetland, you would be well advised to contact him (at Lerwick (0595) 4175).

In 1986, Alex and Joy Whitelaw moved from the Edinburgh area to set up a diving school, Dive Shetland, based at Bigton, some 15 miles South of Lerwick. In addition to diver training they can offer compressed air, equipment hire and servicing along with inflatable boat hire. Contact Alex or Joy at (09502) 295).

THE POTENTIAL number of dive sites in Shetland is virtually without limit. All the islands are liberally endowed with all manner of intriguing stacks, arches, caves, channels, gullies, skerries and shoals. To list these would take very much more space than is realistic. Shetland leaves a visiting diver with a sense of merely sampling the odd known site amongst many hundreds of other equally good, but unknown sites.

There are many other known wrecks relatively close to Shetland in addition to those detailed in this chapter. However, because depths increase so rapidly away from shore these are all well beyond the range of sport diving. These wrecks, with the exception of submarines, have been excluded from this chapter because there are so many sites in it already.

Thanks are due to Andy Carter (Shetland Sub-Aqua Club), Magnus Johnson (Sullom Special Branch), Steve Briggs (Glasgow University Special Branch) and Tommy Watt (Lerwick Museum) for many of the site details in this chapter.

East Mainland

Going North from Sumburgh.

2335 Wreck of "C34". An 807-ton, 44m-long British submarine torpedoed and sunk in 1917 by German submarine U52 at 5951N 0105W, 6 miles East south east of Sumburgh Head. The depth is about 117m, so this is only of academic interest.

2336 Wreck of the "Strathtay", Scatness. HU387080. This lies at the edge of a prominent small geo at the East side of the end of Scatness, between Horse Isle and Scatness peninsula. The spare anchor, chain, engine, brass fittings and valves are to be seen. The seabed is kelp-covered boulders at 14m. Strong tides at all times.

The steep cliffs of the Shetlands make boat diving a necessity in most areas.

2337 Headland South of Ness of Burgi. HU389084. A deep gully which is reasonably scenic. Conger eels noted. Boat access from West Voe (HU393103).

2338 Ness of Burgi. HU387083. Life-encrusted gullies at 20m.

2339 Little Tind, Sumburgh Head. HU407077. There is an exciting tidal race off Sumburgh Head with a maximum tidal rate of 3 knots. Slack at (minus) 0200 to (minus)0130 Aberdeen between end of East-going and start of West-going stream; apparently no slack between end of West-going and start of East-going stream. Adequate boat cover is essential; launch at Grutness Voe (HU404100).

2340 Voe. HU400153. A muddy bottom with peat and weed at a depth of 9m. Poorer visibility.

2341 Wreck of the "Stockholm", Brayfield. HU413183. This vessel was lost in 1745 and its wreck site at Punds Brucie (Bruce's landing place) is protected. Shore access over shelving rocks. An anchor can be seen in a gully and 30 cannon are still to be found.

2342 Wreck of the "Vesper". HU412184 (approx.). This 13m-long British MFV was lost in 1969 when she drifted onto Clumly Baas and sank. The position is 5957N 0115W and depth about 25m.

2343 Wreck of "GK41". A British salvage barge that was stranded at 595937.3N 011445.2W on the rocks on the eastern part of Hoswick Bay,

100m East of the Point of Whilvigarth. The wreck lies in three sections on the high water line.

2344 Cumlewick Ness. HU425221. There is a cave that runs 100-150m into the cliffs here.

2345 Mousa Broch. HU457237. An interesting dive to 20m on kelp-covered rocks. Seals abound and are very photogenic in the good visibility.

2346 Wreck of the "Gratitude". A British fishing vessel lost in 1983 at 595936N 010912W. She lies 500m offshore at Muckle Bard, Mousa in about 46m of water.

2347 Wreck of the "St. Sunniva". HU468234. A 861-ton, 72m-long passenger and mail steamer lost in 1930 when she ran aground on Mousa and became a total loss. The position is 595951N 010924W, at the South east of Muckle Bard just off the point on the North entrance to the Swarf, Mousa. A pleasant wreck dive in 20m. The wreckage lies in a big gully; there is lots of brass.

2348 Wreck of the "Murrayfield". HU468241. Lost in 1942 at 595958N 010930W on Mousa. Ammunition is reported around the wreck and depths vary from 4m to 30m, though are mainly 20m to 30m. A good wreck dive, with lots of seals.

2349 Gruna Baas shoal. A shoal that comes to within 9m of the surface from a depth of over 30m on its North side. The position is 600055N 011054W, 0.4 miles North of Mousa.

2350 Wreck of "UC55". This 511-ton, 53m-long German submarine was sunk by depth charges and gunfire in 1917 at approximately 6002N 0102W, 4 miles East north east of Mousa Light in a depth of about 90m.

2351 Wreck of a pirate ship. This vessel foundered in 1710 near the entrance to Aithsvoe. It is not recorded whether this is Aith Voe, Bressay or Aith Voe, Cunningburgh; I have assumed the latter.

2352 Wreck of HMS "Cheerful". This 30-knot, 307-ton destroyer was mined off Helliness in 1917 and only 18 were saved of a complement of 60. She was armed with one 12-pdr and five 6-pdr guns, together with two torpedo tubes.

2353 Wreck of "Day Dawn". A 14m-long British fishing vessel lost in 1981 at 600300N 010912W about 0.7 miles North east of Helli Ness in about 60m of water.

2354 Bressay Sound. HU482418. A bottom of sand and weed at 15m. Some tide noted, as was a huge fish resembling a catfish!

2355 Wreck of the "Samba", Ruggen. HU471386. This wreck lies about 40m out from the stacks just to the West of Ruggen. She is fairly well broken but still recognisable as a ship. Depths range from 15m to 34m.

2356 Wreck of the "Rangor". HU473391. An Aberdeen trawler lost in 1964 on Munger Skerries.

2357 Wreck of the "Queen of Sweden". HU483407. An area of shallow rocks and weedy gullies about 100m offshore at Twageos Point at the South of Lerwick. The vessel was lost in 1754 when she struck a rock and sank without loss of life. The wreck of the "Drottningen of Sverige" has been substantially worked and little remains to be seen except a few iron cannon. The site was a protected wreck. Occasional artefacts can be located by systematic searching in the crevices. Depths range from 5-15m. See "Scottish Diver" Jul-Aug 1982 and Sep-Oct 1985. Check the latest diving situation with Andy Carter.

2358 Wreck of the "Glen Isla". A 1266-ton, 76m-long British cargo ship lost after a collision in 1917 while bound for Slemmestad with a cargo of coal from the Tyne. About 0.75 mile from Kirkabister Light, Lerwick, the wreck lies on a flat, shingly seabed at 42m, right in the middle of the channel leading South from Lerwick. It gives a splendid dive as the wreck is substantially whole. A large iron prop lies on top of the wreck. Crockery can be recovered from the galley area.

2359 Foul moorings. The foul area marked at 600925.8N 010725.2W, 120m South west from Maryfield Ferry Terminal in Bressay Sound, is actually old moorings at a depth of 12m. There are two obstructions up to 30m long protruding about 0.5m above the seabed. There is also a report of an old coal hulk in this area.

2360 Wreck of the "Wrestler". A British coal hulk at 600943N 010901W, about 350m West of Loofa Baa Beacon in Bressay Sound in 12m.

2361 Wreck of the "Girdleness". An 18m-long barge that sunk in 1941 in 12m of water at 601004N 010853W, 600m North of Loofa Baa Beacon. The holds are open and the top of the wreck is at 7m.

2362 Unknown vessel. A 20m-long wreck stranded at 600914.2N 010652.3W on the West coast of Bressay.

2363 Cro of Ham. HU486392. Rock and boulders leading onto sand at 15m. The wreck of the "Ben Helm" was salvaged from here but nothing remains.

2364 Wreck of the "Brighter Morn". A 15m-long British fishing vessel lost in 1980 when she struck the rocks near the Ord (about HU502365) on Bressay and sank very close to shore.

2365 Cave of the Bard. HU513359. Called locally the Orkneyman's Cave, this site gives an interesting dive. There is an outer cave, followed by an inner cave 30-40m long. Depth of 9-6m. A torch is needed.

2366 Wreck of "H101". A 2886-ton, 85m-long Dutch pontoon that broke loose in heavy seas while under tow, was driven ashore and became a total loss. The tip of the oilwell structure is awash in 18m of water at the base of Bard Head, Bressay at 600612N 010412W (about HU517357).

2367 Noup of Noss. HU551397. This site, 4 miles east of Lerwick, gives superb diving under a 150m-high cliff. At a depth of 30m the seabed is bedrock with huge outcroppings.

2368 Wreck of the "Dovre". A Norwegian vessel carrying 1400 tons of coal lost in 1913 which ran aground at the entrance to Aiths Voe on Bressay when her cargo shifted.

2369 Soldian Rock. HU509476 (approx.). A drying skerry, 1.3 miles North of Aith Ness, with a rapid drop to 24m to its South east.

2370 Nive Baa. A rocky shoal that reaches to within 1m of the surface from a depth of 18m to its North west. It lies about 0.4 miles North east of Green Holm (HU495475).

2371 The Unicorn. A rocky shoal that reaches to within 2m of the surface from a depth of about 25m to its South east. The shoal is a series of rocky ledges and cliffs. A cobble bottom has less life than might be supposed. The Unicorn lies about 0.5 miles East of Hawks Ness (HU463491).

2372 Wreck of the "Unicorn". Unicorn shoal got its title from the vessel of the same named. In 1567 the Earl of Bothwell was fleeing from Scotland aboard the "Pelikan". Bothwell, who had a local pilot, sailed his vessel close by the sunken rock and the pursuing "Unicorn" commanded by Sir William Grange followed almost the same course, struck violently and sank. Several diver searches have been carried out round the shoal to depths of beyond 20m, but to no avail.

2373 Unknown wreck, Lax Firth. This lies at 601249W 011142W on the East side of the firth opposite Black Skerry at about HU447478. The depth is 1m and the wreck dries.

2374 Cat Firth. HU450520. Dense kelp on boulders with some sand patches at a depth of 7m. There is also extensive silty areas in Cat Firth.

2375 Wreck of the "Fitful Head". Lost at 601554N 011142W at the North of Cat Firth at about HU446536. The wreck lies in about 5m and dries with part of her hull intact. This wreck (and the next two) are owned by Hay & Co of Lerwick; their permission should be sought before diving.

2376 Unknown wreck. Lost at 601602N 011136W at the North of Cat Firth at about HU446538. The wreck lies in 2m and dries. The boiler, prop and ribs are to be seen.

2377 Unknown wreck, Cat Firth. A third wreck lies in the middle of Cat Firth in about 10m of water: no part shows above the surface.

2378 Dean Man's Geo. HU475526. For the curious, an interesting name on the map.

2379 Wreck of the "Verdant". HU533624. A fishing vessel lost in 1959 at 602035N 010130W. The position is actually just offshore near Braga to the West of Symbister on Whalsay.

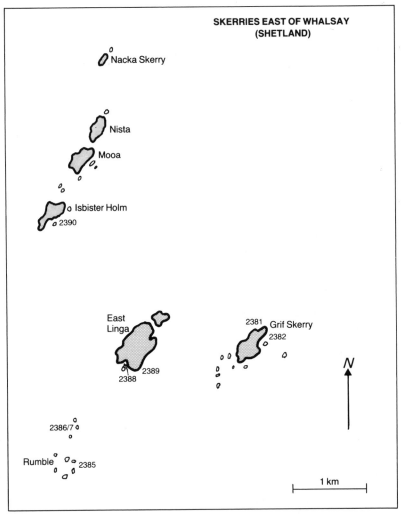

SKERRIES EAST OF WHALSAY
(SHETLAND)

Nacka Skerry

Nista

Mooa

Isbister Holm

2390

East
Linga

2388   2389

2386/7

Rumble   2385

2381 Grif Skerry

2382

N

1 km

DIVE SITES AROUND THE SKERRIES EAST OF WHALSAY (SHETLAND)

2380 Wreck of a Catalina seaplane. This lies off the Point of Gruid, Whalsay at HU533616. The remains, which consist of pieces of aluminium strewn around the bottom, are in a kelp-covered gully on the South east side of the outermost point, just down from a very distinct square shaped rock.

2381 Grif Skerry. Steep-sided, criss-crossed, quite narrow gullies at 22-24m give a very good dive.

2382 Wreck of the "Evstafii", Grif Skerry. In 1780 a 36-gun Russian frigate (a "pink") was lost with 184 people; only 5 were saved. This is a very good site with twelve 2.4m-long cannon in a North gully at 10m. This gully is just to the South of the East skerries. Some of the salvaged guns are built into the pier at Symbister for mooring purposes. Note that this is a protected wreck site.

2383 Shoals East of Whalsay. A shoal with a minimum depth of 38m lies to the East of Whalsay 5 miles East of Grif Skerry. Half a mile West (but separated by a depth of 66m) is a second shoal with a minimum depth of 44m and a depth of 88m to its North west.

2384 East of South east Whalsay. A couple of wrecks supposedly lie in this area. A big drift dive can be made over a bottom of big boulders and cliff faces.

2385 Rumble. Similar to Grif Skerry.

2386 Wreck of the "Jupiter". A trawler lost on the Flaeshans of Rumble. The remains consist of a boiler and steam engine. They lie in 5 pieces on the middle of the inner Flaeshan.

2387 Unknown wreck, Flaeshans of Rumble. An old vessel lost here. Some pieces were salvaged at the time and various items have been found more recently. There were numbered sacks of gold on board and not all of these were recovered from the wreck.

2388 Gun Geo, East Linga. HU613621. The islet to the South has a reef rising to within a few metres of the surface. This gives a spectacular dive down a cliff face to about 25m. There is a cave near the top of the cliff.

2389 Wreck of the "Pacific", Snafa Baa (HU614620). At the South-east corner of East Linga off the islet to the South of in Gun Geo is the well broken wreck of the early steamship "Pacific" of Liverpool. It is well spread out over the flat, kelp-covered, rocky bottom. Wreckage has also filled a wide gully running round the reef.

2390 Isbister Holm. HU604642. Similar to Grif Skerry.

Out Skerries

THIS GROUP of 3 main islands (Housay, Bruray and Grunay) and about 15 islets and stacks lie about 4 miles North east off Whalsay in eastern Shetland. There are three small skerries offlying to the North west of Out Skerries (Vongs, Little Skerry and Muckle Skerry).

2391 Wreck of the "De Liefde". HU664702. A Dutch East Indiamen lost in 1711 on Mio Ness, the South west tip of Housay, the main island of Out Skerries at 602440N 044737W. There were 200 sailors and 100 soldiers lost, and only one survivor. The 500-ton vessel was built in 1698; she was 50m long and armed with 40 cannon. The wreckage actually lies in

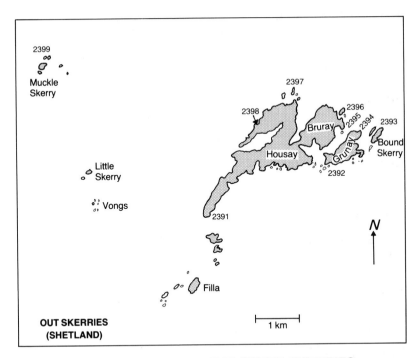

2399

Muckle
Skerry

2397

2398

2396
2395
2394
2393

Bruray

Housay

Bound
Skerry

Grunay

Little
Skerry

2392

Vongs

2391

N

Filla

OUT SKERRIES
(SHETLAND)

1 km

DIVE SITES AROUND THE OUTER SKERRIES

Dregging Geo, just to the East of Mio Ness. It was surveyed, excavated and salvaged by Scientific Survey & Location in 1967 and 1968, then by members of the Home Counties and Kingston BSAC Branches in 1978. It is a protected wreck site. Artefacts recovered included about 300 silver coins and a few gold ducats (out of a cargo os 227,000 guilders, 900 silver ducats and 900 gold ducats). Only 2000 guilders were salved just after the sinking.

2392 Wreck of the "Kennemerland". HU689711. This Dutch East Indiamen was lost in 1664 on the southern side of Out Skerries at the entrance of South Mouth by Stoura Stack. It was surveyed and excavated in the 1970s; the site protected. All that now remains is an anchor and some lead ballast ingots.

2393 Bound Skerry. HU702719. The channel between Little Bound Skerry and Bound Skerry is 15m deep although the entrances are shallow. The site is spectacular above the surface, though somewhat poorer underwater.

2394 Head of Grunay, Grunay island. HU697719. To the North is a steep slope to over 50m after a small cliff.

2395 Unnamed skerry, North East Mouth. HU694719. A good dive over a gently sloping rocky seabed. A 2m-wide gully with jammed chockstones leads North-east from 6m to 24m onto sand at the bottom of a cliff.

2396 Lamba Stack. HU695723. A relatively steep, rocky drop-off down an Alcyonium-covered slope to beyond 30m.

2397 Hevda Skerries. HU684728. Similar to Lamba Stack.

2398 Twin geo by North Ward. HU678725. A nice dive through an underwater tunnel. This runs from 4m to 15m and only allows the passage of one diver at a time.

2399 Muckle Skerry. HU627734. A very good site for those wishing to dive with seals. There is a kelp-covered, gully-riven, rocky slope with lots of small cliff faces but no big drop-offs.

2400 Wreck of the "Ft. La Prairie". A 7138 ton British cargo vessel lost in 1945 at 6029N 0052W, about 0.5 mile South south west of Muckle Skerry Light (HU626734). The depth here is 30-35m.

East Mainland (continued)

2401 Vidlin Voe. HU486677. Weed, sand patches with scallops, and rock at 18m.

2402 Hellam, Lunna Ness. HU485687. Shore access to good underwater scenery at 15-20m. It is possible to swim round the rock in about 20 minutes.

2403 East Lunna Voe. HU488689. Access by going past the church, climbing down the stoney beach of a little bay. Snorkel out then dive to 10-15m. Further out the rock gives way to sand at 25-30m.

2404 Grut Wick (South), Lunna Ness HU505705. A 36" diameter pipeline enters Shetland from the Ninian oilfield. Round the headland to the South there is a sheer face from 12m to 35m then a sandy bottom.

2405 Grut Wick, North. HU506706. Steep, rocky scenery leads to 10-15m, then to 30m and then to beyond 40m. An excellent shore site.

2406 Shoals East of Lunna Ness. There are a series of at least three shoals about 0.5 mile East of Lunna Ness. They each rise to about 20m from general depths of 30m. All are undived. That at 602539N 010230W seems the best, as it drops immediately to beyond 30m to both the North west and South east.

2407 Stour Hevda, Lunna Ness. HU525733. A steep, rocky slope to a sandy seabed at about 20m inhabited by scallops. Lots of crustaceans and fish life.

The breakwater at Grutness Voe, which offers several excellent shore dive sites.

2408 Wreck of the "Margaret Stevenson". This trawler went down between the wars and lies in the Wick of Glenholm not far from the end of Lunna Ness. The boilers, engine, winch, rope locker and anchor are still visible. The wreck is at the edge of the "hard".

2409 Longa Skerry. HU533747. Tidal streams run at up to 8 knots around the Point of Lunna Holm, so take appropriate precautions. Depths of about 25m on a rocky bottom. Beach launch (with four-wheel drive) at Vidlin Voe (HU482654).

2410 Wreck of the "White Daisy". A 79-ton MFV lost in 1940 at 6025N 0100W, 2.5 miles South east of Lunna Holm in 117m of water. In 1980, the wheelhouse of this vessel was brought up in a net several miles off Kirk Baas.

2411 Obstruction, East of Lunna Holm. This foul ground is a 2.5 ton anchor and 1500 feet of cable lost at 602730N 010417W, 0.7 mile North of the Point of Feorwick, in about 85m of water.

2412 Obstruction, East of Lunna Holm. This foul ground is a 4.5-ton anchor lost at 602718N 010515W, 1.2 miles North west of the Point of Feorwick, in about 60m of water.

2413 Hamna Voe. HU235803. Very dense kelp on a rocky bottom at 8m.

2414 Obstruction in Hamnavoe. This is listed at 602558N at the mouth of the voe. It lies in 16m of water with a clearance of 8m.

2415 Little Roe, North west face. HU402795. Weedy with gravel patches at 9m.

2416 Wreck of a boom defence vessel. HU400800. A quantity of unexploded ordnance is located in the vicinity of Little Roe Light, so anchoring and fishing is prohibited withing 500m of the light. While the ordnance was being removed by a bomb disposal team they discovered an old wreck. This WW2 loss is a nice wreck and lies below and to the South-west of the Little Roe lighthouse. There are three sections – cabins with doors, engine room, and the spectacular bows. The quoted position is 603000N 011630W, 160m West south west of the Light.

2417 Little Roe, North east face. HU403799. About 50m offshore a good drift dive can be had along a rock face at 15-20m with sand and rock at the bottom. Tidal streams at 2 knots and more, so plan accordingly.

2418 Underwater discharge pipeline, Sullom Voe. HU400790. Diving is FORBIDDEN here, as the pipeline leads out from Skaw Taing between Little Roe and Calbeck Ness. The seaward side of the discharge point is marked with a yellow buoy.

2419 Orka Voe. HU404773. Shallow rocks covered with kelp leading to a sandy bottom at 18m.

2420 Catalina, Sullom Voe. HU378733. The remains of this seaplane lie in line with the disused runway on Scatsa Ness at about 602633N 011857W in about 20m of water.

2421 The Houb, Sullom Voe. HU362725. A shingle bottom at 9m. Further out the bottom is weedy sand at 18m.

2422 Garths Voe. HU405738. A flat seabed of sand and shingle at 6m.

2423 Voxter Voe. HU365696. A gentle sloping rocky bottom with mud interspersed leading past 15m.

2424 Dale Voe. HU370757. A poor dive with a muddy bottom with lots of dead kelp at 12m.

2425 Gluss Voe. HU366785. A rocky bottom at 15m with boulders and sand patches. Quantities of saltwater mussels noted in the sand.

2426 Taing of Norwick. HU369815. Rocky outcrops at 15m, then 30m, then a sandy seabed. Very rich in life, especially scallops and crabs.

2427 Lamba island. HU386815. The West face has rocky outcrops leading to sand at 20m. A somewhat mundane dive.

2428 Quey Firth. HU360822. Rock to 8m followed by shingle to 12m.

2429 Colla Firth. HU365835. Weed and silt with much dead kelp giving a poor dive.

2430 Wreck of the "Morning Star". A 50-ton, 22m-long British MFV lost in 1982 at 603520N 011727W after a fire in the engine room and while under tow. The wreck lies in 56m of water with a clearance of 40m, 0.9 miles North west of Muckle Holm Light in Yell Sound.

2431 Ramna Stacks. HU375975. A group of 22 islets, stacks and skerries lying at the very North of Mainland. General depths run to 30m, although at the edges of the bank the depths reach about 40m.

2432 Röst off Gaut Skerries, Ramna Stacks. HU373982. Depth of 30-60m together with tidal rips and overfalls should discourage most divers from this site.

West Mainland

THE sites are described going South from Uyea.

2433 The Drongs, Ness of Hillswick. HU260755. This small islet has a very complex underwater rock structure running to 25-35m. The vertical faces are covered with Alcyonium together with many edible crabs.

2434 Geo of Gunavalla (South of). HU326685. This has spectacular rock scenery underwater. Only 25m offshore there is a rock wall running straight to 35m. The underwater gullies and buttresses provide an excellent terrain for divers to explore.

2435 Turvalds Head. HU325682-325675. For about 800m along this headland a very confused bottom of gullies and rock outcrops leads to a seabed of sand at 30m.

2436 Lothan. HU321676. A small skerry at the North east of Muckle Roe. Underwater are a series of parallel ridges, with gullies 15-20m deep in between. The rocks have 10m-high sheer faces rising from the seabed.

2437 Muckle Roe, North end. HU310675. This gives a pleasant dive down cliffs and into small caves. There is a rumour of an old Spanish ship being lost in this area.

2438 Muckle Roe Lighthouse. HU304628. The cliffs drop underwater as cliffs and gullies to 28m and are encrusted with life. To the East of the lighthouse are huge boulders, some with through-passages under them.

2439 Burki Skerries, Muckle Roe. HU315625. A series of very impressive underwater gullies, rock faces and stacks with depths of 15-30m. The rock faces are covered with Alcyonium and anemones. The occasional conger eel may be seen. The visibility is 10m in summer and over 20m in winter.

2440 Ness of Little-ayre, Muckle Roe. HU327627. Snorkel out and dive

Muckle Sound, Shetland, with the Loch of Spiggie visible to the left.

round the headland. Small cliff and a rocky slope lead to sand at 15-20m. Crustaceans noted.

2441 Ness of Gillarona. HU327626. This gives a good scenic dive down boulders, underwater cliff faces and caves until the sand is reached at 30m.

2442 Busta Voe. HU354670. A dive to 15m on to a silty seabed with patches of rocks. Lots of queen scallops. A poor dive for Shetland.

2443 Papa Little. HU332620. A rocky, weedy bottom sloping away at 35° on to boulders then sand. Depths from 15m to 35m, with some rock outcrops to 40m. A wreck is rumoured.

2444 Holms of Uyea-sound, Vementry island. HU310610. A rocky slope from 5m to 25m, then a vertical cliff to 30-35m. The seabed consists of sand and gullies.

2445 Geo of the Ward, Vementry. HU297613. All along the cliff face massive ridges slope away at 45° to 35m. The edges of these ridges are either vertical or overhanging. The rock is quite clean, although there is some encrusting life.

Note: Launches for the Swarbacks Minn sites can be made at Brae Sailing Club (HU351678) or Muckle Roe Bridge (HU341660).

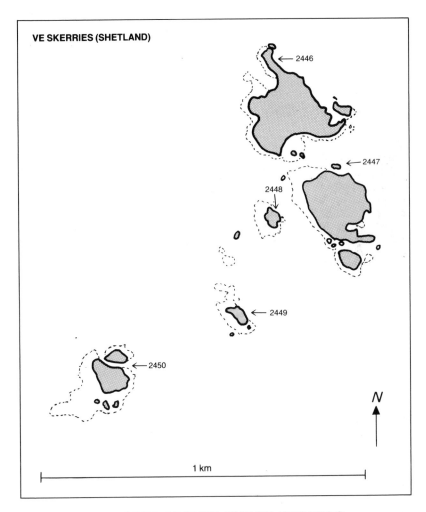

VE SKERRIES (SHETLAND)

←2446

←2447

2448

←2449

←2450

N

1 km

DIVE SITES AROUND THE VE SKERRIES

Ve Skerries

THESE are a group of several skerries that lie about 3 miles North west of the island of Papa Stour in Shetland. The underwater terrain is rugged and all the skerries are frequently penetrated with submarine gullies gull of colourful life. The tidal streams, overfalls and turbulent water are notorious; slack water at about (plus)0150 and (minus)0435 Dover.

2446 North Skerry. HU101658. The West side is similar to the Clubb.

2447 Ormal. HU105656. In the channel between Ormal and North Skerry there is a small wreck of a cargo vessel (the "Turquoise"). Only the anchor and odd pieces are left.

2448 Wreck of the "Ben Doran". HU102655. This lies at the North end of Helligloblo. It is completely broken and only the boiler and engine remain.

2449 Wreck of the "Elinor Viking". HU102652. A 122-ton British trawler lost in 1977 when she ran aground on Ve Skerries in a gale at 602230N 014830W, at the East side of Reaerach. There is lots of wreckage at depths of about 15m, including a large brass prop.

2450 The Clubb. HU096651. All round this site there are large gullies and boulders running to beyond 16m. There are also many small, sinuous cracks that are passable to divers. The walls of the cracks and gullies are lined with sponges and Alcyonium and the larger gullies are frequented by numerous seals. The East-West channel is divable.

West Mainland (continued)

2451 Unknown wreck. This lies at 602036N 014930W, 2 miles West of Fogla Skerry, Papa Stour. The depth is 50m and the charted clearance 40m.

2452 Island West of Brei Holm. HU189613. This gives a good dive through a submarine passage. It is possible to navigate the passage in an inflatable, as the roof is about 5m above sealevel and the passage is illuminated from a vertical chimney. There are two passages underwater and it is possible to swim the entire length of both of these. They are 15-20m deep at the mouth and about 10m deep inside. There are many big boulders strewn around; the life is rather sparse.

2453 Fogla Skerry, Papa Stour. HU467614. This is a total exposed islet to the West of Papa Stour. It gives a superb dive in excellent visibility on great folds of bedrock which slope away to well beyond 40m. The life is somewhat sparse, presumably due to the ravages of winter storms. To the east of Fogla Skerry lies Lyra Skerry; and to the east of this skerry, at about HU142613, is the wreck of the "Juniper", a fishing vessel lost in the 1970s and now well smashed.

2454 Wreck of the SS "Highcliffe". HU188595. A 3847-ton, 111m-long British cargo vessel sunk in 1940 at 601908N 013935W, on the North east of the island of Forewick Holm in the Sound of Papa. She was en route from Narvik to Methil and Immingham with a cargo of iron ore. The "Highcliffe" gives a very good dive with lost of wreckage left, lying on a slope from 6-7m to 26m; the boiler is at 12m. The stern section is awesome, with the gunwhale only 4-5m from the surface. At 20m on the bottom is the stern gland and propshaft. The wreck is broken in the middle, thus forming an underwater cave.

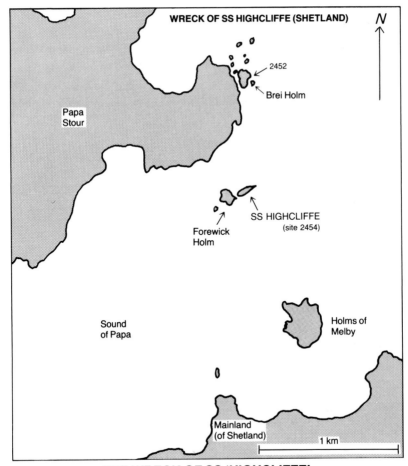

2452

Brei Holm

Papa Stour

SS HIGHCLIFFE
(site 2454)

Forewick Holm

Sound of Papa

Holms of Melby

Mainland (of Shetland)

1 km

THE WRECK OF SS 'HIGHCLIFFE'

2455 North Shoals. An extensive rocky shoal area South west of Papa Stour. The shallowest point is 20m, 9 miles South west of Fogla Skerry at 601510N 015930W. There do not appear to be any steep slopes or drop-offs.

2456 Wreck of a Wellington bomber. This lies off Vaila island (HU223457) in deep water.

2457 Wreck of the "Victory". A 49-feet-long British MFV lost in 1983 at 601103N 014116W, 3 miles South west of Vaila. The depth is 75m, the clearance 60m.

2458 Wreck of the "Avanti Savoyer". An Italian vessel sunk in 1914 while carrying a cargo of saltpetre to Germany for munitions. She lies between two skerries at Giltarump on Culswick. She has been dived and a signal gun recovered.

195

2459 Wreck of the "Ustetind". Lost at 6010N 0129W in 1929, this vessel has broken up and lies near the shore at Sil Wick (HU295418).

2460 Braga. HU316408. This small skerry lies about 2 miles West of the island of Hildsay. The East side gives a rock face to 20m and a rocky, steped seabed. Rocky buttresses and slopes led on to 38m. A good site, though not a vast amount of life.

2461 Snap. HU323420. Pleasant diving in gullies at 20m. Similar to Johnny Sinclair's Nose.

2462 Johnny Sinclair's Nose. HU329436. This provides a spectacular dive on a series of small cliffs and maze-like gullies dropping to below 20m. A very pleasant dive with many big rocks, all covered with life.

2463 Fora Ness. HU353453. Pieces of timber have been dragged up from the South end. There is a kelp-covered rocky slope leading to a sandy bottom inhabited by scallops. At 40m(plus) the seabed slopes gently and is made up of sandy shale.

2464 Sanda Stour. HU345436. To the West of the island of North Score Holm there is a big cliff face in several places.

2465 Skult. HU346434. Similar to Hoe Skerry; a good site for nudibranchs.

2466 Hoe Skerry, near Lunga Skerries. HU344426. An almost vertical rock wall from 14m to 35-40m. Covered with Alcyonium.

2467 Stromness Voe. HU380434. A rather poor dive in poorer visibility over a muddy bottom at a maximum of 20m. Scallops noted. A backup dive for windy conditions. The entrance to the loch, near Jackville, is very shallow and obstructed. It might provide an interesting drift dive.

2468 Silver Skerry. HU378420. This is at the South end of White Ness near Stromness Loch. The West side of the skerry drops rapidly to beyond 30m.

2469 Langa. HU373397. At the North west this gives a poor dive to 10m in disappointing visibility.

2470 Wreck of the "Greyfish". A British trawler lost in 1973 when she was stranded at the Point of the Pund at 6008N 0118W. The quoted position is in the middle of Pund Voe at a depth of about 25m. There is also a report that the wreck may lie on the East side of Shetland off Cunningsburgh district.

2471 Hoe Skerry, near Linga. HU358392. A boulder slope leads to 50m in a series of 3-4m vertical steps.

2472 Setter, Hamnavoe, Burra. HU378358. A rocky slope leads to kelp-covered rock about 50m offshore, then sand at 15m, followed by a gradual slope to 35m. Lots of life.

2473 Steggies. HU348361. This is a small skerry 4 miles South west of

Dramatic caves and windows cleft from the steep rocky cliffs of south-west Shetland.

Scalloway. The North west corner drops very steeply down a series of boulders and small cliff faces to 30m onto a boulder bottom, with another cliff descending from 30m to 38m. An excellent dive, though the faces are somewhat devoid of life.

2474 Burn of Scord, Clift Sound. HU393316. The East side of the sound near the mouth of a burn has a sand and mud slope descending gradually to beyond 30m. Plenty of kelp on boulders in the top 10m, but bare sand thereafter. Scallops, starfish, feather stars, brittle stars and urchins noted.

2475 Wreck of the MV "St. Kentigern". This 469-ton, 50m-long British vessel was lost in 1979 at 699245N 012240W when she ran ashore in a Force 9-10 storm at Kettla Ness (HU348289) on West Burra island. Three days after the grounding there was no sign of the vessel. The quoted position is 100m West of the largest of the islands just off Ketla Head where the depth is about 30m.

2476 Wreck of the "Anna". A 1211-ton vessel lost in 1917 at 6001N 0020W, 500m South south west of Holm of Maywick (HU375264). The depth at the quoted position is 30m.

2477 Wreck of the MV "Goodwill Merchant". HU365237. A 468-ton, 60m-long Dutch coaster lost at 6000N 0121W in 1976. The records show her stranded on the West side of Fair Isle, but the position is on the West coast of Shetland, between the shore and skerry at Burgi Stack. The crew were saved. She lies well broken in a deep gully at 16m. The engine is quite spectacular, but the bronze prop has been salvaged by Shetland Sub-

Aqua Club. The cargo consisted of vehicles, but, only the tyres and axles are left. Beach access at Bigton Wick.

2478 Loose Head, St. Ninian's Isle. HU361219. The West side of the point has rock terraces, gullies and large boulders with holes worn in them by the wave action. Alcyonium carpets the rocks.

2479 Siggar Ness. HU356120. Underwater cliff faces drop to 20m onto sand all round Siggar Ness and its off-lying islets. Tidal streams of up to 3 knots run close to shore, though the gullies and islets are in the lee of the North-going stream. There can be a strong swell through the gullies, which narrows to a few metres at the East end and rise to a depth of 5m. A technically demanding but stimulating dive. The walls in the surge area are covered in sponges and hydroids, the less exposed walls are covered with Alcyonium and tubularia. Large patches of the walls and floor are carpeted with multi-coloured Tealia anemones. Many seals in the gullies. Visibility over 20m.

2480 Lady's Holm, Bay of Quendale. HU374095. A low-lying rocky islet with a craggy coast. Underwater are a series of rocky gullies extending to around 20m. Kelp extends to that depth and the gully walls have the normal northern encrusting life. The site is subject to significant tidal streams and, on the South-going stream, there is some danger of being swept into the Sumburgh Röst.

Wrecks off Cunningsburgh District, South Mainland

A LIST was prepared by R. Stewart Bruce of all the wreckings that he could trace in this part of South Mainland. The list is now in the custody of Lerwick Museum who, for some reason, restrict access to it. (In passing, it is worth noting that certain senior personnel of Shetland Museum can be less than completely helpful to visiting divers planning wreck research amongst the museum archives.) The extracts below have had removed all vessels that were subsequently refloated or salvaged. This list is of little use for diving, but may well be of use to identify remains that are stumbled across while on other dives. The positions given are taken directly from Bruce's list.

2481 1673. Large Dutch ship wrecked at Fladdabister, cloth/linen cargo, 19 men saved.

2482 c.1680 Ship lost and broken up at Aithsvoe, all lost.

2483 1706 Small galliot lost with all hands off Cunningsburgh.

2484 c.1750 Large ship lost in Body Geo, South of Helliness.

2485 1778 "Elizabeth" of Leith wrecked on Sand of Meal, cargo flax/staves/linseed.

2486 1786 Danish East Indiaman "Concordia" wrecked on Taing of Helliness, 900 tons, cargo naval stores, 20 saved out of 52.

2487 1795 "Experiment" of Dysart wrecked on Fat Ayre near Oeraquoy, all lost.

2488 c.1800 Unknown vessel wrecked on Baa of Fladdabister, all lost.

2489 1810 "Gratis" of Drammen, a full-rigged ship wrecked at the back of Cruss outside Aithsvoe, 4 saved.

2490 1823 Unknown vessel wrecked at Seli Geo below Furra Field.

2491 1824 Schooner "Lord Wellington" wrecked at Helliness.

2492 1829 Barque "Henry & Harriot" of Whitby wrecked at Lambastigga near Mokies Geo, 257 tons, 7 saved, 4 lost.

2493 1851 Sloop "Sovereign" of Wick foundered between Helliness and Mousa.

2494 1852 Schooner "Janet Gibson" of Kincardine wrecked on skerry off Taing of Helliness, all saved.

2495 1864 Schooner "Elida" of Christiania lost with all hands at entrance to Aithsvoe.

2496 1876 Topsail schooner "Roshva" of Odense lost rudder, was abandoned at sea and was wrecked at Boga Skerries.

2497 1879 Packet "Victoria" of Fladdabister wrecked there.

2498 1886 Cunningsburgh packet "Sovereign" missed stays beating out of Aithsvoe, became total wreck.

2499 1890 Herring boat "Oriental" went ashore at Fladdabister.

2500 1895 Herring boat "Dolphin" of Arklow wrecked at entrance to Aithsvoe.

2501 1895 Packet "Secret" total loss on shore at Mails Ayre.

2502 1900 Sandwick packet "Heroine" drove ashore at Mail, total loss.

2503 1900 Sandwick packet "Lizzie Jane" drove ashore at Mail, total loss.

2504 1900 "Semper Paratus" drove ashore at Mail, total loss.

2505 1900 Cunningsburgh packet "Harriet & Helen" wrecked Aithsvoe.

2506 1900 "Victory" wrecked Aithsvoe.

2507 1901 "Nicholas Jenkins" of Sandwick totally wrecked at Mail.

2508 1902 "Thunderer" total loss ashore at Oeraquoy.

2509 Viking wrecks, Shetland. The Norse sagas tell of three wreckings in Shetland, but there are no further details, Everything will be long gone. But who knows?

Yell

DESCRIBED West to South to East to North

2510 Gorset Hill, Whaal Firth. HU471969. A rock face runs steeply into the sea to a depth of about 13m, where a sandy seabed with large rocks and boulders gently slopes away to about 21m.

2511 Opposite Longi Geo, Whaal Firth. HU468955. Low cliffs give way to a rock slope into moderately deep water with kelp to 9m. An extensive area of piled boulders is passed just before the sandy seabed is reached at a depth of about 20m.

2512 North of the Crying Taing. HU468944. The seabed is solid rock with a steep slope to about 20m and beyond. Nearby are lesser slopes of boulders and pebbles.

2513 Scarva Taing, Whaal Firth. HU474936. A shallow water silty site with rock outcrops to the East in deeper water. These rocks are covered, unusually, with plumose anemones.

2514 Poita, Whaal Firth. HU467936. A rocky weedy seabed with sand further out.

2515 Graveland, Whaal Firth. HU464944. A kelp-covered boulder and rock slope running onto sand at 20m.

2516 Burka Lees, Whaal Firth. HU464950 (approx.). A seabed of kelp-covered, stepped rock with three level areas. Lots of life.

2517 South of Easter Tammy's Hole, Whaal Firth. HU463970. 200m South of Easter Tammy's Hole there is a prominent surge gully. this has life-encrusted rock faces which are sometimes overhanging. Dense colonies of sponges and tunicates alternate with cliffs covered with crustaceans. A sandy seabed is reached at about 20m.

2518 Wreck of the "Provider". HP435917. An 18m-long British MFV lost at 603630N 011318W in 1976 when she struck a submerged wreck in Yell Sound. The skipper ran the vessel aground but she rolled over and sank on touching bottom. A second report states that she hit a floating object near Sweinna Holm and sank within minutes in 54m. The quoted position is 0.5 miles West of Sweinna Stack in about 57m of water but, in fact, she lies quite close inshore in 10m. A signal pistol and stainless steel portholes have been recovered; a small bronze propeller is still attached.

2519 North of Westsandwick. HU443895. A steep rock slope covered with kelp leads down to very large boulders and isolated rocks in deeper water. Regarded as a good site.

2520 Taing of Nonstigarth. HU442888. A sandy bay with very shallow water and little rock before the sand is reached. Snorkelling only.

2521 Yell Sound. HU408822. Rocky slabs lead down to a hard gravel bottom at 18m.

2522 Ness of Westsandwick. HU438873 (approx.). Shore rocks slope into the sea at 45°. The kelp cover extends to about 20m, just shortly before the sand begins. Large numbers of razor shells noted.

2523 South of Markna Geo. HU449859. A small rocky slope giving way to rock, stone and sand in shallow water. Further out a depth of 20m can be exceeded where the life is worthwhile.

2524 South Wick of Sound. HU451825. A beach located in a sheltered bay almost directly opposite the Shetland oil terminal. Offshore the seabed consists of stepped, kelp-covered rock faces and horizontal rocky areas.

2525 Wreck of the "Robert Lee", Brother Isle. This Norwegian steamer was lost early this century at Collafirth whaling station while loaded with whale oil. The reef at the North end of Brother Isle extends out underwater. The wreckage lies on a rocky and sandy bottom at about 10m.

2526 Geo South west of Clothan. Hu465805. A rocky, kelp-covered slope.

2527 Yell Sound. There are about 20 islands and skerries in Yell Sound. Most of these appear to be undived, yet they have excellent potential. Depths range from about 30m to 70m. Tidal streams run at up to 2 knots in the wide part of the sound and up to 7 knots in the narrow channels; Slacks at +0420 and (minus)0140 Dover.

2528 Black Skerry, Otters Wick. HU530850. Lots of kelp. There is reputed to be a wreck of a Dutch vessel lost in 1737 on this skerry. It could also be the "Joratne" (see later).

2529 Wreck of the "Bohus". HU537853. A steel German training ship wrecked in 1925 on the Groin at the South west of the Ness of Queyon. Much wreckage remains, although the bell was recovered by Shetland Sub-Aqua Club.

2530 Foul area, Colgrave Sound. This charted area, at 603443N 005722W 1.5 miles East of Whitehill Lighthouse, is actually a large pile of chain and an anchor in 53m.

2531 Outer Brough, Fetlar. HU673931. A pleasant dive to 20m with lots of life.

2532 Wreck of the "Wendala". A Swedish vessel wrecked "off Urie Island",

Fetler in 1737. Known locally as the "Silver Ship", the "Wendela" is perhaps Shetland's richest wreck. It has been excavated by Robert Stenuit and is a protected site.

2533 Unknown wreck. An emigrant ship lost at Fetler in 1765 with loss of all passengers and crew.

2534 Wreck of the "Jane". An 840-ton vessel lost in 1923 at 603822N 005625W, 500m South of Sound Gruney island, just North of Fetlar. The depth is 20m with a clearance of 11m. This is the charted position, but the stated position is 70m South of some rocks. The 63m-long wreck is lying on her port side with her keel uppermost without any projecting upperworks, although large parts are intact; it is possible to swim into the engine room.

2535 Wreck of the "Lastdrager". A Dutch East Indiaman wrecked at Crook's Ayre, Ness of Cullivoe in 1653. Some small pieces of wreckage remain, including six iron cannon. The site was excavated by Stenuit and is protected.

2536 Wreck of a Russian trawler. HP502061. This vessel was lost with all her crew in the middle of Scarse Sound, and is sometimes refered to as the "Gloup" wreck. She was a big vessel and it is suspected that she was a "spy ship". She sits upright on a rocky bottom at about 20m. Although well broken, she is still suggestive of a ship. There are pieces of keel, hull and large engines to be seen. Tidal streams can run at up to 6 knots. Launch at Cullivoe (HP545026) and collect divers at Sands of Brekkon (HP526052).

2537 Gloup Holm. HP487064. A flat seabed at 30m; the Atlantic swell reaches 20m regularly.

2538 Wick of Whallerie. HP505052. A spectacular shore dive into 6m deep gullies at a depth of 15m. An ideal second dive.

2539 Outsta Ness. HP523059. Anchor about 30m North east of the channel between the outermost island and the headland. This gives an excellent dive in 15m deep gullies. The scenery is excellent and the life rich.

Old Wrecks of Yell

A LIST of shipwrecks around Yell is held by the Lerwick Museum. The abbreviated version listed here may give some clues to very old shipwrecks you might stumble across. More information may be available from the Museum.

2540 1680 "Thomas & George", ashore at Grif Skerry, towed to Hamnavoe where she became a total wreck.

2541 1681 "Engel Raphael" wrecked Vatsetter Bay.

2542 c.1700 Ship wrecked at Holm of Gloup, several suvivors including an Irishman, hence name of Irishman's Roni.

2543 1701 "Rognvald Jarl" wrecked at sands of Breckin.

2544 1710 Danish vessel from Iceland wrecked on West side of Yell.

2545 1711 Galliot wrecked in Otterswick.

2546 1724 "Clementina" wrecked at Papil Ness.

2547 1731 Log ship wrecked at Whalfirth.

2548 1742 "Elizabeth" stranded at Reafirth.

2549 c.1750 Russian vessel wrecked at Housawick, Hascosay.

2550 1750 "Juffro – Dorothea" wrecked at Ness of Queyhin.

2551 c.1750 A Dutch brig wrecked in the Bay of Houlland (the crew got a hawser to the shore but this was cut by locals!)

2552 1793 "Elizabeth" wrecked at isle of Linga, Bluemull Sound.

2553 1793 "Enterprise" wrecked at Gloup Voe.

2554 1800 "Inga" wrecked at Fugla Geo (between Gerherda and Head of Bratta).

2555 1800 "Mary" wrecked at Cullivoe.

2556 1803 "Jongfrau Rebecca" wrecked near Hesti Geo.

2557 1863 "Krageroe" wrecked on Hascosay after being abandoned off Whalsay.

2558 1807 "Traveller" wrecked at Gloup Voe.

2559 1807 "Glenalmond" wrecked at Gloup Voe.

2560 1809 Unknown vessel wrecked at Baas of Hascosay.

2561 1815 "Wenskabsminde" wrecked on West side of Yell.

2562 1841 "Friends" wrecked at Baas of Hascosay.

2563 1847 "Hunter" wrecked off the Stoal, Aywick.

2564 1847 Unknown vessel wrecked at Gossaborough.

2565 1847 "Harmonic" wrecked at Ness of Queyhin.

2566 1857 "Lerwegian" wrecked at Hermanspea (?), Burravoe.

2567 1865 "Eliza" wrecked at Virdik, Heoganess, Burravoe.

2568 1869 Norwegian smack wrecked at Yell Baa near isle of Orphasey.

2569 1875 "Marie" wrecked South Ayre of Cuppaster.

2570 1886 "Kong Svene" wrecked at Birrier, Vatster.

2571 1897 "Talmerston" wrecked at Tatie's Stane, Cullivoe.

2572 1904 "Ibis" wrecked at Rumble in Yell Sound.

2573 1915 "Jackdaw" lost on Burraness.

2574 1915 "Thors 11" wrecked in Basta Voe.

2575 1935 "Nellie Gardiner" wrecked Burga Skerries, Burravoe.

2576 1941 "Joratne" wrecked Swarta Skerry Otterswick.

2577 1940s. Trawler "Bracken Lea" wrecked Baas of Hascosay.

Unst

2578 West coast of Unst. This appears to be undived. There is an amazing collection of stacks, skerries, geos and their shoreline features – there must be diving of high order to be had, especially as depths seem to fall rapidly to 50-70m.

2579 Bluemull Sound. This narrow sound separates Unst from Yell. It appears largely undived. Depths reach 40m and tidal streams reach as much as 7 knots locally (slacks at (plus)0310 and (plus)0310 Dover).

2580 The Vere. HP646033. A Norwegian coaster was lost here in 1939. It is in good condition with lots of brass, portholes, funnels, engines and prop (6m across) still visible. Depth 15m. Launch with permission of Mr. Peterson (Unst 215). It is possible that this wreck has been confused with the "Tonis Chandris".

2581 Wreck of the SS "Tonis Chandris". A 3161-ton Greek merchantman carrying manganese ore from Narvik that was lost in 1940 when she was wrecked on Vere Rocks at 604207N 004854W, 0.66 mile North east of Ham Ness. The position is 600m almost due South of The Vere island in 20m of water.

2582 Wreck of "E49". An 800-ton, 55m-long British submarine lost by mine at 604414N 004751W in 1917 with the loss of 31 crew. Immediately after the sinking, divers stated that the bows had been blown off. The quoted position is 500m South south west of Balta Light in about 30m of water. Shetland Sub-Aqua Club have searched extensively but unsuccessfully around the charted position.

The small car ferry connecting the islands of Fetlar, Yell and Unst.

2583 South Ship Geo. HP623043. A shore feature named on the map; one wonders why.

2584 Baltasound. HP633087. A muddy bottom with little to commend it except discarded fishing equipment at around 10m.

2585 The Rett, Balta. HP657093. A very good dive in gullies 6-10m deep. There is lots of life and little kelp.

2586 Ship Stack. HP667133. A shore feature named on the map. It is the site of the wreck of the 44-gun Dutch East Indiaman "Curacao" in 1729. She went ashore in a fog; 195 crew saved, 15 lost. This was located at about 25m and excavated by Stenuit. It is a protected site.

2587 Wreck of the "Orel", Crickies Chair. HP673154. A Russian trawler grounded on Skaw Point, Unst in 1967 at 6050N 0046W. It now lies in Crickies Chair and is easy to locate as it is the small inlet beneath the large pill box on the cliff. There is a submerged rock at the entrance to the inlet and it is best to anchor outside. The funnel, engine and anchor are notable, as are large crabs. Depth 12m.

2588 Lamba Ness. HP676155. This is the best site on Unst for Crabs and lobsters though the life generally is rather stunted! There are pieces of wreckage on the seabed from the nearby rubbish tip. Depth 20m(plus).

2589 Wreck of the "May Isle". HU675153. A fishing vessel lying close to the central rocks in the small bay at Lamba Ness. It is extremely broken up and all that remains are the boiler, winches and odd pieces of scrap scattered among the large boulders on the seabed at about 10-11m. The seabed gradually drops to well beyond 20m to the seaward of the wreck.

2590 Hols Hellier. HP627177. On the tip of the eastern shore of Burra Firth, a little seaward of a natural arch running from the firth to the sea. A cave lies to the seaward of the site. Underwater, a vertical rock face drops to 15m then reaches a boulder-strewn, sandy bottom.

2591 Burra Firth, West side. HP615160. Very good diving with lots of crustaceans and fish. The scenery is good with large boulders and 15m drop-offs. Depth 15-30m.

2592 Norwick Hevda. HP624171. Access from lighthouse shore station (The Ness), where the keepers are helpful; boats can be left overnight. A bouldery, kelpy bottom at 15-30m.

2593 Ruska Kame. HP632180. 5 minutes from the slip is a natural arch with some good underwater scenery. Depth 20m.

2594 Muckle Flugga. HP607199. A demanding dive due to the ever present Atlantic swells. Lots of kelp and seals at a depth of 15m.

2595 Out Stack. HP613203. This is the most northerly rock in all Britain. I tried to dive there in 1976 but was beaten back by mountainous seas and strong tidal streams; Dave Holland managed to be the first to dive this most desirable site in 1980. The exposure and frequent occurence of sea-mist demand good planning and experienced divers; SMBs are essential. The depth is 15m by the Stack, but drops away rapidly. The sea life is rich, being most prolific on the more exposed westerly side.

2596 Wreck of "UC43". A 510-ton, 52m-long German submarine tor pedoed and sunk by British submarine G13 in 1917 at 6057N 0111W. The position is now thought to be 605424N 010642W, 7 miles West north west of Muckle Flugga Light in 105m of water with a clearance of 90m.

Old Wrecks of Unst

AN INCOMPLETE list of shipwrecks around Unst from 1600 to recent time, compiled by R. Wilson from the Robert Stuart Bruce Papers and other sources held in the Shetland Room by the Lerwick Museum follows. More information may be available from the Museum.

2597 1600 "Circe", a British (?) vessel wrecked on Vere, Easting.

2598 1600 "The Witte Valeke" of Enkhuizen with general cargo from St. Nicholas in Russia lost on the West side of Unst, crew saved.

2599 1664 British vessel with cargo of Dutch wine lost at Tonga, Her maness; crew perished.

2600 1664 Unknown foreign vessel with a cargo of Dutch hides for the West Indies lost in Lundawick, crew saved.

2601 1700 British vessel, cargo of Russian hides, wrecked near Uyea sound, crew lost.

2602 1705 "Celicia" of Lebe, cargo of Irish hides and tallow, crew saved.

2603 1712 Brig "Fortuna" of Schieswig, cargo of iron and deals, wrecked at Clugan, crew saved.

2604 1713 Dutch East Indiaman "Rijneuburg", 25 guns, general cargo to Batavia, wrecked Muness Ness.

2605 1730 Greenland whaler "St. Helena" of Hamburg, wrecked at the Inner Wick of Skaw, 5 saved, 25 lost.

2606 1737 A German brig lost at Ship Stack, Norwick, cargo of iron and deals, one man lost.

2607 1740 "St. Mathew" of Hamburg, cargo of cereal, wrecked on the Framd, Hermaness, crew saved.

2608 1742 Sloop of Uril, drove from anchor at Uyeasound and wrecked.

2609 1748 Brig "Jenny" of Irvine homeward bound from Germany, cargo of deals, lost on the Holm of Skaw, crew saved.

2610 1763 Sloop "Jhen and Margret" of Lerwick, lost on Uyea Isle, crew saved.

2611 1767 "Seuel" of Skye, from Bergen to Skye, cargo of deals, flax, sugar, gin, lost at Haroldswick, crew saved.

2612 1771 Whaler "Zeerch" of Dordrecht, lost near Baltasound, crew saved.

2613 1776 Greenland whaler "Ceres" of London, outward bound, lost at the back of the Keen of Hamer, Wick of Hagdale, all lost.

2614 1777 "Amity" of Whitby, cargo of timber from Ansagi, lost at Haroldswick, crew saved.

2615 1778 "Tyour", from Leith to Archangel, captured and sunk off Unst by 28-gun American privateer "General Meslin".

2616 1787 Sloop "Elizabeth" of Leith, bound for Lerwick with general cargo, lost at Uyeasound, all saved.

2617 1789 Shetland smack lost at Muness Ness, 5 lost.

2618 1794 HMS "Pylades", 16-gun brig, 450 tons, lost between Brookpoint and Lashamar, crew of 125 saved.

2619 1796 Brig "Speculation" of Drontheim, outward bound for Bilbao, cargo of salt fish and oil, lost at Mel near Colvadale, mate lost.

2620 1796 Danish vessel homeward bound from Iceland, cargo of tallow, wool and stockings, lost at North side of Haroldswick, crew lost.

2621 1798 "Carl Friedrich" of Emden bound from Liverpool to Danzig, cargo 4667 bushels of salt, lost at the Inner Wick of Skaw, crew saved.

2622 1799 Brig "Swan" of Copenhagen, from Faroe to Copenhagen, cargo of fish, tallow, mutton and eiderdown, lost at the Bicht of Sluggins below Maratshonel, two crew lost.

2623 1799 Brig "Thames" of London, captured off Flamborough Head by Dunkirque privateer "Fantasie", driven North in sinking conditions by prize crew, run ashore at Uyeasound, prize crew captured.

2624 1800 HMS "Hound", 18-gun brig of war, 315 tons, foundered about 1 mile East of Easting Vere, 121 men lost.

2625 1805 Brig "Friends" of Montrose, from Christiansand to Ireland, cargo of deals and oil, foundered to North north east of Unst, crew saved.

2626 1807 Brig "Thetis" of Whitehaven, from St. Petersburg to Liverpool, cargo of tallow and flax, lost on island of Balta, one man lost.

2627 1816 Topsail schooner "Fairy" of Dundee, from New Brunswick, cargo of timber, lost at Sand of Lund, Lundawick, crew saved.

2628 1820 Norwegian sloop "Ugland", 70 tons, cargo of salt and deals, wrecked at Burrafirth.

2629 1820 Large vessel driven ashore at Tangwick, Unst, cargo of American timber.

2630 1825 "Resolution" from Hamburg to New Orleans, cargo of linen, bricks, millstones and cats, wrecked at Cruss Geo, near Haroldswick, all lost save master. Known locally as the "Linen Ship".

2631 1826 French vessel "Le Jeane Dataille", cargo of salt fish, driven ashore at Baltasound.

2632 1831 "Barque" of Bergen, 636 tons, in ballast from Bergen to Cardiff, went ashore on the Flaskie, Hagdale. Crew saved. This vessel could also be the "De Lesseps".

2633 1831 Brig "Acasta" of London, homeward bound from Archangel for Britain, foundered off Hermaness, crew saved.

2634 1839 Russian brig "I.H.O.", in ballast from London to Riga, foundered at anchor, West Bight of Skaw, crew saved.

2635 1839 Galliot "Louise" of Stralsund, bound from Riga to Londonderry, cargo of 1300 barrels of linseed, lost at Uyeasound.

2636 1840 Brig "Borussia" of Stralsund, from Archangel to Rotterdam, cargo of mats and 13600 bushels of rye, lost near Haroldswick, 8 saved, 5 lost. Known locally as the "Rye Ship".

2637 1862 Norwegian schooner "Sophia", from Newcastle to Grimstadt, cargo of iron bar and earthenware, struck the "Stack of the Gord", Hermaness and sunk in 15m in what became known as "Iron Geo". 3 lost, 2 saved.

2638 1864 Brig "August" of Christiania, homeward bound from Grangemouth, cargo of deals, lost at Brockpoint, Haroldswick, crew saved. Known locally as the "Rat Ship".

2639 1876 German barque "Emma und Karl", homeward bound from New York, cargo of paraffin oil, abandoned at sea after gale damage and lost on the Nev near Haroldswick. 7 lost, 5 saved.

2640 1880 Barque "Capri" of Nova Scotia, 896 tons, from Norway to New York, wrecked on the Taing of Nustigarth, Muness. Crew saved.

2641 1881 Barque "Henrietta" of Danzig, 347 tons, cargo of timber and black beer, bound for Barrow in Furness, went ashore on Hevdi Grind reef, Foula, got off by rescue crew and put into Burrafirth overnight. Disappeared by morning. Crew saved but rescue crew presumed lost.

2642 1883 Barque "De Lesseps" of Bergen, 636 tons, outward bound in ballast for Cardiff, lost on the Flaskie, Hagdale. Crew saved.

2643 1894 Norwegian barque "Hero", 600 tons, bound from Fleetwood to Russia, cargo of 400 tons of salt, wrecked on the Birger of the Rucock, Norwick. Crew saved.

2644 1902 Fishing smack "King Harold" of Lerwick, 55 tons, was stranded and became a total loss in Baltasound Harbour. Crew saved.

2645 1902 Fishing boat "Nobles", foundered in Baltasound when swept onto rocks. Crew jumped ashore before boat sank.

2646 1903 Swedish barquentine "Nautilus", 384 tons, from Sunderland to Sweden, cargo of coal, sprang a leak and foundered 20 miles South east of Muckle Flugga. Crew saved.

2647 1936 Trawler "May Island" of Leith lost with all hands at Lambaness.

2648 1939 British vessel "Sea Venturer", 2327 tons, 90m long, from Tyne to Tromso, cargo of coal torpedoed 15 miles off Muckle Flugga. Crew saved.

2649 1940 British steamer "Stancliffe", 4511 tons, 117m long, torpedoed off Unst 45 miles North east of Unst island. 15 survivors, 22 lost.

2650 1941 Small boat sunk at Uyeasound by machine-gunning German plane.

2651 WW2 Norwegian vessel wrecked on the Noost Stone at Haroldswick. Crew saved.

2652 WW2 Norwegian vessel driven ashore and lost below cliffs at Burrafirth, near Buddabrake.

2653 WW2 Swedish steamer sunk off Muckle Flugga. Some survivors.

2654 1956 Russian vessel ashore at the Weeting, Bluemill Sound, towed off rocks and sunk. Crew saved.

2655 1958 Russian fishing vessel "SRT4442", wrecked on Outer Flaess Skaw. 22 lost, 3 saved.

2656 1967 Russian trawler wrecked near Holm of Skaw, crew saved.

Area information and services

Hydrographic charts: 219 Western approaches to the Orkney & Shetland islands 1:500,000; 2622 Plans in the Orkney & Shetland islands, various; 3281 Shetland islands – North west sheet 1:75,000; 3282 Shetland islands – North east sheet 1:75,000; 3283 Shetland islands – South sheet 1:75,000; 3290 Lerwick Harbour 1:7,500; 3291 Approaches to Lerwick 1:17,500; 3292 Eastern approaches to Yell Sound, Basta Voe & Bluemull Sound 1:30,000; 3293 Harbours in Yell & Unst, various; 3294 Plans in the Shetland islands – Sheet 1, various; 3295 Plans in the Shetland islands – Sheet 2, various; 3297 Sullom voe 1:12,500; 3298 Yell Sound 1:25,000.
Ordnance Survey 1:50,000 maps: 1 Shetland – Yell & Unst; 2 Shetland – Whalsay; 3 Shetland – North Mainland; 4 Shetland – South Mainland.
Ordnance Survey 1:25,000 maps: HP51/61 Haroldswick; HP40/50/60 Baltasound & Cullivoe; HU39/49 Yell Sound (North); HU59/69 Fetlar (North); HU68 Fetlar; HU28/38 Ronas Hill; HU48/58 Otterswick; HU27/37 Hillswick; HU47/57 Lunna Ness; HU67 Out Skerries; HU26/36 Muckle Roe; HU56 Whalsay; HU16 Papa Stour; HU15/25 Sandness; HU45/55 Nesting; HU14/24 Walls; HU44/54 Lerwick; HU33/43/53 Scalloway; HU32/42 Sandwick (Shetland) & Mousa; HU31/41 Sumburgh.
Local BS-AC branches: RAF Saxaford special, Sullom voe special.
Local SS-AC branches: Shetland (Lerwick).
Dive Centres: Skolla Diving Centre, Gulberwick, Lerwick, Shetland, ZE2 9JX; Lerwick (0595) 4175; Dive Shetland, Jorvik, Bigton, Shetland (09502) 295.
Air supplies: Skolla Diving Centre; Shetland SSAC; Queens Hotel, Lerwick; Dive Shetland.
Outboard motor sales & services: HNP Engineers, Commercial Road, Lerwick – Lerwick 2493/2368 or Scalloway 663 or Weisdale 245.
Boat charterers: 28-ft ex-Police launch – Bernie Edwardson (Lerwick 4320), Jim Manson (Johnson Chip Shop): Lerwick 3125, home: Gott 249); 32-ft wooden vessel – Robbie Leask (Lerwick 4152) – DTI certificated; 40-ft ketch – Sean Milligan (Lerwick 4200) – RYA qualified.
Harbourmasters: Lerwick 3462/2828; Sullom voe, Sullom voe 242551.
Local weather: Lerwick Meteorological Office, Lerwick 2239; Sullom voe Meteorological Office, Sullom voe 2069.

Sea area; Fair Isle.
Tidal constants:

	LERWICK	DOVER
Lerwick	–	−0008
Fair Isle	−0025	+0033
Dury voe	−0015	−0023
Out Skerries	−0025	−0033
Burravoe (Yell)	−0025	−0033
Baltasound	−0055	−0103
Burrafirth	−0110	−0118
Bluemull Sound	−0135	−0143
Sullom voe	−0130	−0138
Hillswick	−0220	−0228
Scalloway	−0150	−0158
Quendale Bay	−0025	−0033
Foula	−0135	−0143

Coastguards: Lerwick RHQ, Lerwick 2976/4600; Sullom voe 2561; Rescue equipment is maintained at Baltasound, Fetler, Out Skerries, Bressay, No Ness, Virkie, Fair Isle, West Burra, Watsness, Papa Stour, Esha Ness and Gloup.
Lifeboats: Lerwick and Aith
SAR helicopter: The nearest is based at Sumburgh Airport.
Police stations: Lerwick 2110; Brae 381; Scalloway 222; Sumburgh 6070; Symbister 432; Cullivoe, Gutcher 222; Baltasound 424.
Doctors: Unst, Dr Karam, Baltasound 318; Yell/Fetlar, Dr McDonnell, Mid Yell 2127.
Hospitals: Gilbert Bain Hospital, Lerwick 5678.
Recompression chambers: Nearest are at Aberdeen. See Appendix 2.
Vehicle recovery: None available.
Ferry operators: P & O Ferries (Aberdeen – Lerwick, vehicular, aboard MV St. Clair or MV St. Sunniva) Aberdeen (0224) 29111 or Lerwick (0595) 4848. Pressure on the ferries has reduced since the introduction of a daily vessel from Aberdeen via Stromness in Orkney.
Inter-island ferries (some passenger, some vehicular) run to all of the main islands: Lerwick – Bressay (V); Bressey – Isle of Noss (P); Vidlin (Mainland) – Whalsay (V); Mainland – South Yell (V); North Yell – Unst (V); Fetler – Yell – Unst (V); Lerwick – Out Skerries (P); Whalsay – Out Skerries (P); Sumburgh – Fair Isle (P); Walls – Foula (P); West Burrafirth – Papa Stour (P); Sandwick – Mousa (P). A timetable is available from the Shetland Tourist Organisation, Information Centre, Lerwick. The ferry charges are subsidised and are extremely reasonable.
There is now a new P & O service between Orkney and Shetland. For divers travelling a long distance to the North of Scotland, this re-opens the exciting possibility of visiting both groups in one relatively extensive northern visit.
Air connections: Lerwick Airport has connections to Wick, Aberdeen, Edinburgh and Glasgow. Operators: British Airways (041 887 1111 & 0856 2233); Loganair (041 889 3181 & 0856 3457). There are several inter-island flights, from Tingwall Airport near Lerwick, between: Tingwall – Fetlar – Unst; Tingwall – Fair Isle; Tingwall – Foula; Tingwall – Out Skerries.

These are not subsidised and are relatively expensive, though an excellent way of seeing Shetland on a clear day.

Car hire: Bolts Motor Garage, Lerwick 2855; J Leask & Sons, Lerwick 3162; MacLeod & Maclean, Lerwick 3313; Station Garage, Lerwick 3315; Scalloway Motor Repair Service, Scalloway 662; AJ Eunson, Sumburgh Airport, Sumburgh 60209; A J Eunson, Sumburgh Airport, Sumburgh 60209; G Stronach, Lerwick 3718. There are several car hirers on Yell and one on Fetlar.

Local tourist information: Lerwick (0595) 3434.

Places of local marine interest: Shetland Museum, Lerwick; Scalloway Folk Museum; The Old Haa Museum, Burravoe, Yell; Unst Visitors Centre, Haroldswick; Bod of Gremista (restored birthplace of Sir Arthur Anderson, founder of the P & O shipping line).

Accommodation: There are hotels in the main centres of population. There are B & B establishments scattered throughout the islands. Queens Hotel, Lerwick offers various packages for divers including accommodation, boats, compressed air etc. Bridgend Outdoor Centre offers cheap self-catering accommodation on West Burra.

Appendix 1: USEFUL ADDRESSES

Dive centres and dive charterers:

Barefoots Diving, Northburn Caravan Site, Eyemouth (08907) 51050;
Scoutscroft Diving Centre, Coldingham, Eyemouth, Berwickshire;
East Coast Divers, West Pitkierie Farm, Anstruther, Fife (0333) 310768;
Orkneyinga Charters, Walliwall Cottage, St. Ola, Kirkwall, Orkney (0856) 5489;
George Litts, Braehead Cottage, Stromness, Orkney (0856) 850434;
John Thornton, The Manse, Palace Road, Kirkwall, Orkney (0856) 4761;
Anthony Duncan, Scapa Flow Diving Centre, Karinya, Burray, Orkney (085673) 225/253;
Robert Swanney, Ayre Mills, Kirkwall, Orkney (0856) 3974;
Steve Mowat, Stromness Diving Centre, Barkland, Cairston Road, Stromness, Orkney (0856) 850624; or Don Temple (0343) 830034;
Sunrise Charters, 22 Slater Street, Kirkwall, Orkney (0856) 3953/78393;
Sands Motel, Burray, Orkney (085673) 298;
Smith Foubister, St. Ola Hotel, Harbour Street, Kirkwall (0856) 5090;
E Jeffrey, 8 Dundas Street, Stromness, Orkney (0856) 850489;
Thomson & Dickie, Roadside, Widewall, South Ronaldsay, Orkney (0856) 83372;
Dive Scapa Flow, Howton Bay (Tel: 0856 2872);
Ferry Inn, Stromness, Orkney (Tel: 0856 850 280);
Taversoe Hotel, Rousay, Orkney (Tel: 0856 82 325);
Skolla Dive Centre, Gulberwick, Lerwick, Shetland (0595) 4175;
Dive Shetland, Jorvik, Bigton, Shetland (09502) 295.

Compressed air supplies

All of the above diving operators have supplies of compressed air. All BSAC and SSAC branches either have compressors or know the whereabouts of local compressors. Compressed air is additionally available as follows:
Swift Diving Supplies (Scotland) Ltd, 11-12 Kittybrewster Centre, Aberdeen;
Sub Sea Services, 21 John Street, Aberdeen (0224) 631362;
Sub Sea Services, 84 Telford Street, Inverness (0463) 223745;
Edinburgh Diving Centre Ltd, 30 West Preston Street, Edinburgh 031 667 7982;
Hunter Diving Equipment, 21 Constitution Place, inside Leith Docks, Edinburgh.

Dive boats

A number of the diving centres and suppliers of compressed air either have boats or know where they can be arranged locally.
The following vessels or organisations are known to operate outwith of Scapa Flow:
"Arctic Star", contact Barefoot Diving
Vessels in the Forth, contact Edinburgh Dive Centre;
"Hamnavoe", contact East Coast Divers;
Balintore vessel, contact Steve Coutts;
Orkneyinga Charters, Kirkwall;
Sunrise Charters, Kirkwall;
Shetland vessels (3), contact Skolla Dive Centre.

Chart agents

Hay & Co (Lerwick) Ltd, 106a Commercial Street, Lerwick, Shetland;
Thomas Garden, Harbour Office, Commercial Road, Buckie, Banffshire;
Burghead Boat Centre, Burghead Harbour, Burghead, Elgin;
Kelvin Hughes, 21 Regent Quay, Aberdeen;
Allison-Gray, 59-63 Dock Street, Dundee;
Chattan Shipping Services Ltd, 5 Canon Mills, Edinburgh.

Coastguard

MRSC Orkney: Kirkwall (0856) 3268;
MRSC Shetland: Lerwick (0595) 2976;
MRSC Wick: Wick (0856) 2332;
MRSC Moray: Peterhead (0779) 4278;
MRCC Aberdeen: Aberdeen (0224) 52334;
MRSC Forth: Crail (03335) 666;
MRCC: Marine Rescue Coordination Centre;
MRSC: Marine Rescue Sub-Centre.

General

Highlands and Islands Development Board, 27 Bridge House, Bank Street, Inverness;
Scottish Sports Council, 4 Queenferry Street, Edinburgh, EH2 4PB;
Scottish Tourist Board, 23 Ravelston Terrace, Edinburgh, EH4 3EU;
Scottish Tourist Board (London Office), 5/6 Pall Mall East, London, SW1;
Countryside Commission for Scotland, Battleby, Redgorton, Perth;
Nature Conservancy Council, 12 Hope Terrace, Edinburgh, EH9 2AS;
Forestry Commission (Scotland), 231 Corstorphine Road, Edinburgh, EH12 7AT;
National Trust for Scotland, 5 Charlotte Square, Edinburgh, EH2 4DU;
Scottish Wildlife Trust, 25 Johnston Terrace, Edinburgh, EH1 2NH;
Royal Society for the Protection of Birds (Scottish Office), 17 Regent Terrace, Edinburgh, EH7 5BN;
Scottish Rights of Way Society, 32 Rutland Square, Edinburgh, EH1 2BW;
Scottish Youth Hostels Association, 7 Glebe Crescent, Stirling, FK8 2JA;
British Sub Aqua Club, 16 Upper Woburn Place, London, WC1H 0QW;
Scottish Sub Aqua Club, The Sports Centre, Eastbank Academy, Shettleston Road, Glasgow, G32 9AA.

Appendix 2: RECOMPRESSION CHAMBER FACILITIES IN SCOTLAND

AS far as I am aware the list of chambers given below is complete. However, there may be others of which I am unaware, and certainly the list will become dated as time passes.

It is prudent to know the whereabouts of the nearest recompression chamber relative to your chosen diving site. However, it would be unusual to go direct to the chamber. The correct procedure to employ in Scottish waters if you suspect you have a case requiring recompression is open to some argument. Probably the best procedure is to phone Aberdeen Royal Infirmary (Aberdeen 871848) and ask for the Duty Diving Doctor if you are anywhere near Grampian Region (or the Northern Isles). If you are in the South-west then the best plan may be to contact Glasgow Western Infirmary (041 339 8822). In any other part of the country it may be best to contact HMS Vernon (0705 818888). In any event, your first contact will be with the Coastguard, and it is they who will coordinate the rescue services and ask the police to assist with transport to the nearest available chamber.

It is worth noting that if you are involved in an incident that may demand recompression after diving at an inland site then you should still contact the Coastguard in the first instance, as they are familiar with the procedure involved.

The chambers below are listed in a clockwise direction around Scotland, starting in the South-west. As far as I am aware, the most informed doctors specialising in diving medicine are involved with chambers at Glasgow, Aberdeen, (Royal Infirmary) and Fort William.

Millport. Scottish Marine Biological Association, Millport Laboratory, Isle of Cumbrae. Tel: Millport (047 553) 581/2 (Out of hours Millport 761/287/835).

Glasgow. Western Infirmary, Dumbarton Road, Glasgow. Tel: (041) 339 8822, ask for Intensive Care Unit.

Faslane. HMS "Neptune", Clyde Submarine Base, Helensburgh. Tel: Helensburgh (0436) 4321, ask for Duty Lt-Cdr. or Duty Diver.

Fort William. Underwater Training Centre, Inverlochy, Forth William. Tel: Fort William (0397) 3786 (Out of hours contact Dr. Douglas at Fort William 3136 or Chris Robinson at Fort William 3773).

Orkney. Occidental of Britain Inc, Oil Terminal Dept, Flotta, Orkney. Tel: Longhope (085 670) 341.

Aberdeen. Royal Infirmary, Forresterhill, Aberdeen. Tel: Aberdeen (0224) 681818 (Alternatively, contact 871848 and ask for the Duty Diving Doctor). Institute of Offshore Medicine, 9 Rubislaw Terrace, Aberdeen. Tel: Aberdeen (0224) 55595/55596 (Out of hours contact Aberdeen 671848 and ask for the Medical Officer in charge of recompression facilities). MAFF Marine Laboratory, Victoria Road, Aberdeen. Tel: Aberdeen (0224) 876544. There are also several professional diving contractors in the Aberdeen area, and some of these have most comprehensive recompression and medical facilities.

These are:–

Comex Houlder Diving Ltd, Bucksburn, Aberdeen. (Tel: 714101);

Oceaneering, Pitmedden Road, Dyce, Aberdeen, (Tel: 770444);

Wharton Williams Taylor, Farburn Industrial Estate, Dyce, Aberdeen. (Tel: 722877).

Rosyth. Marine Services School and Salvage Unit, Dunfermline. Tel: Inverkeithing (0383) 42121 ext. 3127/3527.

NB. Note that there are a number of other chambers in Scotland. Many oil rigs and all oil rig support vessels have recompression chambers. Additionally, there may be naval vessels with recompression facilities operating in Scottish waters from time to time. However, these are not generally available to sports divers.

BIBLIOGRAPHY

MANY general books on Scotland were listed in the first two volumes of this work; these will not be repeated. Appropriate books are frequently referred to in the text of the relevant chapters. In particular, many books on Orkney and Scapa Flow are listed in the chapter covering Scapa Flow. These lists will not be repeated here. What follows is a brief list of books the author has found useful. A very great number of additional books could be detailed and any good library should have the standard reference works on areas of Scotland.

The Diver's Guide to the North East Coast, P Collings, Collings & Brodie, 1986;

A Guide to Diving in the St Abbs & Eyemouth Voluntary Marine Reserve, C Warman, 1987;

Dictionary of Disasters at Sea in the Age of Steam 1824-1962, C Hocking, Lloyd's 1969;

Wreck printouts, from the Wreck Section of the Hydrographic Dept;

North Coast of Scotland Pilot, Hydrographic Dept, 1975;

North Sea (West) Pilot, Hydrographic Dept, 1973;

Pilot Handbook: East Coast of Scotland, ed. N I;

Thomson, Forth Yacht Clubs Association, 1974;

North and North East Coast of Scotland Sailing Directions & Anchorages, ed. G Viycomb, Clyde Cruising Club, 1976;

Orkney Sailing Directions & Anchorages, ed. G Vinycomb, Clyde Cruising Club, 1975;

Shetland Sailing Directions & Anchorages, ed. G Vinycomb, Clyde Cruising Club, 1978;

Orkney & Shetland Tidal Stream Atlas, Hydrographic Dept, 1980;

North Sea: Flamborough Head to Pentland Firth Tidal Stream Atlas, Hydrographic Dept, 1975;

Ordnance Gazeteer of Scotland, 6 vols, ed. F H Groome, Jack, 1886;

North East Scotland, E Peck, Bartholomew, 1981;

Scotland's Eastern Coast, L Scott-Moncrieff, Oliver & Boyd, 1963;

Portrait of the Border Country, N Tranter, Hale, 1972;

The Lowlands, I Finlay, Batsford, 1967;

Portrait of Aberdeen and Deeside, C Graham, Hale, 1972;

The Queen's Scotland: The Eastern Countries, N Tranter, Hodder & Stoughton, 1972;

Portrait of the Moray Firth, C Graham, Hale, 1977;

The Moray Book, ed. D Omand, Paul Harris, 1976;

The Natural Environment of Orkney, ed. R Goodier, Nature Conservancy Council, 1975;

The Orkney Story, Schel & Moberg, Batsford, 1985;

Shetland, J R Nicolson, David & Charles, 1972;

Traditional Life in Shetland, J R Nicolson, Hale, 1978;

The Northern Isles, A Fenton, John Donald, 1978;

The Making of the Shetland Landscape, S A Knox, John Donald, 1985;

A Vertebrate Fauna of the Shetland Islands, A H Evans & T E Buckley, Douglas, 1899;

Birds and Mammals of Shetland, L S & U M Venables, Oliver & Boyd, 1955;

The Shetland Dictionary, J J Graham, Shetland Publishing Co, 1979.

INDEX

This index consists essentially of the names of the dive sites described in this volume. There are also entries covering areas, general points, and individuals. Entries in inverted commas are names of wrecks.